Nothing Down for Women

THE SMART WOMAN'S QUICK-START GUIDE TO REAL ESTATE INVESTING

Robert G. Allen
and
Karen Nelson Bell

FREE PRESS
New York   London   Toronto   Sydney

*f*P
FREE PRESS
A Division of Simon & Schuster, Inc.
1230 Avenue of the Americas
New York, NY 10020

Copyright © 2007 by Robert G. Allen and Karen Nelson Bell
All rights reserved,
including the right of reproduction
in whole or in part in any form.

FREE PRESS and colophon are trademarks
of Simon & Schuster, Inc.

For information about special discounts for bulk purchases,
please contact Simon & Schuster Special Sales: 1-800-456-6798
or business@simonandschuster.com.

Designed by Davina Mock

Manufactured in the United States of America

1   3   5   7   9   10   8   6   4   2

Library of Congress Cataloging-in-Publication Data
Allen, Robert G.
Nothing down for women: the smart woman's quick-start guide to
real estate investing / Robert G. Allen and Karen Nelson Bell
p. cm
Includes index.
1. Real estate investment. 2. Women in real estate. 3. Women capitalists and financiers.
4. Women real estate agents. 5. Real estate business. I. Nelson-Bell, Karen. II. Title.
HD1382.5.A388   2007
332.63'24082—dc22   2006049778

ISBN-13: 978-0-7432-9784-4
ISBN-10:   0-7432-9784-9

Note to Readers

This publication contains the opinions and ideas of its authors. It is sold with the understanding that neither the authors nor the publisher is engaged in rendering legal, tax, investment, insurance, financial, accounting, or other professional advice or services. If the reader requires such advice or services, a competent professional should be consulted. Relevant laws vary from state to state. The strategies outlined in this book may not be suitable for every individual, and are not guaranteed or warranted to produce any particular results.

No warranty is made with respect to the accuracy or completeness of the information contained herein, and both the authors and the publisher specifically disclaim any responsibility for any liability, loss or risk, personal or otherwise, which is incurred as a consequence, directly or indirectly, of the use and application of any of the contents of this book. As the internet is a rapidly morphing technology, the authors assume no responsibility for internet addresses, as not only may the addresses change, but the content may change as well. All addresses are correct at the time of printing.

*This book is dedicated to my late husband, Duncan Guertin,
who demonstrated splendidly that the best way to live a life
is to serve others.*

Contents

Contents

Contents

Contents

Foreword

by Mark Victor Hansen

Karen Nelson Bell and I met in 2001, and I watched her career bloom under the tutelage of Robert Allen and myself, as well as other mentors at our Enlightened Millionaire Institute. She became pretty well known in that environment because she was always popping up to receive another award for excellence and achievement. I referred to her as the Roger Bannister* of real estate, because just as track legend Bannister set the bar when he broke the four-minute mile, Karen set the speed record for ascension from "out-of-work" to "millionaire."

But I really got to know the true essence of "KNB" when she joined the "Inner Circle," a group of 101 people who study, travel, experiment, and do good works with Bob and me at a very personal level for a period of a year. She demonstrated over and over again her willingness to help others, the very quality that the Inner Circle holds most valuable.

If this world is going to change for the better, it's going to take

*Roger Bannister will always be remembered as the man who ran the "Miracle Mile" in 1954. According to *Time* magazine, "When he was asked to explain that first four-minute mile—and the art of record breaking—he answered with original directness: 'It's the ability to take more out of yourself than you've got.'"

people who are willing to do what governments can't or won't do, and it's going to take people who have either money or time or both to implement the changes. Karen's highest purpose is to inspire and enable you to reach your own good and noble goals. She knows that the causes start close to home. Get food on the table. Get a roof over your head. Take care of your children and your family first. Then, as you are able, reach out and help somebody in your neighborhood or at your church or school. Along the way, by all means, buy some "thingamabobs" to celebrate your newfound financial prowess.

But reaching your dreams of freedom, financially and spiritually, will open up your control of your time. KNB, as your "5-Minute Mentor," will show you how to tame time so that you will one day concurrently have the finances *and* the time to do all the things you dream.

Karen, Bob, and I share a love of language, but she and Bob haven't tried to be fancy here. She just wants everyone to "get it." She wants your success as much or more than you do, because she has her eye on the grand landscape, the far horizon. When Bob and I said we wanted to create a million millionaires, KNB said, "I'm in. I'll help."

How can I explain the satisfaction I feel when I see a student of mine who has accomplished so much in such a short time turning around and sharing it with others? Wealth creates a unique power and energy that can accomplish great deeds. And we live in a time when great deeds are a vital necessity to the very survival of our world. I'm happy to see Karen Nelson Bell taking up our crusade as if it were her own.

Maybe one day you'll be joining us in our Inner Circle. You hold in your hands a book that can ignite your heart and empower you to reach your own worthy aspirations. I look forward to meeting you!

A Special Word

from Robert G. Allen

The most treasured moment in the life of any mentor comes when a student not only demonstrates a highly professional application of the subject at hand, but when that student also takes the subject one step further to somehow enhance one's own body of work. Such a moment has come for me now as I watch what protégé Karen Nelson Bell has wrought from her five years under my tutelage. She is no longer my student. Now she is my colleague.

KNB has seen a way to bring my *Nothing Down* brand to women with a gender-specific focus that couldn't be crafted by a man. As a woman, her filters allow her to distill the essence of my teachings in a way that is uniquely suited to the female student. As I collaborated with her on early chapters of *Nothing Down for Women,* I found myself fascinated, as if I were reading about the subject for the first time.

To be candid, Karen's unwavering loyalty pleases me greatly, because instead of "borrowing" my work and claiming it as her own (as others have), she chose to honor the *Nothing Down* tradition I started over twenty-five years ago. In doing so, she has invigorated my own vision of my brand.

Wait until you hear her story—the story I had the privilege to watch unfold. In understanding her journey, you'll also come to appreciate why this book came into being. A woman's way of approaching the topic at hand is indeed different from a man's way. In fact, the science behind gender differences in cognitive learning guided the format of the book in your hands. In an early meeting, I asked Karen to identify why this book would be different and what made it uniquely perfect for women. She laughed disarmingly and pointed out that my question was very, well, manlike. She had never analyzed the why and how of the differences, because she simply lived her story from the only vantage point she could, as a woman. It hadn't occurred to her to prepare an overview of why her own investing was, well, womanlike. It wasn't until she was steeped in the preparation of the *Nothing Down for Women* manuscript that she began to research what elements contributed to her astonishing success. You'll enjoy her story as well as her twenty-twenty hindsight.

By the way, as Karen relates the story, she forgets to brag, and I think you should know that in five years, she amassed a portfolio of real estate valued at over fifteen million dollars. Not only that, she demonstrated uncommon generosity with her money and her time. She clearly duplicated our concepts of "enlightened investing," and for that, I'm personally gratified.

You hold in your hands not only a book, but a portal to some remarkable resources. Sprinkled throughout you'll find references to www.ND4W.com, where we've placed abundant relevant materials that will assist you as you move beyond just reading into actual action.

Karen and her late husband taught for the Enlightened Millionaire Institute as well as for the Robert Allen Institute. She demonstrated admirable capabilities as teacher, persuader, and leader. I trust you'll find her charismatic personality as engaging as her audiences do, and I hope that, ultimately, her clarity of style as well as her clarity of purpose will inspire and enable you to reach your own good and noble goals.

I'm delighted to coauthor this book with a woman who cares so profoundly about your own future.

How Losing My Job Turned Me into a Millionaire

from Karen Nelson Bell

You're probably anxious to get right into the how-to section of this book, but if you'll allow me a few short minutes, I'd like to tell you some of the humbling (and possibly inspiring) experiences I've had along the road to real-estate riches. If you'll hang in there with me for the next few pages, I promise you nitty-gritty investing action coming right up.

In this intro, you'll see how things in life can go so right and then so wrong, and then so right again. The rebound factor has been extremely important in my own life, and maybe if you are having a tough time right now, you'll find a story familiar to your own that will help in the big picture. If you're having financial challenges, I've been there. If you're having relationship challenges, I've been there too. If you're having other personal difficulties, you'll see you're not alone. I've had plenty.

In just a few pages, you'll be diving into details of real-estate investing, but right now I'd like to show you why I believe I've earned the right to be your mentor.

This story has two parts: (1) how I lost my job and got inspired to try real-estate investing, and (2) exactly how I made that first million. (Nobody ever asks me how I made the second.)

Have we met? My full name is Karen Nelson Bell, and you might have seen me somewhere on the Las Vegas Strip performing as a pianist-singer-dancer since 1967. Because I had been raised on classical music, my parents were shocked when I went to Vegas on vacation and immediately got a job opening for comedian Don Rickles in the famous old Casbar Lounge at the Sahara Hotel. Later I enjoyed playing piano and touring with singer Paul Anka for two years, and then performed under the stage name "Kelly Stevens" for a decade in a successful lounge group (our first album resurfaced recently and sold out on the internet). After touring all over the world, I started working as a musical director in the eighties. Then in the nineties, I was hired to create the first country show in Las Vegas at the Aladdin Hotel, "Country Tonite."

If you ever got by to see the show, you know we had a lot of fun! I loved my job, and I thought it would last forever, since I was the creator and ultimately became the producer/director as well. However, I was still an employee working at a J.O.B. (Just Over Broke), working for the people who actually owned the show. When you work for someone else, you end up using *your* talents and energies to make someone else rich. In fact, the show I had created out of thin air made millions and millions of dollars for *other* people!

How Losing My Job Made Me a Millionaire!

I thought my job was secure because I had such a high-up "important" position. What I never considered was that the owners might sell the company and that the new buyers had their *own* producer/director. I did resign, but only moments ahead of a pink slip! I have the privilege to say I resigned or retired, but the truth is that out of work is still out of work, no matter which way you got there.

My late husband, Duncan Guertin, had been working for the show too, doing multimedia productions. So not only was *my* job gone, Duncan's job was gone too. In short order, we had shifted from having two nice paychecks and the *illusion* of affluence to being out of work. We had been living a "rented lifestyle."

Multiple Streams of Income

That August, we went to San Diego for a week, and our idea of a nice trip was always to take a few books and go reading somewhere in nature. We each took three books to the beach, and mine were *Harry Potter and the Sorcerer's Stone, Who Moved My Cheese?,* and *Multiple Streams of Income.* Well, books can change lives, and Robert G. Allen's hit *Multiple Streams of Income* changed mine. When I read it, I thought he had written it straight from him to me. I called his office and alternately begged and demanded that Mr. Allen take me on as a protégé. Something deep in my soul knew this was going to be a great adventure.

I joined his Protégé Program on November 1, and I threw myself into the studies. Everything my teachers suggested, I did without question. I learned the formulas and systems cold. Duncan and I slammed ourselves full bore ahead into putting those formulas into practice, and after resigning from our jobs on January 1, 2001, by March 9—only 129 days after we became protégés—we became millionaires, acquiring over $1 million in equity (the difference between the value of what you own and the cost of what you owe on it).

Identity Theft

Since then, I've worried that my story doesn't have enough "downside" to it. It seems like I don't really have a true *before* story; I only have the *after* story. After all, when I started, I was doing very well. I had a job I loved and was in fact passionate about. I made what I thought at that time was pretty darn good money. I didn't realize that it was an illusion. I actually had very, very little to show for those years of doing well.

What I did have was a wonderful sense of my own importance. Little did I know that it really was a false security.

When I lost the title of director . . . when I lost the title of producer . . . and when I stopped being a musician on a daily basis . . . it was as if someone had come along and erased me. I have experienced identity theft in the normal sense, when my credit was used by someone else pretending to be me. I can tell you firsthand that the experience of losing my work identity was a thousandfold more debilitating.

We are all so wrapped up in what we do, that what we do becomes who we are and defines us. My identity was "the producer," "the one you go to when you need help," "the one who had jobs for everybody." My identity was "the one who won awards for creating standing ovations and created happiness for audiences of all ages."

Now that I had lost my job, I was . . . how can I say this? I was just Karen. I was Duncan's wife, and yet Duncan had lost his job too, so that identity faltered as well.

I would find myself sobbing for no reason at all. Well, actually, in my own heart, I had a reason. I was unbearably sad. It went on for months. I felt as if I were grieving over a lost loved one. Now, looking back, it *was* a lost loved one. I loved that identity of the "important person."

It's embarrassing to think I was so wrapped up in the impression I was trying to make. Most people hope that they can be valuable by being decent and kind. Now I had to see if I had that value in *me*. I understood what the millions of people who've lost their jobs through downsizing or through the change in an industry feel. When we discover that what we *are,* what we *have,* and what we *do* is no longer valued, it's devastating,

That is identity theft of the highest magnitude.

Exactly How I Did It (Millionaire-hood)

We did have a tiny savings set aside. We also had good credit. We had spent the last four years digging ourselves out of the hole. We were so proud to say that we had no consumer debt.

So when Duncan told me that we were going to use other people's money to buy properties, that we were going to go into debt again, I said, "Oh no we're not." It wasn't until gurus Tom Painter, John Childers, and Robert Allen ganged up on me to explain the power of leverage that I got it. Duncan tried to explain it to me, but that was like having your spouse try teaching you to drive a car. I had to hear it from Bob, Tom, and John in order to have the courage to use the equity in our house to acquire more properties.

We learned how to invest with no money and with no credit, but our little savings and our fairly good credit made it possible for us to move quickly.

When we first started, Duncan and I owned three properties. It happened almost by accident. One was the house that I had bought when I was a young woman. We lived in it together when we first got married. Then when my father became ill, he asked us to take over his house. He came to live with us, and we rented out his property. That was a *Nothing Down* deal. He just gave it to us. Now as I look back on it, I see it was an example of how illness can create a motivated seller.

There came a time when Duncan and I wanted to move into a home that we would create together and call all our own. When we moved into our new house, we didn't even have to get a loan, because the seller offered us her own private financing. It was that very house that gave us our nest egg with which to start investing. We got an equity line before we lost our jobs, thinking that we would never again be able to get a loan. Of course, now we know that you can get a loan whether you have a job or not. (You'll be learning how later.)

That equity line was worth just over $100,000, and we learned that you could turn $100,000 into several million dollars' worth of real estate very nicely.

During the first month, we bought a batch of business cards. They weren't especially good cards. We hadn't learned at that time how to create great ones. They were just ordinary business cards, but Duncan began giving them out as if he were on fire. He gave out more than a thousand business cards in November alone. He gave a card to a person at the doctor's office; that person gave it to a friend of hers at church. The friend from church called us up and said, "We're in trouble, we're in foreclosure, can you help us?" That was the beginning of our first-ever deal since becoming students with Robert Allen in his Protégé Program.

Let me tell you about the deal. The house was huge—seven bedrooms, five bathrooms, three fireplaces, pool, and Jacuzzi . . . three-car garage, 5,000 square feet, a little over three years old. The seller was in foreclosure with his second mortgage, and we were able to negotiate a deal with the second mortgage holder, so that instead of paying the mortgage off at $35,000, we paid him only $13,000. We ended up refinancing the property, at which time we got $18,000 cash back at the closing. We had used money from our equity line (so it was other people's money, the bank's money) to catch up the back payments. Therefore, not only did we make the $18,000, the property had $75,000 of equity. It was worth $350,000, and we bought it for $275,000. Today, it's worth almost $800,000. That was from a little business card and word of mouth.

The second deal we did was also word of mouth, from our attorney. He introduced us to some people from Idaho who had a property on a lake near Coeur d'Alene. They had pictures of it, showing that they had been working on renovating this property. They had run out of money due to personal problems and couldn't finish the renovation. They had an appraisal for it at $300,000, and the appraiser said that if we fixed it up, it would be worth $700,000. Wow! That meant that we would have $400,000 of equity minus whatever it cost us to repair it. (There's more to the story in a minute.)

The third deal we did was the story that put us on the map. It was the story that turned us into millionaires. We found this particular house through a Realtor. She said, "You know, I think this just fits your vision. It requires somebody with the right eye to see that this is a sleeper."

The house was a luxury mansion appraised at $1.2 million. It was in a gated community on the first tee of a golf course. It had an absolutely gorgeous structure, but it had been allowed to go into complete disrepair. It was vacant, and the former owner had let the grounds become covered in weeds. Vines were growing all over the entryway. There was cheap tile in the foyer, ugly colors in the cabinetry, and orange and black marble floor to ceiling in the master bathroom. I almost went into a dizzy spell when I first saw it. No wonder it had been sitting on the market for six months. The owner was a motivated seller, because she had already moved on to a bigger, fancier mansion, and was tired of paying the $8,000-per-month payments.

We decided to offer the owner a lowball bid, just to get her used to the idea that she wasn't going to get a lot of money for this house, since it needed so much in the way of repairs. It was a gigantic luxury fixer-upper.

We went in with our first offer of $805,000 on the $1,200,000 house.

Instead of a counteroffer, she said, "Um, OK."

What a shock to us to find that she accepted our offer! Oh, my gosh! Now what would we do?

When we finally closed on that deal, we realized that maybe, just maybe, we had crossed the million-dollar mark in equity.

The day we signed was March 9, which happened to be the day

of our twelfth wedding anniversary. When we walked out of the escrow office, having finished signing the papers, I turned to Duncan and said, "You know, honey, I think it's possible that we might have a million dollars in equity right now. Wouldn't that be some special anniversary present?! Let's go home and find out."

We put together a little spreadsheet of what properties we had bought. We discovered that if you included the house we lived in, we had crossed the million-dollar mark. It didn't mean that we had a paycheck yet. It didn't mean that we'd made up the income we lost from our jobs yet. But we were millionaires. It had such a beautiful sound to it. What a great anniversary present that was! The traditional symbol for the twelfth anniversary is silk, but I think it should be changed to houses! In fact, the symbol for the forty-first anniversary is land, and for the forty-second, it's real estate!

For the next few months, we lived off of the cash-back-at-closing checks that we had received from both properties: $18,000 from the first property and $16,000 from the million-dollar mansion.

We put an ad in the paper saying that we needed $100,000 to renovate a luxury home, and we received many responses. I was amazed that people wanted to give us money. I hadn't realized they were so happy to be making 12 percent interest instead of keeping their money in a 1 percent CD at the bank. We began fixing up the house, which became our new job.

I don't think there are any gurus out there teaching that you should live off of your cash-back-at-closing checks. You should actually be reinvesting that money back into real estate. But we were in a desperate situation. We still didn't have cash flow, so we moved out of the little house we were living in (the one I had bought so many years ago) and moved into the big seven-bedroom house, knowing that we could rent out our smaller home for a good profit. By March 9 we had gone from having the house we lived in, my dad's house, and my old house to having six properties! We lived in one, rented three, were renovating the mansion, and were getting ready to renovate the one up in Idaho.

Then the worst possible thing happened: We found out that the appraiser in Idaho had issued a fraudulent appraisal. The property wasn't actually worth $300,000. It wouldn't have an after-repairs value of $700,000. No, it was actually ready for demolition! Demolition!

The people had lied to us, and because we didn't have a team in place in Idaho, we had no way of knowing that the photographs lied.

What we thought we were going to turn into a wonderful vacation property, a vacation business, making tons and tons of money, was actually a terrible mistake.

Replacing lost income from our jobs was now a huge, pressing issue to us. We were able to walk away from the Idaho disaster with about a $10,000 loss (and with our dignity and pride severely tarnished). We realized then that the only mistakes we had made so far happened when we violated what Robert Allen had so clearly instructed. He always says to buy properties within a fifty-mile radius of your own hometown. Furthermore, he suggests that you get acquainted with the particular zip code of a particular five-mile radius. Get to know it extremely well. We had violated that rule, and we were paying the price.

A side note: I think we got cocky because we had done so well in one aspect. Bob says that you shouldn't become discouraged in the beginning of your investing career if you get turned down on your offers at first, and that you don't get to be discouraged until you've made at least one hundred offers. Well, we got a yes to our first offer, a yes to our second offer, a yes to our third offer, and a yes to our fourth offer. It wasn't until the fifth offer that we got a no, and then it was followed by a long string of yesses. I'm sure those statistics made us think we were infallible. Wrong!

Later on that year, when we finished renovating the big mansion, we discovered we'd violated another one of his rules, which was to buy houses in the price range that people can afford. Right when we were ready to sell the big house and reap our $300,000 in profit, the tragedy of 9/11 took place. What happened on 9/11 changed so many people's lives in such devastating ways, that as I look back on it, our problem of not being able to sell a house was infinitesimal compared to the pain and suffering brought on by that terrible day.

We were stuck with an $8,000-a-month payment that we had no way of paying except to continue eating up the $100,000 we had borrowed for the renovation and carrying costs. Finally, in November we were able to find someone who would lease-option the house, and we leased it for exactly the amount of our payments. At least we didn't have to pay the mortgage ourselves now. But it was very scary. When that renter turned out to be a very naughty renter who never again paid on time, we learned what it's like to have an alligator (investors' slang for a property that eats you alive).

Shortly after that, we began investing in more reasonably priced properties, and we quickly gained back what we had lost from the

Idaho disaster. We had gone down below the million-dollar mark and then risen back up again. Very quickly thereafter, by the end of the first year, we had a dozen properties.

We were still living off of the refinancing of properties, which is not the right way to do it. We felt very uncomfortable when people would congratulate us on our millionaire status, knowing that we were still having cash-flow issues. It wasn't until a year later that we resolved the matter of having enough cash flow and began to have the mind-set that everything was going to be OK.

We spent the whole first year being millionaires but still being so very, *very* worried about money. I wondered if other millionaires worried about money. Were *multi*millionaires worried about money? Could you have a huge net worth and still not have enough cash at hand for the things that carried you through the month?

I heard Oprah Winfrey say that she didn't feel rich until just a few years ago, long after she had in fact become very, very wealthy. It took her that long to stop worrying about money.

Well, that's the story of how we became millionaires in four months and nine days. The record has since been broken by new investor students who made their millions in ninety days or less. I know it can be done. I could do it again too if I had to start from scratch, even faster. We know one gentleman, also a student of Robert Allen's, Greg Warr, who made his first million in one single deal.

We've all been taught that "if it sounds too good to be true, it is." But some things *are* exactly good enough to be true. Robert Allen's gift of explaining *Nothing Down* investing in ways that lay people can understand (and implement easily) isn't too good to be true. It's exactly good enough to be true. It was for me! And remember, "checks don't lie."

If you want to see a fictionalized account of a handful of our real deals, read the right side of *The One Minute Millionaire*. Here's what Bob and Mark wrote on page 379:

"We also want to thank the thousands of our students in dozens of cities in North America who served as the true 'guinea pigs' for this book. Specifically, to Karen Nelson Bell and her husband, Duncan Guertin. All of the fictional properties that the heroine, Michelle, bought were patterned after actual real-estate deals that Karen and Duncan did on their way to becoming real Enlightened Millionaires. Thanks, guys!"

The Devastation of Death or Divorce
(I Never Dreamed I'd Be a Widow)

In the dedication to this book, I referred to my "late" husband. He left this earth too soon. Duncan was only fifty-one years old, and he had never been sick a day in his life. On October 11, 2005, he climbed California's Mt. Whitney with twenty-seven friends, and one month later, on November 11, he passed away, to climb some other mountain on some other adventure. Everyone said he was the very last person they would think could possibly be claimed by cancer. He didn't smoke, he loved to hike, he ate fairly well, and he was the single most positive person anyone ever met. He loved life, he loved helping his thousands of students to learn real estate, he loved me well, and he was poised for even more glorious adventures in his work as an investor, a developer, and a speaker. I miss him every hour of every day. If you are an unwilling widow like me, or a divorcée, perhaps, I pray that you have some financial resources to help you through. The women who have to suffer their grief while working through financial devastation can hardly find time to mourn. They're struggling to survive at the most fundamental levels. If you don't already have some resources in place, then it is all the more vital that you carry forward with this book.

If you're married, and you haven't begun to prepare for the loss of a spouse, I hope you will be inspired (and empowered) by this book to prepare for the stormy day when you may have to cope with death or divorce. Be certain that even though your money umbrella can't turn sorrow into joy, financial security can ease the burden of the practicalities of life's tragedies. Pledge to prepare now, because none of us ever thinks the day will come.

I am so thankful that Duncan and I had already put in place the resources for our future. And thank God we had already embarked on what Bob and Mark call "enlightened wealth." We had begun putting into practice the notion that a person can actually accelerate the arrival of his or her own abundance by consistently giving to others first. Most books on money will advise you to "pay yourself first," and that's excellent advice. But I like Bob and Mark's admonition even better: Pay the *universe* first. Pay with money or with time, give to your church or simply to a neighbor in need.

Bob and I were talking one afternoon, and he said, "Giving your way to wealth is counterintuitive, and that's why women get it quicker than men. Women *are* givers. They always have been. Giving is part of their nature.

"There's a reason why many women are poor. They sometimes possess the character 'flaw' of always giving to others and never thinking of themselves. They're always thinking of others. With our style of doing deals, they can reverse that computation to where helping others enriches and nourishes *them* too."

Bob and I believe that your higher power, however you view that concept, knows that because you are kind and giving, you would be a trustworthy steward of "a good deal."

The last year of Duncan's life was rich and rewarding, and I'm convinced it was largely because we had come to understand the incredible pleasure in being financially able to reach out and extend a hand where it was needed. I look forward to *you* having the same reward.

Thank you for letting me tell you this story. These pages have been about me, but the rest of the book is all about you and your story. Let's get going!

Everybody can be great because everybody can serve. You only need a heart full of grace, a soul generated by love.

—MARTIN LUTHER KING JR.

Introduction:
Nothing Down for Blondes

(Why Women Make Better
Investors Than Men)

When I told my friends I wanted to call this book *Nothing Down for Blondes,* they wouldn't hear of it. They informed me that they were highly offended (blondes, brunettes, and redheads alike). However, blonde Teresa said that even though the title put her off, when she read further, she got the point. It's much more offensive to me that there are still millions of women who have been convinced they can't. Can't what? Just CAN'T, with all caps. Can't do this, can't have that, can't understand, can't accomplish. It's my least favorite word in the English language.

The title above isn't meant to offend, and it isn't another joke about the inadequacies of the blonde mentality. I'm blonde by choice and proud of it. This introduction is about the tacit agreement of many women that they aren't good enough, smart enough, resourceful enough, or clever enough to build a financial fortress for a safe future. They're wrong.

In fact, the very opposite is true.

Precisely because many, many women have been trained to believe some mythical brand of nonsense, I've written *Nothing Down for Women* in a special way. First of all, I don't think you're "stupid," regardless of what any book series might tell you. Would you enjoy

1

reading *Nothing Down for Dumb Women*? While I don't think you're a dummy or an idiot, I *do* think you don't have enough time.

Women I've met all over the country have told me they're exhausted physically, mentally, emotionally, spiritually, and financially. From the industrious women who have corporate executive positions to single moms working two and three jobs to make ends meet, we're all running out of time. I hear the same story from women who are *full-time* moms, working harder than ever before.

You've even told me that you don't have time to read this book!

Well, I hear you loud and clear. So here I am to the rescue: I'm going to be your 5-Minute Mentor (you can refer to me as your "5MM" if you want to)! In fact, just to save time, instead of calling me Karen Nelson Bell, you can call me by my favorite nickname, "KNB." Anything to save another minute!

I think of myself as a "time tamer." My staff has to run fast to keep up with me, and I'm two or three times their age! Taming time may be the best skill you can learn, not just for real-estate investing, but for life itself.

This book comes to you in easily digested portions you can enjoy in little bites. In fact, when one woman told me she was too busy to learn how to invest, the following conversation ensued:

"I haven't even got enough time to read your little five-minute blasts."

"Well, do you go to the bathroom?"

[Puzzled] "Well, yes, of course."

"Do you do it every day?"

"Yes."

"Sometimes twice a day?"

"Yes."

"Would you ever go a day without doing so?"

"No."

"Could you take the book with you?"

"I suppose so."

"Ah, good. Then you can actually get ten minutes of reading done every day, right?"

"Uh-huh."

Did you know that most people read at the same rate they speak, which is 250 words per minute? That's why I've imposed a 1,250 word limit on myself (1,250 words = five minutes). If I can't get the point across in five minutes, the point hasn't been broken down to its simplicities. And that's what *Nothing Down for Women* is all about: getting to the essence of each concept.

This really is a book for beginners. It doesn't matter if you're already successful and looking for a way to maximize your bulging bank account, or you're trying to decide whether to buy Hamburger Helper versus hairspray because you can't afford both. In either case, you're very likely stressed to the max for time, so I'm not going to make it worse. Five minutes is all I ask from you.

Not only that, I'm going to make it easy on your eyes: no long paragraphs with endless blocks of text, but, rather, short sections with easy captions and little headlines to help you identify sections when you go back to reread and highlight. It'll probably drive my editor crazy, but I can write this book to show you how smart *I* am, or I can write this book to show you how smart *you* are! Anything I can do to make it work for you in a way that you can go out and apply what you're reading is the method I'm gonna use. The end result may or may not be fashionable in literary circles, but *you'll* look good with your new MBA (Massive Bank Account)!

You might be interested to know how Bob and I coauthored this book. The process began when I read and assimilated his body of work in a short period of time, reading and rereading everything he ever wrote and immediately putting it into practice. I was a fan. And why wouldn't I be? He turned me into a millionaire. With his permission, I began writing a book about his techniques, strategies, and philosophies, filtered through the eyes of a woman. I used his own words, his famous slogans and mottoes, and quotes right out of his own pages. Then I added my own slant, from the point of view of someone who has succeeded by modeling and molding his training to suit the woman investor.

When we finally sat down together to assemble the book, he often found himself reading his own writing where I quoted him. I asked him to please bring his keen intuition to the writing process to let all our beautiful women readers hear his voice responding to my feminine interpretations of his teachings. You'll see his cogent comments sprinkled throughout in the form of "Bobservations."

Our senior editor asked us, "Why can't women just read *Nothing Down?*" That reminds me of a song lyric in *My Fair Lady:* "Why can't a woman be more like . . . a *man!*" In the very first chapter, you'll easily perceive the answer: We women absorb and apply differently.

Even though I don't know you, my new friend, there are certain things that I can intuit to be true: You may be an intelligent, educated, articulate person, perhaps even an intellectual, with an uncommon awareness of language and vocabulary, plus possibly an easy command of numbers. Your friends and family may be equally gifted. Or you may be a woman who never graduated from high school. Never mind which end of the spectrum you view yourself.

My own personal goal is to bridge the gap between the elite and the common, and to make very clear and simple the things that "intellectuals" may not even recognize as complicated.

In truth, *Nothing Down for Women* isn't just for women, it's for people everywhere who are either intimidated or frustrated by subjects they've been told were complex. At least 40 percent of my students currently using the how-to portion of the book are men, and the response from both genders is overwhelmingly a monumental sigh of relief. People tell me that *Nothing Down for Women* is the first time they've really "gotten it," and many of these people have already been studying real-estate investing for quite a while.

Nothing Down for Women is a codification of Bob's life's work, distilled down to the simplest essences.

It's a sad statistic that many girls are still persuaded that they are less able in every way. There are women who are intimidated before they even open to the first page of a real-estate book. They assume it will be too hard, too confusing, or too math-centric. You may even be one of them.

Or you may be one of the rare women who railed against the low expectations and rose to accomplish great things. You may be a smart, clever, determined woman who made things go right against the odds. You're in the minority, but we love and welcome you in this book.

The pressures on women to be everything, do everything, and have everything result in the fact that now women are multitasking so furiously, there's not one minute left in the day. Delivering the data simply and in short, digestible bits may be the single most appealing reason why women find *Nothing Down for Women* so tasty.

My late husband was an exceedingly bright man, and he had an easy familiarity with the language of real-estate investing. As we taught side by side for four years, I would often have to clean up misunderstood words for the students because he had forgotten that the language he loved was unfamiliar to most. For the students, a simple word like *equity* could cause their eyes to glaze over.

What some people might call "dumbing down" I call "simplifying and clarifying." What may be already conceptually accessible to everyone in Bob's original book may in fact be patently unavailable to countless women (and men) because of their educational limitations. But they nevertheless yearn for a better life through financial independence. This book can empower them in ways that more "sophisticated-sounding" authors will never be able to do. *Nothing Down for Women* is not for elitists. It's for the common denominator of ordinary women. It's for plain people who respond to plain talk. I'm here to demystify the confusion and controversy that can fog up *Nothing Down*–style investing.

Don't Call Me an Expert

Would you be surprised to learn that I don't want people to label me an expert? I'd rather be known as "the megamultitasker." Women are statistically known to be better multitaskers than men, and it's probably because from the dawn of time, we've had a baby on the right hip and our bow and arrow on the other—suddenly we're multitasking.

Some interviewers have called me "the Suze Orman of real estate." I wish I had her depth and years of training. I think my title would more appropriately be "the Renaissance Woman of Real Estate," because I'm so interested in so many different things in this life. Maybe you are too. Maybe real estate will become a passion for you, or maybe it will become a means to a beautiful end, so you can follow *all* your passions.

Believe me, some day some interviewer will challenge me with a question that I won't know the answer to, and I'll have to answer deftly: "Here's how I would *find* the answer to that question." I'm not a professor of real estate, and I'm not "the world's leading expert on real-estate investing." I'm a megamultitasking musician, public speaker, TV producer, and oh, yes, real-estate investor. Doesn't that give you hope that you, who surely are multitasking too, can find your own piece of success in this world of *Nothing Down*? We can both be renaissance women.

Here's what I am an expert on: my own story, my own journey, my own path through the world of investing in single-family homes, based on what I learned from Robert Allen and his friends. I'm happy to share with you how you could possibly improve your personal finances even though you're working two jobs, taking care of three kids, and trying to learn ballroom dancing all at the same time.

Somehow, I've got to find a way to inspire you, or you won't have the desire to move forward. Then I must find a way to enable you to move forward, because inspiration can wear off if you don't have any means to act on it.

That's the game for me; I inherited it from Robert Allen: inspiring and empowering ordinary people to reach extraordinary goals. Ladies, I'm ready when you are!

I'm not offended by all the dumb-blonde jokes because I know I'm not dumb—I also know that I'm not blonde!

—DOLLY PARTON

THE GENDER BLENDER

(Scientific Reasons Why Women Make Better Investors than Men)

It wasn't until Bob asked me why this book is different from a man's book that I gave it any thought at all. "Where's the science behind gender differentials in cognitive learning?" I had figured, I'm a woman, I did this real-estate stuff, women will "get" me. I hadn't thought to ask why it was for women.

To answer his question, I decided to research whether or not there were any real differences in abilities that I could say made this book necessary. Here's the first thing I came up with: Among the experts in the science of gender differences, nobody agrees with anybody.

The simplicity of the disagreement among the experts boils down to this: Until the women's movement came along, it was socially acceptable to say that men and women were created *un*equal. After the movement, it became socially appropriate to say that our upbringing and socialization falsely created the inequalities. Now the pendulum has swung to a predominance of experts saying that men and women are in fact hardwired on a cellular, hormonal basis to have different abilities. What is or is not politically correct fuels the fire between camps. The real argument boils down to nature versus nurture. Neither side disagrees that men and women are different, but they disagree on how we got that way.

Where do I stand personally? I don't have a stand. I can observe that I was different from my husband. I also notice I have some strong characteristics within my womanly personality, while my manly husband was easily in touch with his "feminine side." But I don't know what that *means*.

Today, the emerging science called sociobiology (the study of how behavior is explained by our genes and our evolution) has sophisticated technology available that lets researchers understand amazing details about the human brain. The scientists have spent a lot of energy looking at the differences between men and women, girls and boys, girl babies and boy babies.

Whereas polite society wants to think that we all have the same skills and aptitudes, ironically, science has just turned up new evidence quite to the contrary. And it's got the shiny toys to prove its theories, with brain-scanning computers and genetic-research tools light years ahead of even ten years ago.

Science has irrefutably determined that the two sexes are indeed fundamentally different. What has that got to do with us, we intrepid real-estate investing ladies? It's entirely possible that some of those differences mean we are actually more able, more capable, in some important areas such as verbal and nonverbal communication, and intuition.

Various researchers have noted that women are possessed of decidedly more acute senses than men. In fact, they've revealed that "women's intuition" isn't a myth; it boils down to the female's talent for observing tiny details and alterations in others' appearance and actions. The scientists tell us that our senses pick up and analyze nonverbal communication, and our brain's ability to rapidly transfer between hemispheres makes us more able to integrate and decipher all the signals, whether visual or verbal.

All the researchers agreed that women actually hear better than men, and that we're especially good at distinguishing very high-pitched noises. Our brain is grooved in to hear a baby crying during the night. Not only that, women have better ability to differentiate tone changes in voices. Pitch and volume perceptions allow women to hear emotional changes as well. Often, women think men don't listen, and compared to us, it apparently is true! When success in a business depends on listening, as it does in real-estate investing, women reign. These hearing advantages contribute to the notion of "women's intuition" and are part of the reasons why women are capable of "reading between the lines." Go ahead and trust your women's intuition in your investing career. You've got science backing you up!

Have you heard that we are either left-brained or right-brained? Our estrogen causes nerve cells to grow more pathways within the brain and between the two sides. Many studies say that the more connections you have, the more fluent your ability to speak. With that abundance of fiber connections for faster relay of data between the hemispheres, women can make many fast, accurate judgments about people and situations on an intuitive level. Aren't you glad to know you don't have to wonder whether or not to trust your instincts?

Here's an interesting point you may have thought was a negative trait: Research has determined that women are more indirect than men. We're always trying to create rapport with other people, avoiding aggressive, confrontational interactions. We love harmony. This gentler style of communication is especially helpful when dealing with sellers traumatized by a pending foreclosure, for example.

Do these gender differences actually exist? Today's science says yes. I don't necessarily like thinking that my personality, abilities, and successes have got only to do with hormones and genetics; I personally live by the thought that those characteristics are driven by the *spirit*. However, I get a kick out of hearing that my women's intuition isn't imaginary.

Some people will have a hard time seeing the correlation between these assorted facts and women's superior abilities in the people business we call real-estate investing. Those people are (you guessed it) men!

Your income can only grow to the extent you do!

—T. HARV EKER, AUTHOR, *SECRETS OF THE MILLIONAIRE MIND*

'Cause I'm a W.O.M.A.N

(You Got a Problem with That?)

When I was a teenager, Peggy Lee had a hit song, "I'm a Woman," which boasted about all the ways that a woman was amazingly powerful. It finished with "'cause I'm a woman, W.O.M.A.N." With this classic ringing in my ears, and with my parents' constant reassurance that I could do anything that I set my mind to, I entered my young-adult years blissfully unaware that I would ever have a need to be "liberated."

I've been blessed all my life *because* I was a W.O.M.A.N. I've traveled all over the world, dined with presidents and celebrities. I've lived and worked all over Africa, Southeast Asia, and Scandinavia, just because I was a W.O.M.A.N. And finally, I have a chance to write this unusual book from this unusual point of view, and once again it's because I'm a W.O.M.A.N. So what makes real-estate investing so especially good for women?

Well, I'm going to speak in generalities for a bit. Generalities are never completely correct, but if you remember that they're generalities, you'll see what I believe are the benefits women bring to the *Nothing Down* system of investing. These points are different than the "science" we discussed in the last chapter.

In general, women care more about human issues, and in this system of investing, it's all about people. It's all about solving problems for people who can't solve them for themselves. Women traditionally position themselves as nurturers, and that's what this whole *Nothing Down* stuff is all about: helping people through tough times. It's about helping that desperate seller find a place he can actually afford to live in instead of the place he's losing to foreclosure.

I'll never forget the first time we had a "Buy a House Boot Camp" weekend, and all of the students attending got the chance to listen to the negotiations with a wonderful woman we'll call "Janie." She was kind enough to allow us all into her home while we figured out how to help her out of her pending foreclosure. Everyone was sitting around her living room while she sat at the kitchen table with her back to the students.

Her situation was terribly sad. Her husband had discovered he only had a month to live; he was dying from cancer. In a crazy and regrettable response, he went out and maxed out all their credit cards, drove to the casinos and gambled it all away. If he weren't already dying, Janie could have killed him!

For some strange reason, one thing Janie wanted most was to keep her brand-new refrigerator. She wanted to take it with her to her daughter's house, where she would stay until she could join her husband back in Kentucky, where he was being treated near his children.

I said, "Janie, look, we usually keep the refrigerator, but we can see it's so important to you, of course, you just go ahead and take it with you. In fact, we'll even help you move. If you'll pack up all your things, we'll hire a crew and come put everything on our truck and help you get it over to your sister's house."

"Well, how much will that cost me?"

"Nothing, Janie, we're going to do that for free. You don't have to pay a thing. We're going to help you move because you clearly need the help. It's free."

With that, Janie's shoulders began to shake, and she wept unashamedly. She finally realized that someone was going to relieve her of an intolerable burden, and the floodgates opened. Of course, all the students on the couch were quietly sobbing by then, because they finally understood that helping people out of their desperate situations was a kind and generous thing. We weren't out there taking advantage of people, we were giving them hope. We were giving them help.

Hope and help. There's our real product. In real-estate investing the enlightened way, we can become their guardian angels.

Hope and help. That's what women have been dispensing for centuries. We are able to tap into our feelings in order to figure out what someone else is feeling. We rely on our intuition out of habit.

At almost every seminar we've held since we met Janie, I always tell her story, and, invariably, I end up crying. It just gets to me when I remember her shaking shoulders. Then the ladies in the class start tearing up too. That's when they tell me they don't think they can invest, because they're too softhearted.

But, no, I say, you're perfect hearted. It doesn't mean you'll throw all the analysis and good investing sense out the window to help people. It means you'll really understand their problems at a core level. And they will know that you understand them, because it will be organic, not forced.

Trust between the seller and the buyer is all-important, and trust is best developed by being trustworthy. Just genuinely understanding and genuinely caring will put you a good distance down the road to a trusting relationship.

Did you know that 54 percent of all real-estate agents are women? Women dominate that field, and the same attributes that make them good at it make women naturally good at investing too. What's the common wisdom concerning "who" buys houses? It's said that *women* buy houses. That's not a sexist comment, it's just the statistical fact of which gender predominantly drives the choice of where a family lives.

And now, 18 percent of all first-time home buyers are single women (versus 8 percent of single men). That's staggering.

But surprisingly, many women real-estate agents rent rather than own their personal homes. That means they're out there selling and making other people wealthy, and they're not buying for themselves. Also, most women agents earn less than $5,000 per year from real estate. Perhaps they get their license with the notion that they'll dabble in it as a part-time job or even a hobby, because they like houses a lot, they like homemaking and designing the interiors, so real estate sounds like a compatible activity.

Here's my dream: I'd love to permeate the investing world with kind, caring, spirited women who care for others with generous hearts. Let's be so wise in our investing that we're able to create stable wealth for ourselves and our families and then help others create stability in their financial futures too.

One seller came back to us a year after her foreclosure, with her credit all cleaned up, asking us to help her buy a home the right way. What a pleasure! Women helping other women to clear a confident path to a better future!

The thought I want you to remember is this famous and accurate insight:

> *If you think you can, you're right. If you think you can't, you're right.*
> —MARY KAY ASH, FOUNDER OF MARY KAY COSMETICS

So make sure you're right on the "I can do it" side! And remember, I'll be there to help you. I'm ready when you are.

Men: Stop! Don't Read This!

(Unless You Want a Sneak Peek at How Women Think)

OK, the title was a trick. I actually *do* want you to read this. In fact, you probably borrowed this book from your wife, your sister, your mother, or your girlfriend. And *they* want you to read it too.

They want you to read it because they want you to support their intentions. They even may want you to partner with them in the adventure they're undertaking. Most of all, they don't want you to be a dream stomper.

In order for you to get a feel for their newfound enthusiasm, take a look at module 1, helping 1. It's called "The Truth behind *Nothing Down* (To Be Blunt, Is It a Scam?)." If you'll read that short section, you'll have a better grasp of what we're doing. The next section you should read is "Turning Naysayers into Yea-sayers." Please scrutinize it for your own attitudes. Thanks!

If you're one of the rare men who picked up this book in order to get some fresh insights into the minds of women (or some new viewpoints on real-estate investing), congratulations! *You have courage and wisdom uncommon to your gender.*

In reality, that last sentence doesn't reflect my true opinion. I think that last sentence smacks of the very sexism women have had to fight for too long. My original intent was to write this book for anyone who needed some assistance in extracting the fundamentals and clarifying the basics of *Nothing Down* investing. I intended it to empower anyone who desired to change the condition of his or her financial future.

My purpose was to write this book for anyone overworked and overwhelmed, anyone with too little time to create a quality life. Are women the only ones who feel stressed to the limit? Probably not. Are men less busy than women? *You* can answer that.

Maybe the publisher should release a version of this book in a plain brown wrapper, so that no man would have to withstand the indignity of reading a *women's book,* but something tells me you don't care.

Money is like people. It only goes where it feels welcome.

—DAN KENNEDY, AUTHOR

The 5-Minute Mentor Presents Sixty 5-Minute Helpings

(Getting the Best Results from This Book)

Does the 5-Minute Mentor method have everything you'll ever need to know about real estate in it? No! It just has everything you need to get *started*.

Lali, the Underwater Wonder Dog

I had a Labrador retriever named Lali, and she loved the water. I got the notion that she would enjoy diving underneath the surface, so I set out to train her. I'd place kibble on the first step of the pool, where there was only two inches of water. She'd follow my hand into the water to grab it. We only "worked" a few minutes a day—it was definitely playtime. Then we started trying it on the second step, where there was five inches of water. I had to use little bones, because the kibble floated. Little by little, we got deeper into the pool, and by the end of two weeks Lali was a dog that Jacques Cousteau would have loved. She could fly off the side of the pool and do grand belly flops to retrieve anything I'd throw; she'd wiggle down to the bottom, staying long enough to scare the dickens out of me sometimes. Other times, she'd slide in from the side of the pool, as quiet as a Navy Seal. She loved performing for everyone underwater! Rainbow the cat was the only one who wasn't impressed!

While you're studying with the 5MM method, you're going to feel me cajoling you, helping you take your time, going easy into the shallow water first. We'll only work a few minutes at a time. You'll be able to guide how much time you spend on the action steps, but the actual pages of text you'll absorb shouldn't take more than five minutes!

Here's How the *5MM Method* Works

It's all about gradients (like Lali and the steps of the pool), it's about not skipping stuff you don't get, it's about not getting overwhelmed and giving up.

The "5-Minute" part should be easy for me to describe: This book is going to present you small portions you can digest in five minutes. A "mentor" is a wise and trusted guide and adviser. There you have the 5-Minute Mentor.

There are ten "modules" (like parts) divided by broad topics. Each module has a buffet of "helpings" (chapters, or lessons). We called them modules to differentiate them from the chapters before and after, because they are the main course of the book, the real skinny on how to do this *Nothing Down* stuff. The modules are the empowerment, and the chapters are the "inspirement"!

We named the individual lessons helpings because that's what we dream of doing: *helping.* Let us know if we succeed, will you? When *your* dreams come true, *our* dreams come true. We love hearing about it.

There are sixty helpings, and if you multiply sixty by five minutes, that's three hundred minutes, or five hours of your time. You could read the book in a weekend.

Each helping is divided into quick little clumps of information. It's short enough that you can read it in five minutes. Then following that data, you'll find a really, *really* simple list of important words called the "Word Wizard." Each of those words is identified in the text by a symbol (❖) and explained in the Word Wizard. I'm never going to let you get bogged down with fancy, special language.

If you see some words that you don't understand, be sure to look them up in a regular dictionary. You don't want to start feeling foggy and sleepy just because you passed over some words you didn't really know the definition of.

Following the Word Wizard, you'll find a quiz, the "Quiz Wizard," with a few questions that you can use to see how well you understand what you've read.

I Know You Don't Have Time—I Didn't Have Time to Write This Book!

I know you don't have time to do even one more thing. *I* didn't have time to write this book. I had to sneak in an hour in the morning and an hour in the evening. I had to learn to procrastinate the way Bob teaches (good procrastinating, where you put off what you can so that you are able to do the truly important thing). I had to shut off the ringers on my phones during the weekend so I wouldn't be tempted to answer them. I had to turn off the TV.

Please don't think that I'm promising you'll become a successful investor if you just read the book in a weekend. Yes, the lessons take five minutes, but you will need to carve out some time to work the Wizards for the results to show up in your bank account.

I know it would be nice to think that just reading a book could make us rich. The truth is, you'll have to sneak some time to do some action steps in the real world. That's when you'll have a real chance at a new financial future.

The Word Wizard, the Quiz Wizard, and the Whiz Wizard

You've already heard about the Word Wizard and the Quiz Wizard, but what is this "Whiz Wizard"?

It's the 5MM method of whizzing you on your way toward speedy success. We want you to reach your dreams, we want you to get your goals, and we want you to exceed your own expectations for yourself. Therefore, the action steps have been designed to work the same way I got Lali to dive underwater.

The Whiz Wizard gives you action steps to keep you moving forward in the real world. You may not have liked "homework" before, but I think you're going to like it now. I've designed it to be so easy, you can't help but do it. Each Whiz Wizard will ease you into the next one, so that nothing is ever hard to do. You'll be whizzing along in no time!

I designed the whole process to be easy and fun.

I'm Just Trying to Get You off Your, Um, *Couch*

1. Sample the helping.
2. Check the Word Wizard.
3. Answer the Quiz Wizard.
4. Do the Whiz Wizard action steps.

Four little steps—what could be nicer?

By the way, the Word Wizard will have nuggets that you need to know, so even if you understand all the words, be sure to check the Word Wizard for usages you might not have heard before. The Quiz Wizard may deal with something that appears only in the Word Wizard.

At the end of every module, you'll get a "Time Capsule" that you can use to see if you really got all the important points. Also in the Time Capsule, Bob presents his Bobservations on the preceding module. You'll be amazed at yourself and how much you know at the end of each module!

I've come to realize that teaching all this *Nothing Down* stuff has really helped me understand it myself at the most fundamental level. The saying about how the teacher learns more than the student—I think it's really true. I've gained a certainty and confidence, plus I have a broader and deeper view of the subject just from having to get it across to my students.

Well, if that's the case, why don't I give *you* the chance to teach it? If teaching is all that great for a person's understanding, is it possible that it's a missing element in training programs? OK, you're going to find out for yourself. After every helping, you'll take one key element and teach it to someone else. It'll be a short piece, something that should take you only a few minutes to explain.

If you can get the other person to understand, you're going to know for sure that you yourself have grasped the concept fully. This can be the way you get your spouse or partner to get with the program, because he's "only doing it to help you complete your home-work"! Yea!

When you see that you've been able to teach someone else, your confidence is going to soar!

Would you like for me to take the job of kicker-of-the-behind?

Some women may read this book and simply go out and "do it." For me, I needed Bob Allen, Mark Victor Hansen, John Childers, and Tom Painter to simultaneously push me and hold my hand. I needed accountability with a capital *A*. Maybe it's something built into me from childhood days, when I wanted to please my mom and dad. I seem to thrive when someone is expecting me to meet a challenge.

OK, do you want me to push you? Yes? Do you want our team to stand with you, looking over your shoulder, helping diminish those fears, day by day?

If you would like for us to be your real 5-Minute Mentor, then go to www.ND4W.com/5MM and check out our special offer for our loyal readers!

On the website, you get your next helping when you've demonstrated your completion of the previous helping! If you're working with me as your 5-Minute Mentor on the internet, you'll receive the next video or the next sound file when you've proved you understand and can teach and apply the prior helping! Built-in accountability! Plus, you'll have the daily Power Hour so you can call up and ask questions.

Now, if you decide you'd like to work with this book alone on your own, promise me you won't even dream of cheating and reading ahead until you can apply what you've already read. Promise? Good.

You know, if a person can't apply what she's just learned, what's the point? Why spend all that time reading, listening, reading, listening, and not applying? It's time wasted. Instead of "self help," it becomes "shelf help," as the books pile up. Application, that's the thing. Can you apply this stuff?

Well, I've thought up everything I can to help you apply it, to help you stay on the path, to help you succeed in your goals. You just have to take the pledge to actually work with the Wizards!

Did you say you want me to push you?

All right, I accept the job. Here we go.

MODULE 1

FIRST THINGS FIRST

HELPING 1

The Truth Behind Nothing Down

(To Be Blunt, Is It a Scam?)

Let's talk honestly about the phrase nothing down❖. When Robert Allen used it for the first time, *wow,* the concept seemed so radical, it almost sounded impossible. What if I told you that "nothing down" doesn't mean—and has *never* meant—that no money is transacted? What it does mean is that it isn't *your* money! It doesn't come out of your purse or wallet; it doesn't come out of your savings. It comes out of *someone else's* pocket!

I'm going to show you how to identify the places where that money is waiting for you.

That's the story that RGA told in his revolutionary book! That's the story I'm going to distill and simplify for you here! By the way, do you think Robert would have had a huge hit if he had called the book *How to Invest in Real Estate Using Other People's Money*? I'm sure he would have had a few interested readers, but that title would never have ended up as the all-time bestselling book on real estate!

OK, so *nothing*❖ means "not yours." What does *down*❖ mean? Some of you already know the answer, but if you don't, know you're not alone.

In this case, *down* refers to down payment❖, or the money a buyer usually has to come up with before a lender will give you a home loan.

21

Most people think that you have to come up with 10 percent or more down to buy a house, and that used to be true. So if you could buy a house without having to come up with that money, buying a house would be a lot easier, right? People who thought they'd never be able to save enough discovered they could actually move out of their apartment as long as they didn't have to come up with a down payment!

You're Uniquely Qualified!

That's what's so exciting about investing in houses the *Nothing Down* way. The number-one thrill is: You can afford to do it! If you have *nothing* to put *down* right now, you're actually uniquely qualified for this style of investing! Sometimes people with a little bit of money available to use on the down payment don't get as good a deal as people with no money, because they haven't been forced into more outside the bun❖ thinking.

When someone tells you, "This *Nothing Down* stuff doesn't work," it means that he doesn't understand the real meaning of *nothing down*. You can ask him if he's ever heard of a Veterans Administration loan (VA loan❖), where the vet only has to pay one dollar for the down payment. You can ask him if he knows that mortgage companies are currently giving people (even first-time home buyers) loans for 100 percent of the value of their home. You can even inform him that some lenders are loaning more than 100 percent—even up to 125 percent in some cases—so that the buyer doesn't even have to pay any closing costs❖ associated with the loan and may have money left over for home improvements.

You Could Go Even Faster

Do you *have* to buy properties *Nothing Down*?

No, if you have some cash, you could use a little for part of the down payment to reduce the amount of your monthly payments. Then it would be a "Low-Down" deal. However, I suggest that you challenge yourself to do *Nothing Down* deals for your first year because you're in the building stages of your investing career. I didn't use my own money for the first five years. That's right, everything was bought using other people's money (what investors refer to as "OPM"), because it was my "game." And believe me, it's a really enjoyable game to play!

So *Nothing Down* isn't a scam after all, it's the legitimate use of techniques for finding resources outside your own.

OK, time for you to check out some words, take a little quiz, and perform some action steps to get you whizzing on your way!

The less we stress, the more we soar.

—KAREN NELSON BELL

Word Wizard

___ Nothing	In this context, *nothing* means "not yours."
___ Down	See *Down Payment,* below.
___ Nothing Down	No down payment paid by you, but paid by some other resource.
___ Down Payment	The cash money that lenders often require before they will give a home loan.
___ Closing	The time when all the paperwork is finished, all the signatures in place, all the details worked out, and the money that has to change hands has done so.
___ Closing Costs	The expense of creating and completing a home loan, paid when the loan is done; has different meaning in a different context.
___ Outside the Bun	A play on "outside the box," from a commercial for Taco Bell, meaning creative and innovative thinking.
___ VA Loan	A home loan given to a veteran that doesn't require a down payment except for one dollar. It has various rules and regulations for eligibility.
___ OPM	Other people's money. Not your money. Bank's money, friends' money, relatives' money, mortgage company's money, and so on.

Quiz Wizard

1. What does *Nothing Down* really mean?
   a. No money changes hands
   b. No money comes out of your pocketbook
   c. Nothing gets written down
   d. Nothing comes out of your savings or checking account
   e. Using other people's moola

2. What do most people think is the normal down payment for purchasing of a home in regular retail real estate?
   a. 5 percent
   b. 10 percent
   c. 15 percent
   d. 20 percent
   e. 30 percent

3. What are some samples of OPM?
   a. A loan from a friend or relative
   b. A loan from a mortgage company
   c. A line of credit on your home
   d. A credit card
   e. A fifty-fifty partner
   f. Seller financing

Turn to page 435 for the answers.

Whiz Wizard

1. Look in your local newspaper and on the internet to find at least three ads for mortgage companies that say they will do loans for 100 percent of a property's value. You can use www.Google.com to search for 100 percent real-estate loans. You also can also go to www.ForSaleByOwner.com and click on the tab called "Mortgages." When you get to that page, look for a heading called "No Money Down Mortgage Financing," and click on that one. Remember, websites change from time to time, so be a sleuth, and find as many resources for *Nothing Down* financing as you can on

the internet! Today, I found over 33,000 references. How many do you need?

Done_____

(Note: The world of computers and the internet changes so frequently, that by the time you read this, the internet might be holographic! Just stay determined to search for resources similar to the ones I describe here and elsewhere in this book. For sure, there'll be even better ways to do things as time passes!)

2.   Call on the ads to find out what the guidelines are. For example, (1) what credit score does the borrower have to have, and (2) will the lender grant mortgages to investors or only to people who plan to occupy the residence? Don't apply for a loan online, by the way. Those lenders submit your application to multiple funding sources all over the internet, and all the inquiries on your credit can pull down your credit score. Just call the phone number and get your questions answered.

Done _____

3.   Teach the concepts of *Nothing Down* and OPM to someone else so that he or she understands it.

Done _____

Three Platinum Rules

(For Successful Investing)

There are three fundamental aspects to any real-estate investment, and you have to consider all three principles as essential parts of the whole deal. You have to *find*❖ a property, you have to *fund*❖ the property, and you have to *farm*❖ the property. "Find 'em, Fund 'em, Farm 'em" has long been Robert Allen's motto.

Finding the property means making contact with someone who wants to sell. Funding the property means getting for all parties involved what they want. (It could be money, mortgages, other kinds of property, like cars and boats, or even good will.) Farming it means finally making a profit for you.

Find it, Fund it, and Farm it are the most basic elements of every project.

Find 'em, Fund 'em, Farm 'em

To invest using *Nothing Down for Women*'s 5-Minute Mentor method, with little or nothing down out of your pocket, you have to find properties that fit certain criteria: (1) they have to be owned by people with problems, (2) you'll fund them with very little or none of your own money, and (3) you'll farm them either by "flipping"❖ them (selling them to another buyer) or "keeping" them (to rent for a positive cash flow).

In the beginning, you're going to be talking with private individuals who are selling their houses by themselves without a Realtor❖. That process is called "For Sale by Owner," or "FSBO"❖ (pronounced "Fizz-Bo").

There are some basic rules that the 5-Minute Mentor method wants us to follow, and we're going to discuss seven of them over the next three sections. Here are three of the rules for you to consider today:

1. Never try to do a creative deal❖ with someone who isn't a "Don't-Wanter❖." A Don't-Wanter has some kind of a problem that you can solve. Always do business with someone who has a problem that you can solve by buying his or her property.

As you begin to develop your investing abilities, you're going to focus on FSBOs. Later on we'll learn how to use real-estate agents❖ to expand our reach, but for now you'll want to talk to the seller directly. You want to become able to really listen to someone so you can find out why he or she is a Don't-Wanter.

Why *Nothing Down* Doesn't Work

Every time I hear people say that *Nothing Down* investing doesn't work, I always ask them what has been their challenge or barrier. Every single time, I've found out they're trying to do a deal with someone who isn't motivated. Sometimes they ask a real-estate agent to make offers to sellers for a price that's way under asking price. They've never even talked to the seller; they have no idea if the person is motivated or not.

Our style of investing is very different from regular retail real estate❖, where people are just out looking for houses. Always remember, we're not looking for houses, we're looking for people with problems that we can solve by helping them get out of their houses (which have become a burden for some reason).

2. Never buy a property based on emotion. Always buy a property based on sound financial analysis. Will it make money? If the answer is yes, then it's a valid prospect to be researched further.

If you fall in love with the antique ceiling fans, if you're drooling over the custom-built stone fireplace, if the lilacs blooming remind you of a scene from your childhood, you might not notice the water stains on the ceiling where the mold is hiding.

3. Never harm another in a real-estate deal. Always go in with the viewpoint of helping. Be willing to walk away from a deal. Remember what famed speaker Zig Ziglar always taught: that the best way to get what *you* want is to give someone else what *they* want.

Listen carefully to what the seller says in general conversation, and you'll find out what he or she really needs and wants! Not only will the deal turn out great, you'll get a flowing river of wonderful referrals. This isn't the real estate business; we're not looking for houses. We're looking for people who have problems that we can solve by buying their house.

Always remember, *we're not looking for houses, we're looking for people!*

If you feel you can't help the sellers, maybe you can direct them to someone who can. Being kind is a wonderful business strategy, even when there's nothing in it for you.

Come to think of it, "Never harm another in a real-estate deal" could be boiled down to a simpler phrase: "Never harm another in a deal," or even "Never harm another."

That's good business, good sense, and good living. Let's take a pledge that the 5-Minute Mentor method of investing is the same enlightened method of investing that Robert Allen and Mark Victor Hansen propose in their books. Believe me, it makes all the difference in the world, not only to your success but to your heart.

We're not in the house business; we're in the people business.

—KAREN NELSON BELL

Word Wizard

___ Find	To locate motivated sellers. In our way of investing, it's not finding houses, it's finding people with problems.
___ Fund	To gather all the financial resources necessary to transact a deal, and in the 5MM Method, using OPM.
___ Farm	To communicate to potential sellers, buyers, renters; to do the necessary marketing in order to find, fund, flip, rent, and so on.
___ Flip	To buy a property under its real value and sell it for more than you bought it.
___ FSBO	For Sale by Owner, a designation that means the seller is not using a licensed real-estate professional to help him sell his property.
___ Don't-Wanter	A seller who has some kind of problem that makes him more anxious to sell than a typical home owner; he doesn't want to own that house anymore.
___ Creative Deal	A real-estate deal that doesn't follow the typical retail real-estate world's pattern; a deal where other people's money is used in inventive ways that are not common knowledge except to smart real-estate investors.
___ Real-estate Agent	A person who has gone to school to learn how to help people sell their homes; a salesperson who connects sellers and buyers.
___ Real-estate Broker	A real-estate agent who has taken more training to learn how to run an office with other agents working for her.
___ Realtor	A trademarked word for a real-estate agent who belongs to the National Association of Realtors.
___ Retail Real Estate	The normal real-estate market, where people buy and sell homes using traditional methods; the focus is typically more on the house itself and not the unusual circumstances of the sellers and buyers.

Quiz Wizard

1. What are the first three platinum rules of real-estate investing?
   a. Always do business with a motivated seller.
   b. Never buy a property based on emotion.
   c. Never harm another in a transaction.
   d. Always do right.
   e. Only do business with FSBOs.

2. What's the fundamental difference between *Nothing Down* investing and regular retail real estate?
   a. *Nothing Down* investing involves using creative financing.
   b. Retail investing involves going to a bank.
   c. *Nothing Down* investing is all about people, whereas retail investing is all about houses.
   d. *Nothing Down* investing is with FSBOs, whereas retail investing is done with Realtors.
   e. Retail investing always costs more.

3. What's the most important concept you learned in this section? Write a short paragraph to explain your most important aha! from this section. (An *aha* is a recognition of some truth or the satisfaction of some success or win.)

   _____

   _____

   _____

Turn to page 435 for the answers.

Whiz Wizard

1. Look in your local newspaper and on the internet to find at least three FSBO ads for sellers that say they will do loans for 100 percent of the value of a property. If you don't find an ad in the classified area, look at the regular advertisements as well. The ad might say "zero down" or "nothing down." Also look for "low down." These ads will almost all be for properties owned by investors, mortgage companies, or banks. A typical home owner

wouldn't think to use the *Nothing Down* language. You can use Las Vegas's local newspaper on line, www.ReviewJournal.com, if your own local paper comes up lacking.
Done _____

2. Call on the ads to find out what the guidelines are; for example, what credit score you have to have, what percentage rate will the loan be at, and do you have to live in the home. Since these people will most likely be experts in some way, ask them to help you understand their ad.
    Done _____

3. Teach the difference between *Nothing Down* investing and regular real estate to someone else so that he or she understands it.
    Done _____

HELPING 3

Bubble Schmubble

(Make Money in Real Estate No Matter What "the Market" Is Doing)

Let's dig into some more fundamental rules. The first three were conceptual, and these next three are more down-to-earth "nuts and bolts."

> 4. Focus on purchasing properties that you can buy at a price that is substantially below market value❖. That way, you already know what your profit potential❖ is, and you're not speculating❖; you're not wondering and worrying if the value is going to go up or not.

When you buy at a discount, you don't have to worry about the market going up or down, or whether or not a "bubble"❖ will burst. Market analysts worry about prices going up too fast and then going back down too fast. If you bought at a deep discount, you won't be concerned about those matters, because you'll already have a bargain, which means that if you decide to sell, you can make money.

Later, you'll be learning how to rate properties depending on how far below market value they're priced, but for now, try to purchase at a 10 percent discount or more. In regular real estate, the general public thinks that if they get a $5,000 discount, they got a great deal.

The $5,000 Rule

There's a secret unspoken rule called "the $5,000 rule"❖, which says that the Realtor can raise the seller's asking price by $5,000, then discount it for the buyer by $5,000, and everyone walks away happy, even if ignorant of the fact that there was no real bargain. But, in fact, experienced investors look for at least a 10 percent discount, so on a house worth $100,000, that would be a $10,000 discount.

More aggressive investors actually seek 20 percent to 30 percent discounts, and, frankly, we've personally had discounts over 50 percent.

Imagine buying an $85,000 townhouse❖ for $35,000! Think that's not possible? Well, it's one of my favorite stories. The lady was elderly; she was in preforeclosure❖, highly distressed, and about to lose her home. We helped her find a senior apartment that she could afford, we helped her move, and we gave her money she didn't even ask for or expect in order to get her started in her new life. But $35K❖ for an $85K condo! That's more than half off!

Even after we put in $5,000 for repairs and gave her $5,000, we still had about a 50 percent profit, because we sold it for $90,000. Just think, $45,000 in profit by helping someone in trouble. She was so grateful, it was heart wrenching.

We had a fifty-fifty partner❖ on that one, so we ended up doing pretty well. The partner put up all the money, and we did most of the work. So you see, we ended up making about $22,500 without using any of our own money or any of our own credit. We just put in some "sweat equity"❖.

Is *Nothing Down* starting to make more sense?

5. Target properties that you can buy without having to get a loan in your name. Seek out sellers who are willing to work with you so that you don't have to come up with a down payment. Then you are buying with no cash or credit of your own.

Some real-estate gurus think that you shouldn't ever buy a property at market value. In fact, some investors won't buy a house unless they get a 30 percent discount. I think that's pretty shortsighted; they're missing out on some incredible opportunities.

For example, what if you could buy a $180,000 house for $180,000, and the seller told you he would let you pay him interest-only❖ payments for five years at 5 percent? Your payments would be only $750 per month. You'd be paying full value, but watch:

Now, if you could rent out that house at $1,150 for the next five years at a positive cash flow❖ of $400 per month, and in five years you could get a new loan with a regular lender and take some cash out❖ of the value of the property, wouldn't that be great? You would have made $4,800 per year—more than $24,000 total over five years—and then you would have a property that was worth more than when you began. And you got it for no money out of your pocket.

That's my idea of heaven. I'd like to have ten of those, and then I'd be making $4,000 per month. That's $48,000 a year, last time I checked. Hmmmmm, do you think those investors who passed up the deal because it wasn't discounted would like to have a $48K yearly salary coming into their mailbox?

So, to recap, let's look at these two rules. You either want to get a good deal on the price, or you want to get a good deal on the terms. Price❖ or terms❖. Discount or financing. Or as Bob calls it, wholesale❖ or retail❖. (A wholesale seller is the one who is so motivated that she's willing to bring down the price. A retail seller is the one who is so motivated that she's willing to work with you on the financing terms.)

The Dream Seller

Sometimes you may even find somebody who fits into both categories. That's a real dream come true when it happens. He's motivated every which way! Don't expect it in general, but be very glad when you find him. Usually the person willing to go down in price wants you to get your own financing, and the person willing to work with you on financing wants the full asking price. Don't take it as a defeat. You've still got a motivated seller, even if it's only on one aspect, price or terms. When one comes along that will work with you on both, smile all the way and say a little prayer of gratitude!

By the way, remember that neither of these rules will work if you're dealing with a seller that isn't motivated! Always keep rule number one in mind. If you don't remember rule number one, go back to helping 2 and reread it. It's that important!

6. In negotiating, never be the first one to mention a number. The first one to state a figure loses the game.

Always let the seller talk first; let the seller tell you the numbers. You may get a real nice surprise! If you get a yes to your first offer, you may have offered too much!

This is one of Robert Allen's favorite rules, and I love it too. However, don't be rigid. If someone just won't give up a number first, you can assume he's playing the same game and knows the same rules. Just offer a real lowball❖ figure, and let him come back with a counteroffer❖. You *want* a no, because you want to find out the true low point. If you get a yes, you'll never know how much lower the seller would have gone! Rejection on your first offer means you won't be leaving money on the table when you get your yes. Isn't that an interesting switch? You actually want to get rejected!

I don't believe in miracles, I depend on them.
— SUZAN HUDSON, MULTIMILLIONAIRE INVESTOR

Word Wizard

___ Market Value   The amount people are actually willing to pay for similar houses.

___ Profit Potential   How much money you predict you'll make when you sell or rent.

___ Speculation   Buying a property that you predict (and hope) will grow more valuable.

___ Bubble   Markets in which speculative investment drives prices higher than usual demand can sustain; the prices go up, and when the bubble bursts, they go down.

___ The $5,000 Rule   The amount of money the general public considers a great discount on a house.

___ Townhouse   A property that is connected to other ones like it; not a separate single-family home.

___ Foreclosure   What happens when a home owner doesn't pay the mortgage over a period of time, and the lender takes away the house and sells it by auctioning it off to the highest bidder.

___ Preforeclosure   The period of time when the home owner who hasn't been paying the mortgage has the chance to make up all the payments and avoid having his house sold at auction.

___ K — A slang term for "a thousand"—as in "$10K," or "ten thousand dollars."

___ Partner — A person who supplies something you don't have: money, credit, time, knowledge.

___ Equity — The difference between the value of a house and the amount of the loans on it; if a house worth $100,000 has a loan on it for $60,000, then there's $40,000 of equity.

___ Sweat Equity — The value a person puts into a property by doing labor herself.

___ Interest Only — Home loans that let you pay a payment of interest only, with no amount going toward paying off the loan. This kind of loan makes the payments very low in the early years; it generally is interest only for a limited number of years.

___ 5 Percent — A number that tells how much percentage is being charged to borrow money; like the rate on a credit card or the percentage rate on a bank savings account.

___ Positive Cash Flow — When rent comes in, the amount of money left over after all the expenses, including mortgages, are paid.

___ Cash Out — Money you can get back when you get a loan on a house that has sufficient equity.

___ Price — The amount agreed upon between the seller and the buyer.

___ Terms — The arrangements concerning where, to whom, and how payments get made.

___ Wholesale Seller — A seller who wants to sell so badly that he's willing to reduce the price.

___ Retail Seller — A seller who wants to sell so badly that she's willing to work out special terms in financing.

___ Lowball — A really low offer, such as 20 percent to 30 percent off the market value.

___ Counteroffer — What the sellers might say if they want to sell but don't quite like your offer yet.

Quiz Wizard

1. What are the second three platinum rules of real-estate investing?
      a. Find 'em.
      b. Try to buy below market value.
      c. Fund 'em.
      d. Let the seller be the first to mention a number.
      e. Farm 'em.
      f. Try to get the seller to let you pay him instead of getting a new loan.

2. When would be a good time to pay full price for a property?
      a. When the market is going crazy hot.
      b. When the bubble is about to burst.
      c. When you can get good terms and make a positive cash flow.
      d. When you can get the seller to finance.
      e. When you can't get a discount.

3. Which is better to find, a motivated wholesale seller or a motivated retail seller?
      a. A motivated wholesale seller.
      b. A motivated retail seller.
      c. Neither.
      d. Both.

Turn to page 435 for the answers.

Whiz Wizard

1. Look in your local newspaper and on the internet to find at least three FSBO ads where the sellers use the word *motivated* and three where the sellers say they would give you seller financing. If you can't find any in your own area, look in other areas. Try www.reviewjournal.com, and you'll find a lot of sellers who advertise that they'll do owner financing. These are mostly investors themselves. Just call them and talk to them to get the hang of it. Don't worry about whether it's in a neighborhood you're going to invest in, just start talking to people for practice!
      Done _____

2. Call on the ads and say the following: (1) "Could you help me understand what 'motivated' means, and does it mean that I can get an especially good deal?" (2) "Could you help me understand what 'seller financing' means, and does it mean that I can get an especially good deal?"

   Don't try to make a deal, don't try to be "smart," just be a person who wants to buy a house and doesn't quite understand the ad. Remember, most of these sellers will actually be investors who know how to write an alluring ad. They'll possibly be very glad to show you how "smart" *they* are. Once they explain to you how seller financing works, thank them for their time and tell them that you'd like to discuss it with your spouse (or mom, son, sister, partner, lawyer, and so on). Some sellers on these FSBO ads will be very kind and helpful, and others may not. If they don't seem helpful, just use my favorite four-letter word: next.
   Done _____

3. Teach the concept of price versus terms to someone else so that he or she understands it.
   Done _____

HELPING 4

The Seventh Commandment

(Thou Shall Not Be a Know-It-All)

Whew! That last one was a big lesson. To get some relief, let's do a shorter one this time. (Shorter, but no less important.)

7. Always keep adding to your knowledge base. The more tools you have in your array of strategies❖, the more you'll find a deal where no one else can. The best way to broaden your abilities is to find a mentor❖ you trust and let her guide you through any mine fields by stepping exactly into her successful footprints.

Here's the deal: Real estate is constantly changing. The same technique that worked last summer may not work in the same part of town next winter. Laws change. Cities change. Job availabilities change. Styles change. The IRS codes❖ change. Interest rates❖ change. Lending guidelines❖ change. People change.

All of those changes mean that *you* have to change too. You have to analyze the scene with a fresh eye every month.

Well, what's going to keep you on the cutting edge? Keep studying. Don't ever get to the point where you think you know it all. The biggest barrier to study is thinking that you know everything. When you already know everything, there's no room to squeeze in the new stuff! Robert Allen and I still go to seminars and study to expand our toolboxes all the time.

Keep Your Thingamabobs Ready

John Childers says that he used to have a huge, fancy toolbox in his automotive repair shop. It had every kind of gadget in the world in it, so when he would buy yet another gizmo, his wife, Brenda, would ask him why he needed another one, when the tool chest was already full. His answer was always, "I don't know what problem the next customer is going to have. I may not use this thingamabob for five years, but when that customer walks in, I'll be able to solve his problem."

That's what we have to do: keep studying so that we'll have the exact right tool to solve the exact problem that shows up tomorrow.

Another reason to keep studying is that the subject of real estate and real-estate investing is vast. One person can't know every single thing there is to know, especially since it's always changing.

I'll never forget when Tammy Billington came to study with me at our weekend seminar. She's an experienced real-estate broker, a professional property manager, and a multimillionaire investor with over eighty properties to her name. I was very nervous for her to attend our weekend, because I couldn't quite picture her getting anything new out of it. She said, "If I can pick up one or two new ideas, it will be worth the time and money."

At the end of the weekend, she was blown away by how many new viewpoints she absorbed. I was blown away too, because I had been investing for only four years, whereas she had been investing for decades. It taught me that you can learn something from anyone, and through the years of teaching, I've learned tons and tons from the students themselves.

Take the Pledge

Let's take the pledge together. I'll pledge it myself if you'll pledge it too. Let's do it:

I pledge to keep learning enthusiastically for the rest of my life! Great!

Ultimately, the product you sell is love—manifested and materialized.
—ROBERT G. ALLEN

Word Wizard

___ Strategies   Specific plans for buying real estate.

___ Mentor   A teacher who will tell you how, show you how, and monitor how you do it; a person who cares about your results.

___ IRS Codes   Regulations having to do with real estate; tax liabilities or tax benefits having to do with real-estate investments.

___ Interest Rates   How much money you have to pay to borrow the money you need; the rates change slightly every day, and they vary up and down through the years. The higher the interest rates are, the more clever you have to be in your strategies.

___ Lending Guidelines   The points of interest that matter to lenders when they look at you and your ability to pay back a loan; the guidelines change whenever the lenders feel like it, so you'll need to know what the prevailing guidelines are. Years ago, investors had to put down 20 percent to 30 percent in order to get a loan. Now even an investor can find 100 percent financing on residential properties. More commonly, investors can get loans with only 5 or 10 percent down. That's a big change from fifteen years ago.

Quiz Wizard

1. What is the last platinum rule of real-estate investing?
   a. Always do right.
   b. Never use an attorney unless you own a gold mine.

       c. Always keep adding to your knowledge base.

       d. Never use Realtors.

       e. Always use other people's money.

2.   What pledge did you take today?
Write a paragraph that explains your new pledge to yourself:

_____

_____

_____

3.   Why do you need new tools all the time?

       a. To stay ahead of other investor competitors.

       b. To keep aware of new laws.

       c. To keep aware of new strategies.

       d. To keep from becoming mentally stagnant.

       e. Because learning new things keeps you young.

Turn to page 435 for the answers.

Whiz Wizard

1.   Obtain a copy of Robert G. Allen's *Nothing Down for the 2000s* and read the introduction and first chapter, "You Can Still Make a Fortune in Real Estate." You don't have to buy the book; you can get it from the library or borrow it from a friend, but do yourself the favor of reading one of the most important books on money ever written. (P.S.: Just for fun, check out the back cover!) Done _____

2.   Write one sentence that describes the most important point you learned in this section. Done _____

3.   Teach the concept of why ongoing education is so important in real-estate investing to someone else so that he or she understands it. Done _____

Three Little Questions

(The Perfect Script for Novice Investors)

What's the one thing that will stop you from succeeding as a real-estate investor?

I thought the answer would be "lack of money," but virtually 100 percent of the time, I hear the answer "fear."

It's my job to help you remove some of the fear. By the way, courage isn't the *absence* of fear, it's doing the thing *in spite of* the fear.

One of the things that many people are afraid to do when they're learning how to invest is to call someone up on the phone and make an offer❖ on a property. To tell you the truth, I was scared to death. That may seem surprising to you, because I'm not shy, and I've been onstage all my life. However, I felt like I just didn't know enough to have the proper conversation. I really, really, *really* didn't want to do it.

Tom Painter was the Protégé Program mentor that insisted we call sellers on the phone. I did it every week, just like his homework said, but I hated it in the beginning. Little by little, it did get easier. Would you like me to make it really easy for you right from the start?

I've got a script for you to follow. We're not going to call to make deals in the early stages, we're only going to call to get used to calling.

I'm going to give you the script now and walk you through the logic behind it. I suggest you take out a piece of paper and write down these three questions.

Question 1: "Is this a good time to talk?"

Don't you wish everyone would use this question as an opening line on the phone? How many times does your best friend start blabbing without realizing you were just on your way out the door? This little question is simply common courtesy.

However, for the investor, it's more than a courtesy. It's a way to subliminally✧ reinforce the notion that *you* are the one caller who understands that the person has a life that you don't know anything about. You are acknowledging that he may have problems that you are respectful of. It's the beginning of establishing trust between you and the seller. It's the beginning of a relationship in which you actually care about what's going on in the seller's life. Get it? It's not just a formality.

Question 2: "What can you tell me about the property?"

When you're the buyer, you call it "the property" or "the house." When you're the seller, you call it "the home." So use the above sentence verbatim! Now, if the seller says, "Well, can't you read the ad?" then you know he's not very motivated. But normally, the person is very anxious to sell, so he'll rattle off all the things he thinks would persuade you to buy the house. Once you ask the question, just hush up and listen!

Take notes the whole time, because you may learn something that will help you if you end up in negotiations✧. Take down how many bedrooms, take down the name of the seller's dog, take down the address and zip code, and take down his favorite food if the subject comes up. You're building a profile. You can do it on a legal pad, or you can do it on your computer, but get a file going.

If a seller wants to know why you asked that question, when all the details are in the ad, just say that you would like to hear about the house from his viewpoint, to get a feel for it. Usually, people love talking about their houses. You may be surprised at how much they want to tell you!

Question 3: "Wow, that sounds so nice— How can you bear to part with it?"

First of all, when people tell you all about their home, what are they going to talk about: the good things about it or the bad things about it? The good things, of course! (If they talk about how the roof is caving in and the sewer is backed up, this question won't work, will it?)

So when they're through telling you all about the wonderful features, you say, "Wow, that sounds so nice." (Or "so appealing" or "so perfect.")

When you say, "How can you bear to part with it?" what are you really saying?

Why are you leaving? Why are you selling?

But if you actually say, "Why are you selling?" you could end up with a nasty response like, "It's none of your business," or "Why do you need to know?" It sounds somehow rude when you say it directly. However, if you say it my way, you're complimenting them. You're developing an affinity between you. You could even say something like, "Wow, I don't think I could walk away from a house like that."

Now when they answer you, you've got a chance to find out what's really going on. If you're talking to an investor who is just selling because that's her business, you'll find that out. If you're talking to a distressed single mom whose ex-husband is stalking her, and she needs to move *tonight,* you'll find that out.

And all of that helps you to understand what kind of a problem you are going to help them solve. Now, you can get your thinking cap on for solutions. By the time you're through with this book, you'll have tons of bright ideas.

By the way, don't be discouraged when you find out you're talking to an investor on the phone. Many times, investors will help you structure a great deal. Tell them that you're just starting your portfolio and ask if they could use their "vastly superior expertise" to help you both structure something where you both can win. All of the houses I've sold except one, I've sold to other investors. And I've always given them good or great deals!

OK, there you go; you've got a script to get you started. You don't need to know any more than those three questions. When you get the answers, you can say, "Thanks for taking the time to speak with me. I'd like to tell my spouse [or son, mother, partner] what we talked about." And if you tell them you're going to call them back, call them back no matter what! It demonstrates that you are a person of your word. You may not do the deal today, but a month from now, who knows if their motivation might have changed, and they remember you as the one person who actually did what they said they were going to do.

> *Don't wait to buy real estate; buy real estate and wait.*
> —ROBERT G. ALLEN

Word Wizard

___ Offer — What you say when you tell the seller you would like to purchase the property and for how much and under what circumstances.

___ Subliminally — Communication that gets received slightly below the analytical awareness of the person receiving it.

___ Negotiations — The communication back and forth between the sellers and you as you try to figure out how to solve their problem at the same time as making it a worthwhile investment for you; win-win is your goal.

Quiz Wizard

1. Does it really matter if you start off with "Is this a good time to talk?"
   a. Not really.
   b. Only if they're in a hurry.
   c. Yes, because you should be polite.
   d. Yes, because you can subliminally let the seller know that you realize he has a life with problems you haven't got a clue about.
   e. No, because every other investor asks the same question.

2.   What's the difference between a *house* and a *home*?
        a. A house is made of stucco; a home is made of stone or wood.
        b. A *house* is something you say when you're selling; a *home* is something you say when you're buying.
        c. A *house* is something you say when you're buying; a *home* is something you say when you're selling.
        d. A *house* is what an investor calls a property; a *home* is what a Realtor calls a property.
        e. A house is not a home unless someone is living there.

3.   What does "How can you bear to part with it?" really mean?
        a. Are you feeling sad because of selling?
        b. Why are you selling?
        c. Do you have other plans if you can't sell it?
        d. How can I help you?
        e. How much of a discount can I get?

Turn to page 435 for the answers.

Whiz Wizard

1.   Call up a FSBO (no Realtors for this exercise) and ask the three questions. Write down what the seller says. If you only get answering services, keep trying until you get to talk to a live person. It's just for you to practice talking, not to make a deal. No fears, OK?
Done _____

2.   Analyze if the seller sounded motivated or not, and write down your observations.
Done _____

3.   Teach the three questions to someone else so that he or she understands them.
Done _____

HELPING 6

The Money Pause

(How to Make $60,000 in Five Seconds!)

What kind of aha's did you get from doing the Whiz Wizard in the last helping? Did you discover that you could actually call someone up and not die? Are you still with me? Great!

Now that you've done that, I want you to do it again (and again and again), but I'll give you two more wonderful questions.

Question 4: "What are you hoping to get for it?"

Yes, the seller may already have a price listed in the paper. But look at the word *hope*. We're subliminally stressing the concept that what he's *asking* and what he's *hoping* are two different numbers!

Now, there's more to this question, and it lies in how you ask it. Here's what you do:

Ask "What are you hoping to get for it?" Then let the person answer, and no matter what he says, *pause* for five seconds! It'll seem like an eternity for both of you, it'll be uncomfortable for both of you, but *you* will know exactly what you're doing, so you'll stay zipped for five full seconds!

If the seller hasn't said anything by the end of the five seconds, you say, *Shzzschhhh.* I really don't know how to write that down, but it's air being sucked in between clenched teeth!

In that five seconds, there's a high probability that the seller will fill the silence with, "Uh, I'd be willing to negotiate," or "Um, I could come down a bit." One of our Robert Allen Institute students in Denver got a $60,000 reduction in price in that five seconds, and another in Phoenix got a $100,000 discount in that five seconds. That's why we call it "the Money Pause❖." This is pure Robert Allen at his finest!

If the seller doesn't respond the way you want, then say something along the lines of, "Well, I guess I was hoping for a little better discount to match my budget."

The statistics on this strategy are about 49–51 in favor of the discount. OK, I made that statistic up, because there aren't any available, but that's my own personal observation. (Aren't statistics all skewed to make whatever point the writer wants to make? I hope you like my statistics here! I'd be OK if your own statistics on it are 80–20 in favor of the discount happening.)

Question 5: "How low could you go if I could *close*❖ fast and give you *all cash*❖?"

This is the question where you're going to find out the truth of just how motivated the seller is. If he says he wants to close in four months because his new house won't be built until then, switch it to "close in four months" instead of "close fast." You have to listen to the seller, remember, and figure out a way to solve his problem.

I realize you don't know how to close fast yet, and you sure must be thinking, "How the heck does KNB expect me to give all cash? I haven't got a dime!" but hang on. All you have to do is use these questions to find out how flexible your seller really is. Then, if you've got a live one, you call up one of your mentors and say, "Help! What do I do next?"

And remember that the cash isn't going to be *your* cash, is it?

This question is going to let you know if you have no deal, a mediocre deal, a good deal, or a great deal. If you've got a good or great deal, then you move forward by asking your mentors to walk you through the necessary steps to close fast and pay in cash. (Or whatever it is the seller needs to solve her problem.)

In sales, this would be considered a "qualifying question." You're letting the seller qualify himself as a prospect, whether hot or cold. If he gives you a figure at all, then let the negotiation games begin! You've got someone who wants to do a deal.

Here's a thought: If you have a great deal, and you call up one of your mentors, it's even possible that the mentor may want to do the deal with you. Great deals are what we're all looking for. They have to be great deals, but when one comes along, we love it! Feel better? More confident? Good. Let's get out there and offer fast closings and all cash, and find some motivated sellers to work with!

> *Good money flows to good deals. Great money flows to great deals. What kind of money flows to mediocre deals? Mediocre money? No. No money flows to mediocre deals. So your job is to find good deals and great deals, and good money and great money will flow to them.*
>
> —KAREN NELSON BELL

Word Wizard

___ The Money Pause   The five seconds of silence after you ask a seller what he's hoping to get for the property, followed by *Shzzschhhh* and possibly followed by the seller expressing a willingness to negotiate.

___ Close   Get the deal all finished, all wrapped up, completely done.

___ All Cash   Some wealthy investors have big bank accounts, and when they say "all cash," they mean that they're going down to the bank to withdraw the amount of their offer and fork it over to the seller. *We* mean that you're going to pay "all cash" for some part of it from *somebody else's* bank account! You'll learn how in later chapters.

Quiz Wizard

1. Why wouldn't you say, "What are you asking for it?"
    a. Because it's rude.
    b. Because the seller might say, "It's none of your business."
    c. Because the seller's asking price may be higher than what he really expects to get.
    d. Because the seller's asking price may be lower than what he really expects to get.
    e. Because you might get a discount if you ask what he's *hoping* to get.

2. What is the Money Pause?
    a. When you wait for the money.
    b. When you cough up the dough.
    c. When you wait five seconds after asking the seller what she's hoping to get.
    d. When you wait five seconds after asking the seller to tell you about the property.
    e. When you press the pause button on your CD player while listening to "If I Were a Rich Man" from *Fiddler on the Roof.*

3. How can you give a seller all cash if you don't have any money?
    a. I don't know.
    b. Ask Karen for the money.
    c. Use OPM.
    d. I don't know right now, but I'll find out in the chapter on *Nothing Down* funding.
    e. It's just a way to buy some time with the seller.

Turn to page 435 for the answers.

Whiz Wizard

1. Call up three or more FSBOs (no Realtors for this exercise) and ask them the five questions. Write down what they say. If you only get answering services, keep trying until you get to talk to live people. You're not really trying to get a deal yet, you're just prac-

ticing talking to strangers. No worries, mate! Analyze if they sounded motivated or not, and write down your observations right here:

_____

_____

_____

Done _____

2.   Write down your aha's from the calls.

_____

_____

_____

Done _____

3.   Teach these two questions to someone else so that he or she understands them.
Done _____

HELPING 7

I.D.E.A.L.S. = L.A.D.I.E.S.

(Why Real Estate Beats the Stock Market)

What kind of aha's did you get from doing the homework in the last helping? Were you able to get a very clear picture of your seller's motivation or lack thereof? Did you by any chance actually go further than the homework and talk about how a deal could be done?

Why do you like the idea of investing in real estate? Is it because you've heard that 95 percent of the wealthy people on this planet got that way from real estate? Is it because you heard someone say, "You can't get hurt with dirt"? Maybe you're not clear why you want to invest, you just heard it was a good thing to do. Let me show you a famous acronym❖ that beautifully explains the advantages of investing in real estate. The word is *IDEAL. I.D.E.A.L.*

I	=	Income
D	=	Deductions❖, Depreciation❖
E	=	Equity
A	=	Appreciation
L	=	Leverage

Let's compare real-estate investing to, say, stock-market❖ investing:

The *I* Stands for "Income"

Does the stock market give you income? On the happy days, it sure does. Some might tell you right now that it doesn't, especially when they're looking at their 401(k) like it's a 201(k). If you really know your stuff, though, the stock market can give you income, no doubt about it. Does real estate give you income? When you do it right, it sure does.

The *D* Stands for "Deductions" and Also for "Depreciation"

Does the stock market give you tax deductions? Yes, when you lose. Does real estate give you tax deductions? That's a big yes. Not only does it give you stellar deductions, it also has this funny deduction called depreciation.

That's when the IRS says that you can get a deduction for the fact that your house is depreciating in value every year. "But wait," you may think, "I know my house is *appreciating.* Is the IRS just stupid?" (Don't answer that!) They actually do indeed know that the values are going up, but it's a deduction they created to stimulate real-estate investing. They want people to invest in real estate. It keeps America strong. Real-estate investing kept America from terrible financial ruin after 9/11 (just one woman's opinion). So take your cool depreciation deduction and enjoy it.

Oh, yeah, there are rules and regulations, but it's still very, very cool. It can save you a lot of money in taxes over the years if your tax preparer knows his stuff. (Be sure to ask him, because I'm definitely not a tax expert. My own adviser has used this deduction for me, so I'm passing on the hint to you.)

The *E* Stands for "Equity"

Remember from your glossary that equity is the difference between the amount your property is worth and the amount you owe on it? Does the stock market have equity? Some say yes. I wouldn't care to argue the point, but I think maybe the answer is "not really." Does real estate have equity? If you buy it right, it sure does. Give me equity in real estate any day. Values of homes nationwide have gone up overall since 1931.

The *A* Stands for "Appreciation"

That is when something goes up in value. Does a stock❖ or bond❖ appreciate? Yes, it sure can. Does real estate appreciate? Yes, it sure can. I personally favor real estate because the trends of up and down are broader, longer, easier to see.

What's another word for "appreciation"? How about "inflation"❖? Isn't that when everything is going up in price? The price of milk, the price of gas, the price of a vacation, the price of a big-screen TV, and the price of a house are all going up during inflation. Well, isn't that the same as appreciation?

Think about this: Do rich people look at inflation differently than poor people? Well, does a real-estate investor want the values of her properties to go up? The answer is yes.

Now, let's take a little quiz. What's the one thing that is not adjusted upward during a period of inflation? Usually, someone in my audience will say "my salary"! Well, actually, salaries are supposed to go up during inflation through a cost-of-living❖ increase. That's where you get 2 percent to 3 percent more in your paycheck to cover the fact that living life costs 2 to 3 percent more.

That's not the answer. The answer is this: *debt.* Your debt doesn't go up during inflation; it keeps going down. Even if you're in the first year of your home loan, when most of the payment is going toward interest, your loan is still going down, even if slowly.

And what's another word for "loan"? "Leverage.❖"

The *L* Stands for "Leverage"

That means the money you've borrowed on the house. It means OPM. The term *leverage* comes from the concept that you can move something heavy if you can use leverage, like using a crowbar and a rock to move a Jeep stuck in the mud. Other people's money lets you buy things you couldn't buy without that extra push. Donald Trump probably didn't get rich without OPM. Robert Allen didn't succeed as the world's most famous real-estate investor without OPM. I used OPM every step of the way. Leverage of money is one of the most beautiful aspects of real estate.

Does the stock market use leverage? Yes, there are some ways you can borrow the money that you're going to invest. However, real estate is where leverage really is king. I borrowed my way to millionaire. So can you (real soon).

The *S* Stands for "Safety"?

Just for fun, let's add an *S* to the acronym. *I.D.E.A.L.S.* Real estate has long been known as the safest investment on earth. One reason why is that "they're not making any more of it"! By the way, if you switch around the letters in *I.D.E.A.L.S.,* it spells *L.A.D.I.E.S.* (John Childers came up with that clever observation. Thanks, John!)

L	=	Leverage
A	=	Appreciation
D	=	Deductions, Depreciation
I	=	Income
E	=	Equity
S	=	Safety

John always asks, "Which sentence is better? 'If I can work out the details, I'll take it,' or 'I'll take it if I can work out the details'?" The answer is the second one. If you're focused on working out the details, someone else will swoop in and buy your great deal while you were thinking and figuring. Tell them, "I'll take it," and get yourself the chance to work out the details. If they don't work out to your liking, then you won't take it. Simple, huh? And beautiful. Simple is often beautiful. Let's all say it together: "I'll take it!"

I'll take it. I'll take it (if I can work out the details). I'll take it!
—JOHN CHILDERS, KAREN NELSON BELL, AND YOU

Word Wizard

___ Acronym	Letters that stand for something besides the word itself.
___ Stock Market	The place where people trade stocks and bonds, and so on (see below).
___ Deduction	Amounts of money that you can legitimately remove from your total income for the year so that you end up paying less taxes.
___ Depreciation	A unique type of deduction that the IRS lets you take regarding your real-estate investments; subject to rules.
___ Stock	A piece of paper that represents a piece of ownership in a company's worth.
___ Bond	A piece of paper that represents a piece of ownership in a city, county, state, or nation's worth.
___ Inflation	A time in the nation's economy when prices are going up, up, up.
___ Cost of Living	What it costs to live in America; there's actually a cost-of-living index that takes into account the price of everything we buy and figures out if we're paying more or less than we did last year or last month.
___ Leverage	A way to get more power to move things; a way to get more power to buy things. The money lent on something, the loans on something.

Quiz Wizard

1. What does the acronym *I.D.E.A.L.S.* stand for in relation to real-estate investing?

    I = _____

    D = _____

    E = _____

    A = _____

    L = _____

    S = _____

2. What's the one thing that doesn't go up in price during a period of inflation?
   a. Wages
   b. Debt
   c. Taxes
   d. Gasoline
   e. College education

3. Which sentence is better? If I can work out the details, I'll take it, or I'll take it if I can work out the details?
   a. If I can work out the details, I'll take it.
   b. I'll take it if I can work out the details.

Turn to page 435 for the answers.

Whiz Wizard

1. Say "I'll take it!" out loud three times. Tell someone else to say it with you three times! I'm dead serious about this step, by the way. Don't you dare pass this one up! LOL—abbreviation on the internet for laughing out loud! Yes, you can laugh, but don't even think of passing up this step!
   Done _____

2. Call up a FSBO seller, go through the five questions with the person, and tell her, "I'll take it if I can work out the details." Do you have to take it? No, not if you can't work out the details. This exercise isn't for you to actually *take it,* it's just for you to get used to saying it! It's to help remove fear and give you confidence that it's OK to say "I'll take it." Write down how saying "I'll take it" made you feel. Remember, you're just practicing your scripts, so it doesn't matter what happens; therefore, no fears!
   Done _____

3. Teach the concept of I.D.E.A.L.S. to someone else so that he or she understands it.
   Done _____

100 Percent Rate of Return

(Make All Your Mutual-fund Friends Jealous!)

Let me give you a really fun example of leverage in action.

First, I'm going to give you $100,000 in cash! How do you like that? I hope a big cheer went up at your house!

The only thing is, you have to do with it exactly what I tell you, OK? Excellent.

I want you to pretend that you live in a city where you can still buy houses for $100,000. If you *do* live in a city like that, well, great! I chose that amount because it makes the math easy to understand. I'm not very good at math (that's what calculators are for), but I want you to be able to see this example very clearly.

Steps to Take

Step one: Go buy yourself a house worth $100,000 with the money I just gave you. Buy it in an area where the houses are going up in value each year by 10 percent. That should be pretty easy to do across America today. If you have to go to another city, OK.

Step two: Keep the house for at least a year. You can rent it out to someone who will pay you every month, or you can leave it vacant.

Step three: If the house grew in value during that year by 10 percent, how much money is that? Ten grand, right? Right.

Step four: What was the rate of "return on investment," or "ROI"❖? The answer gets expressed as a percentage, like the ROI on a bank savings account.

If you spent $100,000, and you made $10,000, what was your ROI? Ten percent, right? Right. Ready to go on?

Another $100,000 Gift from KNB

Let's do this all over again. That's right, I'm going to give you another $100,000 (and the crowd goes wild).

Step one: Go buy another house, just like the first one, but this time, tuck $90,000 of the money into your back pocket for a rainy day. Go out and find a lender who will loan you $90,000 on this $100,000 house. We know that's going to be easy; we have already met lenders who will even lend $100,000. But we're just borrowing $90,000 and putting down $10,000.

Step two: Keep the house for at least a year and rent it out to someone who will pay you enough to cover your mortgage❖ payment every month.

Step three: If the house grew in value during that year by 10 percent, how much money is that? $10,000, right? Right.

Step four: What was the rate of return on investment, or ROI? Once again, the answer gets expressed like the ROI on a bank savings account.

If you spent $10,000, and you made $10,000, what was your ROI? Wow! That's kind of hard to figure out—you might have to use a calculator.

It's *100 percent*! "Wow" again! Let that soak in. You just learned how to earn 100 percent return on your investment. You doubled your money. And you did it by using leverage. You used other people's money so that you could earn a higher ROI. Let's say it together: *wow!*

By the way, this isn't some trick I'm playing with words. Do you think your friends who are watching their bank savings earn 1 to 4 percent interest would like to know that you've just earned 100 percent? And you, would you rather earn 10 percent or 100 percent? By the way, you still have $90,000 in your back pocket. How many more times could you do this deal? Nine more times. And you'd have bought $1 million of real estate. How many times could you do this deal if you were putting down only 5 percent, or $5,000, on each house? You could buy twenty houses with $100,000. Would you rather buy one house or twenty houses? Me, I'd rather buy twenty.

There's another point you need to think about: The money you were using wasn't really yours. You didn't come out of pocket for one penny; it was *my* money. I was your source of OPM. So let's recalculate the ROI.

If you spent zero dollars, and you made $10,000, what's your rate of return?

Some of you may know the term for it: It's *infinite*. I had never heard of that before I learned this example. "Wow" one more time! An infinite rate of return❖. And you get that rate by using other people's money. This *Nothing Down* stuff is really starting to sound better and better, isn't it? When we get to the chapter on how to actually get other people's resources, you're going to be completely ready, I'll bet!

Well, I've been getting 100 percent, to 1,000 percent, to infinite rates of return for the last six years as I buy properties. By the way, you don't have to have appreciation for this strategy to work. All you have to do is buy the properties at a discount, and you'll get the same benefit.

I hope you've enjoyed this little demonstration of the power of leverage!

Motto for the day: Rule out the phrase "I don't have enough money"❖. Strike it from your vocabulary. If you hear yourself say it, snap a rubber band around your wrist to associate a little pain and punishment with the phrase (Bob's trick). It's very hard to remove this phrase, and it's equally hard to remove the thinking.

Let's find something to replace it with, something that will be congruent❖ with your core beliefs. If you really believe you don't have enough money, just saying you do have enough won't be believed by the core-level you. Let's replace it with this:

"Where can I get it?❖"

This phrase flips your mind into problem-solving mode. It takes away the victim mind-set and replaces it with the problem-solving mind-set. "Where can I get it?" isn't a phrase that your core self will have any trouble agreeing with—it's congruent.

Never: I don't have enough. Always: Where can I get it?

Where can I get it?
—KAREN NELSON BELL

Word Wizard

___ Congruent | When things seem to be in alignment, when they correspond, when they match; when what you say matches what you do.

___ ROI | Return on Investment; the rate of benefit you get from an investment, expressed as a percentage.

___ Mortgage | A home loan; it's called different things in different states. For now, just know that it's a loan on a house.

___ Infinite Rate of Return | The incredible kind of ROI you can get when you use *Nothing Down* strategies, where no money at all comes out of your pocket.

___ "I Don't Have Enough Money" | Something you don't ever say, something you don't ever think, something you don't even understand anymore—something you've replaced with "Where can I get it?"

___ "Where Can I Get It?" | The sentence that instantly transforms you into "Super Solver," the super heroine that goes around finding solutions everywhere.

Quiz Wizard

1. If you could get a home-equity line for $100,000, how much real estate could you potentially buy?
   a. $100,000
   b. $500,000
   c. $750,000
   d. $1,000,000
   e. $2,000,000

2.   What's ROI? And what's the highest ROI you can get?
    a. Rate over income   100 percent
    b. Royalty on interest   200 percent
    c. Return on investment   Infinite

3.   If you were in the building stages of your investing career, would it be smarter to pay cash for a house or to get a loan and make a small down payment?
    a. Pay cash.
    b. Make a little down payment and get a loan.

Turn to page 435 for the answers.

Whiz Wizard

1.   Say "Where can I get it?" over and over until you feel it replacing "I don't have enough." Yes, you know the drill, really do this step. Do it out loud, and get your family and friends to join you in your new mantra. Do it for me. Do it for you.
Done _____

2.   Call up three more FSBO sellers, go through the five questions with them, and see what happens. There's no pressure to make a deal, just do it for fun!
Done _____

3.   Teach the concept of 100 percent rate of return to someone else until he or she understands it. If this helping tripped you up at all, be sure to go back and diagram the steps on paper. Or use Monopoly money to do a little demo of the steps until you get it.
Done _____

Retire in Ten Years with Ten Houses

(And Let Someone Else Pay for Your Kids' Education!)

I'm going to show you how to retire in ten years just by buying one house per year! Of course, you can speed it up and get there sooner, or you can buy more houses per year and have a more luxurious retirement. The thing is, you're not going to be one of the folks worried about Social "Insecurity"❖—oops, Social Security❖.

Take These Steps

Step one: Buy a house this year and rent it out. Buy a house next year and rent it out. Do that every year for ten years. I don't care how you buy it—*Nothing Down,* creative financing, discount or retail, from a FSBO or a Realtor—just get out there and buy a house every year for ten years.

Step two: Wait. Wait for ten years. In that time, will the property value probably have gone up? Will the mortgage probably have gone down? The answer to both is probably yes.

Step three: In the eleventh year, take the property you bought in the first year and refinance❖ it. Don't take a lot of money out of it, maybe 60 to 70 percent of its value, and do what's called a "cash-out refi"❖. This means taking a loan against the new, higher value of your home. Make sure that the rents can still cover the payments. Of course, rents will have probably risen in that decade too.

Step four: Enjoy that tax-free money during year eleven. Yes, it's tax free❖ because the money you get from loans is not considered income. Ask your tax preparer. I met an accountant one time who insisted this plan was illegal. He was a former IRS agent turned CPA❖. Well, when he called up all his friends to verify that I was doing something wrong, he got the thrill of his career. "Wow, I never heard of it before," he said, "but this is totally legal and, yes, tax free. What a plan!"

Step five: In the twelfth year, take the property you bought in the second year and refinance it. Now you're getting the picture: You're going to do this every year. And when the twenty-first year rolls around, you can start all over again, because the houses will have appreciated another decade! That's a better retirement than any government plan I ever heard of.

Free College for Your Kids

You can let someone else pay for your kids to go to college with this same strategy. Buy a house for every child that you have to send to school. Buy it *now*. By the time he's ready for the university, just refinance the house, and let the renter pay for your Johnny to go off to campus. Johnny can live in a condo❖ that you buy for him, and his rent can be covered by his roommates, who pay enough to cover the mortgage. When Johnny graduates, he'll understand property management, and he can keep it, sell it, and pay you back, or you can gift it to him. I just love the part about someone else paying for his tuition and someone else paying for his housing. Johnny will be the only one of his friends who doesn't have to worry about paying back all those student loans.

One Simple Step to Security

Here's another nifty plan:

If you ask one hundred people to name the best investment they ever made, almost all of them will say their home. If it was such a great investment, why didn't they buy two?

Let's check out the actual investment:

1. Did they earn any income from it? No.
2. Did they use creative financing? No.
3. Did they get any special training to buy it? No.
4. Was it an asset❖? No. It was a liability, at least until they paid it in full, because they had to pay the mortgage every month. Some investment!

I can remember my dad at the end of his life, when he still had about four more years left on his mortgage. He had run out of dough, and when he became ill, Duncan and I brought him to live with us in our home. We rented out his home to cover his medical expenses. What if Dad had bought just one more house and put a renter in it?

Well, in thirty years, his house would have been owned free and clear. Also, the house that had the renter in it would be free and clear too, because the renter would have paid off the mortgage. Then he would have had a place to live with no expenses except utilities, and he would have had income from the renter to cover those utilities, plus enough to pay for gas, food, and an occasional movie. That's a better life than most Americans achieve.

If all you do with this book is find a way to purchase your own home and one other, you'll be ahead of the game. You'll be in the top 5 percent of Americans who won't become a burden to their families and friends, and you won't be begging for handouts from the government. You might even find yourself in a position to help others in need. All because you bought one house to live in and one house to rent out!

These two strategies sure give a lot of hope to a lot of people who don't know what's coming around the bend.

Our fundamental products in the real-estate investing game are hope and help.

—KAREN NELSON BELL

Word Wizard

___ Social Insecurity	A play on words, suggesting that Social Security might not be there for the younger generation to enjoy.
___ Social Security	A government program designed to give secure retirement funds to people who have paid into its program during their lives; mandatory investment taken out of a person's paycheck.
___ Finance	To obtain a loan for a property.
___ Refinance	To obtain a new loan on a property that you already have a loan on.
___ Refi	Short for *refinance*.
___ Cash-out Refi	A kind of Refi where you can get money—actual cash—if you have enough equity in the property.
___ Tax Free	Money that comes into your account that you don't have to pay taxes on.
___ CPA	Certified public accountant; a person who has been certified by the state and is able to do accounting and tax preparation.
___ Accounting	Keeping financial affairs accounted for in an orderly fashion.
___ Condo	Short for *condominium;* housing similar to apartments, but owned by the tenants instead of rented. Sometimes apartment complexes are converted into condominiums.
___ Asset	In this context, something you own that produces income.

Quiz Wizard

1. How soon can you retire if you follow my nifty plan? What year?
    a. Twelve months from now
    b. Five years from now
    c. Ten years from now
    d. Fifteen years from now
    e. Twenty years from now

2. What's the minimum number of houses you should own?
    a. Two
    b. Three
    c. Five
    d. Ten
    e. Twenty

3. How can you get someone else to send your kids to college? (Pretend you have kids if necessary!)
    a. Write a paragraph to explain this concept:

    _____

    _____

    _____

Turn to page 435 for the answers.

Whiz Wizard

1. Explain my Buy-a-House-Every-Year-for-Ten-Years Retirement Plan to someone else. As you know by now, your homework always includes teaching something to another person. If you can teach it, you get it. I've learned so-oooooo much from teaching, and I want you to feel the satisfaction of it!
    Done _____

2. Explain my Get-Someone-Else-to-Pay-for-Your-Kids'-College-Education Plan to someone else.
    Done _____

3. Call up a three more FSBO sellers, go through the five questions with them, and see what happens. Do you get the idea that you're going to be making phone calls for a while? Bob Allen says that you need to call at least one hundred people before you'll know what your average results are. If you know you always get one yes out of every one hundred people you call, you'll be ecstatic after that ninety-ninth no, because the next one is your big yes. That way, you'll never be discouraged by a rejection! It just means you're that much closer to the real deal!
    (Pretty soon, you'll be getting some new twists to use on the calls! Hang in there with me, OK?)
    Done _____

HELPING 10

It's All about You

(Your Own Dreams and Goals)

This helping is all about you and your own personal real-estate investing. What's more fun to talk about than yourself (LOL)?!

Robert Allen stresses the fact that all the strategies and techniques in the world will not overcome a "losing mind-set." In his books, he offers up an abundance❖ of ways for a person to begin shifting from a scarcity mentality❖ to an affluence mentality❖.

When people ask me what enabled me to succeed so rapidly in my investing career, I think of several things. One was that Duncan and I got ourselves a $100,000 equity loan to use as other people's money; another was that we had very good credit. If you have ready access to OPM, and you also have good credit, it does speed up the process. You don't have to have money or credit at all to make this work, but I believe you can go faster if you do.

However, looking back, I think the most important element that put me on the fast track was that I had been working on the abundance mind-set for years. I knew that before I could change my finances, I had to change me.

This book isn't essentially about mind-set, but one thing is sure: The clearer you are about what you want, the more able you will be to have the physical universe agree with your intention.

Vivid Vision

Robert Allen challenged me on my first training conference call with him, when I was just learning about the Protégé Program. He said that whoever wrote the best "Vivid Vision❖" would get a special tape set. I decided to organize my goals with every tool he had to offer. I spent a couple of weeks inventing my new life. When I wrote my Vivid Vision for five years into the future and sent it in, I could see everything with perfect clarity.

About a year later, I ran across the Vivid Vision, and I was astonished. So many of the details had come true. My favorite point that I had written in my vision was that Robert would mention Duncan and me in his new best seller, and we would celebrate its ascent to number one. How amazing it was when I realized that Bob and Mark actually did give us a paragraph in their best seller that year.

I want you to have that same chance to predict the future—to create the future. Enjoy the fact that there is no real quiz in this helping and that your homework is all about you!

Always do right. It will gratify some people and astonish the rest!
—MARK TWAIN

Word Wizard

___ Scarcity Mentality	The trick your subconscious mind can play on you that causes you to operate on old and useless programming, saying that there isn't enough.
___ Affluence Mentality	The mind-set that it is your responsibility to develop, so that you can create a wonderful affluence that will allow you to do great and noble things for yourself, your family, your community, and your fellow man (one woman's opinion).
___ Abundance	The concept that there is so much good in the world, all intended for us to enjoy and to share; that there is more than enough to go around for everyone forever.

___ Vivid Vision   A beautiful technique I learned from Robert Allen that lets you luxuriate in your perfect future five years down the road in order to begin actually creating that very future.

Quiz Wizard

1. Didn't I say there wouldn't be a real quiz? Yes or no?
   - a. Yes
   - b. No

2. What's the most fun thing to talk about and to think about?
   - a. Yourself
   - b. The weather
   - c. Yourself
   - d. Real Estate
   - e. Yourself
   - f. Philosophy
   - g. Yourself

3. This isn't really a quiz, is it? Yes or no?
   - a. Yes
   - b. No

Turn to page 435 for the answers.

Whiz Wizard

1. You'll write your Vivid Vision statement as a letter to someone you love, living or dead. Fill it with sensory details, as if you are already living in your beautiful future five years from now. There is an amazing power in writing your statement to another person. It has to do with the fact that this planet is a two-pole universe, negative and positive, male and female, north and south, yin and yang. You can send it or not send it, but if this person really sup-

ports you in positive ways, getting her agreement that your future is what you've written can be very powerful. The Vivid Vision that helped bring me so much happy success was written to my dear friend from my college days, Rita Harrington, as if five years had passed. Go to www.ND4W.com/vision to see that actual Vivid Vision statement I had written then.

Enjoy this step; there is no right or wrong.

Done _____

5MM Time Capsule 1

5MM Module 1, Helpings 1–10

Here's what we covered in this module. By now, you should feel very comfortable explaining these points to someone else. Check off every point that you feel absolutely certain you understand. If there are points you don't really feel good about, please, please, *puleeeeeeez* go back through the materials on a hunt for any words you didn't get cleared up. Promise? Great!

When you come back a year or two from now and look at this list in your Time Capsule, you'll be amazed at how comfortable you are with the data. Here's the checklist of what you've learned. See how smart you are?

Helping 1:
___ The secret of what *Nothing Down* really means.
___ A few places where you can find *Nothing Down* money.

Helping 2:
___ What *Find, Fund, Farm* really means.
___ The one thing that would guarantee your failure in *Nothing Down* investing.
___ What investing in real estate the *Nothing Down* way is really about.

___ The big difference between *Nothing Down* investing and the regular world of real-estate agents.

Helping 3:
___ The difference between price and terms when negotiating a good deal.
___ When to pay full price for a house.

Helping 4:
___ The Seventh Commandment in real-estate investing.

Helpings 1, 2, 3, 4:
___ The seven platinum rules for real-estate investors to ensure your success.

Helpings 5, 6:
___ Five specific things to say when you call on a FSBO that will let you know if the person is motivated and get you started on a good path to negotiating.
___ How to ask "Why are you selling?" in a way that doesn't come across as rude.
___ When you should wait to buy real estate.

Helping 6:
___ The magic of the Money Pause.

Helping 7:
___ The power of leverage.
___ What *I.D.E.A.L.S.* stands for in real-estate investing.

Helping 8:
___ How to get a 100 percent rate of return—or more—when everyone around you is getting 10 percent or less.
___What to do the minute the thought "I don't have enough money" crosses your mind.

Helping 9:
___ How to retire by buying one house a year for ten years.
___ How to retire by buying two houses.

Helping 10:
___One special trick to make your Vivid Vision goals for your real estate work even better.

___ I understand all the above points so well that I have taught them to someone else.

Wow, if you saw those points in a promotional marketing piece, you'd be blown away. Just think! You've finished only ten helpings of data in module 1, and you already know that entire list! Because you're in this to win all the way, you're building a strong foundation. Demand excellence from yourself!

Bobservations

Ladies, I've seen the future and it is *you*. The very qualities that define your sex, even according to the contentious science of gender differentiation, predispose you to the characteristics of a good real-estate investor. We're in the people business. Houses and money are the ancillary by-products of the activities you'll undertake. If it's true that men (in general) care more about things, and women (in general) care more about people, then women have a great advantage with people-centric *Nothing Down* strategies.

Take as an example KNB's phrase "How can you bear to part with it?" We men barge right in and ask, "Why the heck are you selling?" Five times out of ten, we get a resistive response like, "None of your business." The womanly way of not creating an adversarial stance really is more effective, I think. The seller ends up pouring out his heart to you. In fact, I'm going to try it next time!

As another example, I, Bob Allen, would like you to firmly refuse to be the first one to mention a number. Karen Bell would like you to go ahead and mention a number if you're pushed into it, hoping you'll get a no. Instead of ending up in a testosterone-driven battle, you get straight to the seller's true bottom line. I think I'm going have to "get more in touch with my feminine side," because I love where you're headed as investors.

After years of defending the concepts of *Nothing Down* against criticisms of doubting reporters, I see a new wave of women demonstrating how the techniques really do work, and how they work best when applied with kindness, empathy, and intuition. The future really is *you*.

MODULE 2

FIX YOUR CREDIT NOW!

HELPING 11

Fix Your Credit Now

(Your Get-out-of-Debt Mind-set Is Stopping You)

This is going to be a very short module with only one crucial helping!

Yes, I could save this topic for later in your lessons, when we're studying all the ways to fund real estate with little or no money of your own, but it's better to get you going on repairing anything negative in your credit❖ now, just in case it'll help you later.

I'm going to show you how to invest without any cash or any credit, no doubt about it, but if you have good credit, it makes things easier and faster. You'll have more resources for other people's money if you've shown that you're trustworthy with other people's money! That's what credit is! It's somebody wanting to do business with you because you've demonstrated that you know how to handle your finances. "I gotta give him credit, he's really got a way with animals." That sentence didn't refer to financial credit, it was personal credence. However, it's that personal credibility that's at the core of financial credit.

It's Easier to Borrow $10 Million Than to Earn It

About a year ago, I was attending Mark Victor Hansen's annual MEGA Speaking Event in Southern California, and as I walked toward the back of the room to stretch my legs on a break, I glanced down at a book on a table in front of another attendee. The book cover was shiny and bright red, like a big, inviting candy apple, and it said, *From Credit Repair to Credit Millionaire.*

That book winked at me and said, "Take me home." It wasn't even published yet. I didn't even have bad credit. I just had to have the glossy red candy apple. The title was so-ooooo appealing. I introduced myself to the author and asked if I could buy one. She hadn't sold any yet, and she wasn't ready for my order, but Donna Fox said yes, and we became friends on the spot. I wrote her a check, and I received the delicious book in the mail a week later.

Donna has written what I believe to be the best book in the universe on the subject of credit. It's not just the best for credit repair from a consumer-credit❖ point of view, but also the best for credit borrowing for business people, especially real-estate investors. She goes deep into techniques for using other people's money that no one else wants you to know. She teaches you how to fix things you thought couldn't be fixed. She teaches you how to get dough out of thin air for your business.

I Did It!

Well, if I sound like a living, breathing testimonial, it's because within one week of reading her book, I had removed a very damaging item from my business credit report. That removal paved the way for me to get a $20,000 line of credit❖ for my corporation❖ without having to put up any collateral❖ whatsoever.

Then, about three months later, I needed some money for a big property I was making an offer on, and using Donna's techniques, my company qualified for a $4.5 million loan! That meant it wouldn't even show up on my personal credit report! Whew, was I ever grateful to Donna!

Aren't books amazing? Robert Allen changed my whole life with his book, and Donna changed my whole business bank account with *From Credit Repair to Credit Millionaire.*

Donna's website is filled with great tips and great resources, so your homework for this chapter is to pay her a visit. Even if your credit is superb, you're going to find information that will pave the way for you to do what she did on her first loan ever: She borrowed $5 million to invest in real estate. Even if your personal credit score is at the very top, wouldn't you love to know how to parlay that advantage into great business credit, so you could do what Donna and I did?

My first puny little $20,000 seemed humble by comparison, but then I received an invitation to apply for a $50,000 credit line for the biz. Hmmmm, that took care of a few down payments on a few properties, and it was other people's money! It didn't even show up on my personal credit report! Yea!

The book is so hip that I've been giving it to all my team members. My personal banker has a copy; he loves it and sends his customers to the website. My mortgage broker said it had stuff she'd never even heard of or thought of, and that it rocked. In fact, I've given away a whole box of books just because it helped my team members to all think congruently from Donna's unique and creative viewpoints.

OK, I'll say it: Donna Fox "rox"! Let's get your credit strong enough to borrow your way to "credit millionaire"! I asked Donna to contribute a "helping" to give you enough data to get started. Here's what she wrote just for you:

> Dear Karen,
>
> I've prepared this explanation especially for your readers because they probably aren't the typical credit consumers, since they're going to be looking at things from a professional investor's viewpoint. I hope you enjoy the way it's presented, in alignment with your 5-Minute Mentor principles.

(The Get-out-of-Debt Mind-set Is Holding You Back) by Donna Fox

"Who wants to be debt free?" I often start my speaking engagements with these words. Usually, the entire audience raises its hands. Do *you* want to be debt free?

The next statement out of my mouth astounds the

room: "I don't want to be debt free at all. In fact, I have a goal to be $100 million in debt."

I continue. "Of course I want to be $100 million in debt someday, because, after all, you are what you owe." Jaws drop, and a nervous murmur begins in the room.

"Now that I have your attention, let me explain."

I then continue to tell the audience that the get-out-of-debt mind-set may really be holding them back.

Why do some people work all their lives and retire in debt, and others become millionaires seemingly overnight? We don't know all the reasons, but we do know one of the secrets that creates millionaires.

You could become a millionaire working at a job. Let's say you have an above-average salary, earning $50,000 annually. Further, let's imagine that you can work miracles and save every penny of that salary. In twenty years, you will be a millionaire! Can you wait?

You already know the secret to being wealthy; it's the reason you bought this book. You know it's the power of leverage—using other people's money and doing deals with *Nothing Down*.

Good Debt—You Are What You Owe

You are what you owe only if you go into debt to buy assets that pay for themselves. Eventually, the loan is paid off, and you own the asset free and clear, as well as the income from the debt. For example, let's say that you buy a $100,000 property, and the mortgage and expenses on that property are $1,000 a month, and you can rent the house for $1,300 a month. The numbers may be unrealistic for your area, but the concepts still apply.

If you hold on to the property for thirty years, you'll have earned $3,600 annually in income from the property (let's assume no rental increases), and the loan will have been paid off entirely. What do you own now? You've got a $100,000 home (also assuming no appreciation!), $1,300 in income each month, and no debt. Do this ten times, and you're a millionaire.

See, it's easier to borrow $1 million than it ever is to earn it. And when you borrow smart, for the purposes of accumulating asset-backed debt❖ that pays for itself, soon you'll have made your $1 million.

But why stop there? I want you to be one of KNB's megamillionaires❖. If you can use the power of leverage—taking a small amount of your money and using it to move a whole lot of other people's money—to buy asset-backed debt that pays for itself and grows your personal fortune, wouldn't you want to do that over and over again? Unlike working at a job, you can easily generate this kind of wealth in your life ten times over, or even hundredfold.

Why Stop at One Million? Go for Megamillionaire!

I want to be worth $100 million one day, so the necessary stepping stone to get there is to have $100 million in asset-backed debt, just like the kind of situation described above.

If you take a cross section of the world's most affluent people, you will find that they all used the power of leverage to grow their personal and business fortunes. They know it takes money to make money, and they know that the easiest money to have access to is other people's money!

To obtain access to other people's money, you need good credit.

But wait a minute! Isn't it a classic *Nothing Down* position that you can buy property with no credit?

It's true, my mentor Robert Allen told me that you can buy property with no credit. However, when I really dug into the subject of credit and what it meant, I realized he wasn't exactly right.

What Bob really means to say is that you can buy property without a good credit *score*. And he's right about that. See, there are dozens of strategies that you can implement from this very book to purchase property where no one will take a look at your credit report or care one bit about your credit score. As I like to say, you don't have to drop your financial drawers and have your assets examined.

But they absolutely require credit.

What Is Robert Allen's Credit Score?

Confused? Consider Robert Allen.

What's Robert's credit score? I don't know either, but what I do know is that Bob tells the story onstage of how he lost everything due to a devastating avalanche and how he had to climb back from the very depths of financial ruin. So his score most likely stunk. It may still stink, yet he can get all the financing he needs for his business activity.

It's because Bob has good "credit." Because good credit is so much more than credit score. What Bob has is one of the Five C's of Credit❖, which are the only five factors that a banker can use to make a lending decision. The C that Bob has is Credibility—and he has that by the truckload.

Credibility is your reputation in the community and the financial marketplace. Your credit score is part of your credibility, but only a very small part of it. It's also part recommendations that you receive, testimonials from satisfied customers, and referrals.

When you're getting started in real estate and you work with an owner in foreclosure and "get the deed," or buy a property where you pay the seller directly, you aren't using your credit score, it's true. However, you are absolutely using credit. Your ability to develop a rapport with someone, and get him to trust you, so that he eventually agrees to sell his property to you is a sign that you've convinced him you are credible. And credibility is the most powerful C of credit.

As you can see, credit score really doesn't matter when you're getting started. Good credit makes things easier, but it's not necessary—at first.

There comes a time in an investor's career, and it's

usually sooner than she realizes, when she will want to tap into some of the sources of other people's money that are available to her. When this time comes, credit score is highly important.

Banks, credit card companies, the U.S. Small Business Administration (SBA), and other easily obtainable and ready sources of unsecured cash will all want to see a good credit score. It's unavoidable in your investment career if you want to keep growing and succeeding in business. You must go through the bank-funding phase before you reach the next level.

Eventually, like Robert Allen, and yes, Karen Nelson Bell, no one cares about your score any longer. When you reach these levels, it's your credibility that gets you the loan. It's your reputation and track record. You become a good credit risk simply because of who you are.

Most new investors don't really know how close they are to this level. Just starting out, it's hard to imagine making $1 million in real estate. However, I did it in my first year, and so did Karen.

Which is why it's important to start now to build your credit, and your credit score!

Sincerely,
Donna Fox

It's easier to borrow ten million than it is to earn it.
—DONNA FOX

Word Wizard

___ Credit

In this chapter, *credit* means how you rate in the eyes of lenders, as represented by an artificial number known as your "score."

___ Consumer Credit

The credit that most Americans have in the form of credit cards, gasoline cards, department store cards, and so on, which they use to buy consumable goods or services.

___ Line of Credit — A form of credit that lets the borrower use any portion of the whole amount and then pay it back, then use it again and pay it back again, in whole or in part, over and over.

___ Corporation — A business structure.

___ Collateral — Something a person pledges when he borrows money; something valuable that the lender can keep if the borrower doesn't pay back the debt.

___ Asset-backed Debt — A loan that is secured by something tangible owned by the borrower.

___ Megamillionaires — People who have a net worth of $100 million or more, coined by KNB.

___ Five Cs of Credit — Character (Credibility), Capacity, Collateral, Capital, and Conditions.

___ FICO Score — Fair Isaac & Co.; it's the most recognized firm that uses fancy computer measuring tools to recommend to lenders whether you're a good credit risk or not. FICO assigns your credit a score that gives the lender an idea of how likely you are to pay back the loan you're seeking.

Quiz Wizard

1. What is consumer credit? (This is a trick question!)
   a. Credit for things you consume.
   b. Credit for things that go down in value.
   c. Putting a vacation on your Visa.
   d. Putting a down payment for a house on your MasterCard.
   e. Putting an equity line of credit on your house.

2. Why would a person who already has good credit research the subject of credit repair? (This is a trick question too!)
   a. To find out her credit score.
   b. To create ways to get credit for a business to use to purchase real estate.

    c. To show up her neighbors.

    d. To keep her credit from going down in the future.

    e. To help sellers who are in foreclosure with their credit problems.

3. What is the core foundation of financial credit?

    a. Credibility.

    b. Your FICO score.

Turn to page 435 for the answers.

Whiz Wizard

1. Go to www.ND4W.com/credit and take a look around. Enjoy the data prepared for you there!
Done _____

2. If you don't know what your credit score is, go to www.creditexpert.com to find out what your score is with Experian, one of the three major credit reporting agencies. The others are TransUnion and Equifax. You can get your scores for all three for about $40, but you can get a good idea of your score by just checking for free on Experian. You can also try www.MyFICO.com or others.
Done _____

3. Teach the concept of "It's easier to borrow $10 million than to earn it" to someone else so that he or she understands it.
Done _____

5MM Time Capsule 2

5MM Module 2, Helping 11

Here's what we covered in this module. These are the points that you should feel very comfortable with, and by now you should be able to explain these points to someone else.

Helping 11:
____ What the core of financial credit is.
____ The concept of "It's easier to borrow $10 million than to earn it."
____ When it would be good to be in more and more debt.
____ Why you are what you owe.
____ One cool reason why a person wouldn't need a good credit score.

Word Wizard:
____ The Five Cs of Credit.

Whiz Wizard:
____ I went to www.ND4W.com/credit and looked around.
____ I know my credit score, and I'm beginning to develop ways to get business credit for real-estate investing.

When you're done checking off every item, you can get started on module 3!

Bobservations

When you really understand the difference between *good* debt and *bad* debt, and when you can envision and demonstrate that you have no difficulties whatsoever exerting conscientious control over the use of the good debt, you're on the road to real wealth. I do see many people, and yes, many of them are women, who fit the common caricature of credit captives. We all probably have been deep in consumer debt at one time or another, struggling to break free of that pecuniary prison. Good debt is vastly, astonishingly different.

Whereas bad debt will take you hostage, good debt can set you free. If you borrow money to pay for an asset that goes up in value year after year, and if someone else pays the payments on the loan, you've created a triple-win situation. The lender is happy to make all the interest, the person paying the payments is happy to have a wonderful home with an enlightened landlord, and you're especially happy when you see that "Paid in Full" at the end of the loan, when you now have an asset with no loan on it and with all the payments going directly to *you*.

Ladies, if you'll take the time and energy to learn to become highly effective borrowers, you'll create a legacy for you and your family that reaches far beyond the normal definition of retirement. Let's call it "re-*fire*-ment." You'll be fired up for living, emblazoned with bountiful passion for whatever you were DNA-encoded to do in this life.

MODULE 3

FINDING DEALS

Why Sellers Become Motivated

From my experience in teaching over the years, I've found that certain specific issues account for most of the students' fears and concerns. One of them is incredulity❖ regarding the availability of good deals. When I say incredulity, I mean the lack of ability to believe that there are any deals such as Robert Allen describes as desirable. Some students feel that there simply aren't any motivated❖ sellers. Some others refuse to believe there are any deals in their own hometown, because their town is somehow different in one way or another. Before we're done here, we'll address those issues and more.

This module's title is plain: "Finding Deals." Not only is that a title, it's also your job description. Remember the motto we learned in module 1 about great money flowing to great deals? Well, your new job is *finding* good deals and great deals. Once you've done that, the rest will fall into place.

Here's the scenario: You find a great deal; you don't know what to do next. You call up your mentor on Monday for help; your mentor gives you the next few steps of homework that will get you going. You do the steps and call her again on Tuesday; more steps. You call on Wednesday; more steps. You call on Thursday; even more steps. And voilà! on Friday you share with everyone how you just finished a really, really good deal. How much did you have to know to get started? You only had to know how to ask the "Fave Five." Let's call them that from now on, OK?

The Fave Five

1. "Is this a good time to talk?"
2. "What can you tell me about the property?"
3. "Wow . . . that sounds so nice. How can you bear to part with it?"
4. "What are you hoping to get for it?" (Pause) *Schzzssssshhh.*
5. "How low could you go if I could close fast, and I give you all cash?"

Motivations

Now all you need to do is discover where to look for people to talk to. Exactly where is one supposed to find these "motivated" individuals? First let's think up all the reasons that somebody might become motivated. You know, when people first buy a house, they probably think they're going to stay there forever and live happily ever after. Whenever I ask a class what they think are some reasons for people to become motivated, there's one word that always gets shouted in unison: divorce. Is there divorce where you live?

The next most common answer is "loss of job." Sometimes a whole city can experience job losses when an industry changes its needs. Try making a mortgage payment when you haven't had a paycheck for six months. Just knowing that you can't pay the mortgage puts a mental, emotional stress on you that says, "I gotta move. I gotta live someplace I can afford. I gotta get outta here now!" Do people ever lose their jobs where you live?

Maybe the seller didn't lose his job. Maybe his company was downsizing and asked him to take a reduction in pay. Maybe he had to move to another city. Any of these things can cause a person to become very motivated to make a change in his living environment.

By the way, if a person had to be transferred, it's possible that he might not have been able to sell his house in the first city before he moved to the second city. Now he has two houses and two mortgages. The first house is vacant and draining his pocketbook. You will look at vacant houses in a new light from this day forward. Vacant houses equal potential motivated sellers. If you see one, stop the car, take out your pad, write down the address, and look up the owner's contact information from county records❖. Yes sir, those vacant houses are gonna be very, very interesting from now on!

When a reduced paycheck or an out-of-work status has gone on too long, how easy would it be to go into debt overload? Overwhelming consumer debt is making financial prisoners out of millions of Americans. Then, when the debt gets too enormous, calls from cranky creditors❖ are followed by bankruptcy❖, foreclosure❖, or both. Are there bankruptcies where you live? Are there foreclosures?

What about gambling problems? It used to be that Las Vegas was the only place where that might be a real issue. Years ago, there were only two states with gambling. Now, all but three states—Tennessee, Hawaii, and Utah—have some form of legal gambling. With gambling on the internet, it's really every place you look. Don't ever discount the particular motivation that a compulsive gambler in trouble might feel. Is there gambling where you live?

Here's a motivation you may not have thought of: The home owner has a nasty loan with a too-high interest rate; the rates go up even higher, and now his paycheck doesn't even come close to covering the mortgage payment. He doesn't have good credit, so he can't refinance, especially since he was late three months in a row, scrambling to get the darn thing paid.

What about illness? What about a death in the family? These are times when people must make life changes. They can become very motivated overnight. Families that have to deal with issues of caring for mom and dad often have high motivation. Honestly, do people get sick or die where you live?

Ah, then there's the IRS. What happens when someone gets into a problem or disagreement with the IRS? Tax problems can cause a seller to become *highly* motivated.

Some people just don't want to take care of their "deferred maintenance"❖. That's a fancy way of saying they didn't keep the place up. Now they just want to move away from the problems. It could be a landlord, or another investor who has the problems too. Maybe it isn't just the fix-up, maybe it's problem renters. The investor could be getting older and just wants to cash out.

Wow, all of these problems seem so sad. I'm getting a little teary eyed, aren't you? Are these all the folks we're going to take advantage of? No, no, and *no*. Remember module 1: We're going to *help* them. They truly do need and deserve our help, don't they? They're going to remember us as their guardian angels if we do our investing the right way.

Merry Motivations

Are there any happy reasons why people become motivated sellers? Of course there are!

What about someone who wants a bigger, nicer home? (That's how we got the $1.2 million mansion that turned us into millionaires. The gal wanted a $5-mil pad.) Maybe they want a smaller home for less upkeep. Maybe it's an older couple who are experiencing empty-nest syndrome! Maybe it's a younger couple and there's a new baby on the way! By the way, are babies being born where you live?

Here's my personal favorite, because the motivation is such a nice circumstance: retirement! Yes, I love, love, *love* dealing with people who are motivated because they're getting ready to retire. They're often not only motivated to do a discount (they own the property free and clear and have a lot of wiggle room for negotiation), but they also may not want to have a lump-sum payment and are ready to discuss seller financing so that they can give themselves an ongoing income stream in their retirement! Nice for them, nice for you—it's just nice all around! Are there any people retiring where you live?

Here's a list to keep handy:

- Newspaper (houses for sale and houses for rent)
- Notice of Default (NOD) list at the county court house or Notice of Default letters
- Divorce notices
- Bankruptcy notices
- Internet sites
- For Sale by Owner signs (FSBO)
- For Sale by Owner lists and websites
- Vacant houses
- Bank REO departments ("Real Estate Owned," or re-possessions)
- County court house sales of foreclosures
- Call real-estate management companies

- For Rent signs put up by management companies; find the owner
- Drive around different neighborhoods
- Advertise in newspaper
- Advertise on billboards
- Give out business cards
- Word of mouth
- Tell everyone you meet your sixty-second "elevator speech"
- Out-of-state owners
- We Buy Houses billboards and ads (other investors)
- Advertising on your car
- Your ad saying that you buy houses (to find them *pre*default)
- Title companies
- Realtors who can look up motivated people on MLS, as well as seller financing, out-of-state owners, and so on.

You can think up more reasons for motivation. There are as many motivations, as many problems, as there are people. You'll definitely call me up someday and tell me about a really unique problem your seller had, and how you solved it! It's this really great game: You listen to what the person is saying, you come up with a solution, you solve the problem, and everyone benefits.

Now that you've got the idea that someone actually could possibly be motivated, even in your own hometown, in the next helping we'll talk about where to find these people. At least for now, would you agree that there could possibly be a seller where you live who could possibly be motivated? Great, my mission's accomplished.

The best tool an investor can have is her ability to listen.
—KAREN NELSON BELL

Word Wizard

___ Incredulity	The condition or quality of not being able to believe something.
___ Motivated	Having an urgent reason to do something. A seller could be motivated to sell either at a better price or better terms

because he has a big problem of some kind. A real-estate student could be motivated to study because she has a problem (like not enough money) or because she is passionate about something (like keeping her family's financial future safe).

___ County Records

Public records held at the building of the county's court house, viewable by the general public; records such as property ownership, divorce decrees, bankruptcy proceedings, and so forth.

___ Creditors

Companies or individuals to whom you owe money.

___ Bankruptcy

A legal procedure that allows a person in debt the chance to wipe out all his bills; other kinds of bankruptcies allow a person to reorganize his bills so he can have a chance to pay them.

___ Foreclosure

A legal procedure that happens when a person doesn't pay his home loan over some months' time, and the lender either threatens to take away the house or actually does end up taking away the house; there are four stages of foreclosure, which you'll be learning later.

___ Deferred Maintenance

A fancy name for fix-up work that hasn't been done; procrastination of the proper upkeep of a house.

Quiz Wizard

1. What are three of the most common reasons a seller might be motivated to come down in price or help with terms?
    a. Divorce.
    b. Hunger.
    c. Loss of job.
    d. Sleep deprivation.
    e. Overwhelming consumer debt.

2.   What are three of the nicest reasons a seller might be motivated?
    a. Moving to a bigger, nicer home.
    b. Keeping up with the Joneses.
    c. Having a baby.
    d. Trying to be helpful to the buyer.
    e. Retiring.

3.   Why is it a win-win situation when you find a motivated seller who's retiring soon?
    a. The sellers could possibly view you as an offspring of their own and give you the house.
    b. The sellers could save on their taxes, get a stream of income, and you could get a property without going to the bank.
    c. The sellers might pay you to stay in the house and take care of it while they're in Florida, or wherever they retire.

Turn to page 436 for the answers.

Whiz Wizard

1.   Call your county court house and ask where they keep the public records. Also ask what you would have to do in order to view something that was a public record. Ask if the records are available any other way than personally visiting the courthouse, like subscribing to a legal paper or going to a website.
    Done _____

2.   Use some method that you've discovered in the previous step to view some records. They could be any one of the following: (1) public notices that people haven't paid their mortgage, (2) divorce decrees, (3) bankruptcy filings, (4) tax delinquencies, (5) public auctions (sales) of properties that are in foreclosure.
    Done _____

3.   Teach the concept of "what causes motivation" to someone else so that he or she understands it.
    Done _____

Exactly Where to Find Them

We've figured out *why* folks might become motivated. Now let's figure out *where* to *find* them!

Here's a list for you, and it's going to be listed in order of cost to you:

Free:

1. Local newspaper (houses for sale and houses for rent).
2. Newspapers online. (I love this one; most have a clipboard feature so that you can get a nice, clean list of the properties that interest you. You don't get any ink on your fingers! And you can look up most metropolitan areas all over the country!)
3. Small newspapers like *Nifty Nickel, Thrifty Nickel, Shifty Nickel* (?), *PennySaver,* and so on.
4. Notice of Default (NOD)❖ list at the county court house.
5. Divorce notices.
6. Bankruptcy notices.
7. Internet sites (here are a few samples out of the hundreds of thousands).

    www.ForSaleByOwner.com
    www.eBay.com
    www.fsbo.com
    www.CraigsList.com
    www.Realtor.com

8. For Sale by Owner signs.
9. Vacant houses.
10. Bank "REO❖" departments ("Real Estate Owned❖," or repossessions❖).
11. County court house records, in addition to Notice of Default: sales of foreclosures, divorce decrees, bankruptcies.
12. Lists of Notices of Default (NOD) from free sources (I get mine from a title company❖).
13. Call property-management companies.
14. Call title companies where you have a contact or team member.
15. Call mortgage companies where you have a contact or team member.
16. Call attorneys who are team members of yours.
17. Drive around different neighborhoods on your way to work.
18. Call on For Rent signs by management companies.
19. "Bird dogs" (people who scout for you for a fee), postman, gas-meter reader, teenage neighbors, friends, business associates, church members, the list goes on and on!).
20. Word of mouth.
21. Tell everyone you meet your sixty-second "elevator speech❖."

Some Cost:

1. Give out business cards (don't worry, next chapter is all about *your* business card).
2. Realtors who can search (look up) "motivated" people on the MLS❖, or they can search for seller financing❖, out-of-state owners, REOs, foreclosures, new construction❖.
3. Letters to out-of-state owners.
4. We Buy Houses type billboards and ads placed by other investors.

5. Small We Buy Houses type signs of your own.
6. Notice of Default lists that cost a fee.
7. Letters to people on Notice of Default lists.
8. Advertising on your car, vinyl letters or magnetic signs.
9. Flyers.
10. Postcards.
11. Door hangers.
12. www.LandVoice.com❖.

LandVoice.com is one of my very favorite finds. We met them through one of our 5MM Action Weekend graduates who happened to be a Realtor. He called it "the best kept secret" in the world for real-estate agents. For my money, he was absolutely right.

LandVoice.com searches every day for all-new FSBO listings. They look in the regular newspapers, little newspapers like the *Thrifty Nickel,* and all FSBO websites. Then they send you the data every morning in your in-box as a list or as an Excel spreadsheet❖. Not only that, LandVoice.com keeps a database of all the listings for six months on its website, and you can search it using special criteria like price or style of property. I use the database more than the daily emails, because I like to go back in time and find people who haven't sold yet and are discouraged.

The service has an affiliate program, so if you sign up and you spread the word to other members, you can end up getting the service for free. You can sign up for two cities, but you can always add more, and if you go on a vacation, you can route your account to the vacation city if you're thinking of investing there!

Go to www.ND4W.com/LandVoice. It really is the best kept secret in real estate. When people find out about it, they don't want anyone else to know!

High Cost:

1. Your newspaper ad saying that you buy houses
2. Radio advertising
3. TV advertising
4. We Buy Houses type billboards of your own

Here are some statistics on how I found good and great deals: About 40 percent have been found through word of mouth (business cards, bird dogs, friends, relatives, students), another 35 percent have been done with our wonderful Realtors, and the other 25 percent have come from LandVoice.com, letters to people in foreclosure, calling on ads, and running our own ads in the newspaper.

You'll find some of these ways that suit you more than others (and ways that suit your city more than others). You may even find some new ways of your own, and I hope you'll let me know when you do!

> *The more communication you* outflow, *the more communication you*
> *will* inflow. *The more communication you* inflow, *the more* deals *you'll*
> *find. Therefore, communicate!*
>
> —KAREN NELSON BELL

Word Wizard

___ Default	In this section, the meaning refers to a situation where a person hasn't paid his home loan in a timely fashion; he's usually ninety days late, and the default would start on the ninety-first day. The time a home goes into default differs according to locale.
___ Notice of Default (NOD)	A public statement by letter and/or newspaper to home owners, letting them know they've gone too long without paying their home loan, and now they'll have a certain amount of time to catch up their payments or else lose their home in a foreclosure auction; also known as NOD.
___ REO	Short for Real Estate Owned.
___ Real Estate Owned	REO, the actual real estate that the bank owns; technically, there's another acronym, OREO, Other Real Estate Owned, which means all the properties that the bank *repossessed*. REO actually means the properties the bank owns; in other words, its own assets, like the bank building. Most people just use the term REO.

___ Repossess	A legal process used by lenders to take back a property. The owner possessed it to live in, then when he didn't pay, the lender re*possessed* it.
___ Title	A piece of paper that confirms the true owner of a piece of property; it could be a piece of paper that confirms the true owner of other items as well, such as a car.
___ Title Company	A company that provides title insurance (actual insurance that the title is free and clear and can be transferred from the seller to the buyer); a title company performs many other services for Realtors, investors, buyers, and sellers.
___ Elevator Speech	What you would say about your business if you met someone in an elevator and only had sixty seconds to get them interested in your product or service.
___ MLS	Multiple Listing Service, the place where the normal retail real-estate world lists all the houses that are for sale. Realtors can search this database using special search criteria; you can find all the properties listed on the MLS by going to www.Realtor.com, and you can search, but not in as detailed ways as a Realtor. These will *not* be FSBOs; you may still find motivated people who have listed with a Realtor.
___ Seller Financing	An arrangement between the buyer and the seller where the buyer pays the seller for all or part of the amount owed for the home; the buyer doesn't have to go get a bank or mortgage company to lend them the money; often the buyer doesn't even have to have good credit.
___ New Construction	Homes being constructed by builders right now; never been lived in; may be in the beginning stages, and the house isn't a house, it's dirt; new communities or

developments where you can buy a home before it's built, pick out the carpet colors and design upgrades. Some builders won't let investors buy and some will.

___ www.LandVoice.com   A company that delivers FSBO leads to your in-box daily.

___ Excel Spreadsheet   A nifty way of keeping track of stuff, especially when there are lots of numbers involved (Excel is a particular brand of spreadsheet made by Microsoft); if you haven't learned how to work with spreadsheets, you may want to have a friend teach you how. It's easy once you learn it, and it'll help you a lot in your future real-estate investing career; a great way to track Notice of Default lists and FSBO lists.

Quiz Wizard

1. What are three *free* ways you could find a motivated seller today?
   - a. Radio shows
   - b. Word of mouth
   - c. Newspapers
   - d. Vacant houses
   - e. Flyers

2. What is an NOD list?
   - a. Not on Demand
   - b. Not Overdue
   - c. Never Over Draft
   - d. Notice of Default
   - e. Nine Other Dogs

3. How many methods of finding motivated sellers should you use? (Answer not given in the text.)
   - a. At least six
   - b. More than ten

    c. As many as it takes

    d. Less than one hundred

    e. All the free methods

Turn to page 436 for the answers.

Whiz Wizard

1.   Using your local newspaper, whether the real paper or the online paper, call on three FSBO ads that appear to have some motivation. Ask the Fave Five questions. Write down the sellers' responses. You don't have to make a deal, just find out if anyone you call is actually motivated.* If you can't find them in your own paper, call on leads from www.ReviewJournal.com. Don't worry if you don't plan on buying in Las Vegas; you're *practicing* talking to people. Then when a deal does come in your area of choice, you'll be confident and smooth.

    Done _____

    *OK, you can start to make a deal if you feel like jumping ahead or if a seller is so motivated that you have to act right now, but you are not obligated by the terms of this action step to do so!

2.   Write down what you might say to someone for your elevator speech, and read it to another person. Begin memorizing it and saying it as often as you can to your friends.

    Done _____

3.   Teach the concept of where to find motivated sellers to someone else so that he or she understands it.

    Done _____

HELPING 14

Biz Cards,
Your Minibillboards

In the last section, you heard about my statistics, and maybe you were surprised that 40 percent of my deals have been found by word of mouth. Well, to be fair, I counted deals that came from other forms of word of mouth, like business cards and elevator speeches. A business card is something you hand to someone you're talking to, so in a way, it's a *symbol* of word of mouth.

Here's the story of the first deal Duncan and I found after we joined the Protégé Program. We had just bought one thousand business cards because it was part of our homework for John Childers' class. At that time, there were only two real-estate classes, one taught on the phone on Saturday morning by Tom Painter, and one taught on Tuesday evening by John. I attended both of them, and I treated every bit of homework as if I were back in high school and my parents were watching me like a hawk.

Biz Card Homework Worked!

So of course, when John said to go hand out one hundred business cards, I did so without question. They weren't very good cards, not like the ones I'm going to show you in this chapter. They were just plain old cards, like everyone else's business cards. That makes this story even better, I think.

Duncan was waiting for me while I was in a doctor's appointment, and he struck up a conversation with a lady in the waiting room. She was, coincidentally, a wealthy real-estate investor herself, and she sure didn't need our services. But she specialized in a different style of investing, so Duncan's elevator speech about helping people in foreclosure kind of piqued her interest.

She took Duncan's card, but we never thought she'd call. Well, she didn't call, but she *did* give the card to a friend of hers at church. That friend was in a bad foreclosure situation, about to lose his home. He called us up and asked, "Can you help?"

The rest is history. We bought the house for nothing down, and it had $75,000 worth of equity. We got $18,000 cash back at closing, and we moved into it! The house was huge, almost 5,000 square feet; it had seven bedrooms and five baths, plus three fireplaces, and a gorgeous pool and spa! We had never dreamed of living in such a nice home. Boy, this homework landed us in a great circumstance! We never suspected that over the next four years the home would soar in value and its worth would become $450,000 more than what we paid for. We were making money just by going to sleep at night! Wow!

OK, that was one little step of homework with one simple business card. Are you itching to go get your own cards and start handing them out? Great! Let me give you some ideas on how to create an even better card than the one we used.

Fluffy Versus Stuffy

By the way, I do think you need two different cards. One should be a more formal one, suitable to present to bankers, lenders, or other professionals. It should be made with raised black letters on white linen paper. I never knew this until recently, but some more conservative professions throw away your card if it doesn't conform to these standards. Whew! The other one should be a minibillboard telling people what's in it for them. It should *not* be conservative! It should let them know that you're the one person they can trust to help them with their problem. You'll have two cards; you could say there'll be a stuffy card❖ and a fluffy card❖.

Below, you'll find a sample of the fluffy card.

You'll notice that I don't bother including the name of the company or the address. It's a waste of space, in my opinion. Motivated sellers don't care where your company is, because they're not going to go there or send any mail there. You'll be going to them! You can see I've put the main concept of what we do in big, bold letters in the center.

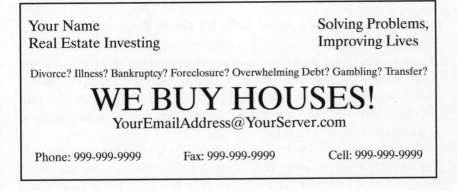

Your Name Real Estate Investing	Solving Problems, Improving Lives

Divorce? Illness? Bankruptcy? Foreclosure? Overwhelming Debt? Gambling? Transfer?

WE BUY HOUSES!
YourEmailAddress@YourServer.com

Phone: 999-999-9999   Fax: 999-999-9999   Cell: 999-999-9999

I've been testing different phrases for a pretty long while, and "We Buy Houses!" still wins out. I put little one-word questions above that, because it conserves space, but it puts a lot of information there in a short, concise way. I do make sure the cards have a phone number and a fax number, since people in foreclosure will be faxing you documents. I also put the email address, but honestly, people in trouble often don't have internet service at the moment—it's just a courtesy to put it there.

Solving Problems, Improving Lives

While I don't think it's important to have your company name, I do indeed think it's important to have your company *slogan*. There should be some quick and easy way for people to get a feel for what kind of a person you are. My motto is "Solving problems, improving lives." You're very welcome to borrow that slogan, but the best thing is to find something that truly expresses your own core values.

There are lots of variations on the We Buy Houses business card. Some people put more information on the back. Some turn them into minibrochures by using a fold-over kind of card. I like those very, very much. However, you need to get started right now, and you may not have the big bucks for those fancy cards. You can go to your office-supply warehouse and get one thousand blank business cards that you can bring home and print to your heart's desire. You can experiment and see what works best for you, using only one hundred at a time.

If It's Good Enough for Bob, It's Good Enough for Me!

Bob wrote a story about an investor who puts an offer of a $1,000 finder's fee on the back of her business cards. I thought, "If it's good enough for Bob to put in a book, I'll do it!" I tried it out, and so did some of our personal students, and guess what amount worked the very best? Guess!

Yep, $100 got us the best response. Why do you suppose that is? Do you think it's because $100 is more believable to most people? I do. Now what I do is *not* print anything on the back. I write it by hand and say, "Look, I don't want you to throw my card away, so I'm going to write a dollar figure here on the back, and if you give my card to someone I end up doing a deal with, I'm going to send you a thank-you check for that amount!" Then really do that. You'll be very tickled with the look on the person's face when they get the check, because they never expect it. It's great fun!

Now, here's the most important thing I want you to learn out of this section: Give the cards out. If you don't give them out, there's no communication. Cards represent contact betweeen one human and another. Give them out. Cards are a symbol of energy, *your* energy, energy that you're willing to expend on someone else's problems.

Did I mention that I want you to give them out?

And oh, by the way, the last thing I want to say is, *"Give them out!"*

Motto for the day: Give them out!

—KAREN NELSON BELL

(WELL, IT'S NOT EXACTLY A MOTTO, IS IT? JUST DO IT!)

Word Wizard

___ Stuffy Card   The kind of formal card you would give to a professional in a conservative field like banking, lending, title insurance, and so forth.

___ Fluffy Card   The kind of informal sales-y brochure card you would give to a potential motivated seller or someone who might *know* a motivated seller; a card that tells recipients what's in it for them.

Quiz Wizard

1. What's the most important thing to know about business cards?
    a. Give them out.
    b. Hand them out.
    c. Distribute them.
    d. Disseminate them.
    e. Give them out.

2. Who might receive your stuffy card? (This is a trick question.)
    a. Your stuffy Aunt Effie.
    b. Your banker.
    c. The people on your NOD list.
    d. Your title-company rep.
    e. Your mortgage-company president.
    f. Your minister.

3. What is the one thing a person needs to do to insure that their business card will be effective?
    a. Hand them out.
    b. Hand them out.
    c. Hand them out.
    d. Hand them out.
    e. Hand them out.

Turn to page 436 for the answers.

Whiz Wizard

1. Design a fluffy card for yourself, or have someone do it for you.
    Done _____

2. Get your fluffy card printed, either with your own printer or at a
    professional shop like Kinko's or OfficeMax.
    Done _____

3. Hand out ten cards to ten people.
    Done _____

4. Teach the concept of why and how to use business cards to some-
    one else so that he or she understands it.
    Done _____

If you'd like a free copy of a template you can use in MS Word to create your own card with a simple design described here, go to www.ND4W.com/bizcard.

Rate the Ads

(How to Laser-tune Your Call List)

If you look in the newspaper ads, and you see language like the following, you can guess that the sellers might be Don't-Wanters:

- Transferred
- Must sell
- Quick sale
- Priced for quick sale
- Owner desperate
- Vacant
- Owner will carry (OWC)❖
- In over our heads
- Fixer-upper❖
- Divorce forces sale
- For sale by owner
- Nothing down
- Low down payment
- Seller financing
- Bad credit OK
- Bank repo❖
- Will consider any offer

- Make offer
- OBO❖
- As is❖
- Handyman special
- Butt ugly (a real ad)
- Immediate occupancy❖
- Great investment
- Foreclosure
- HUD foreclosure❖
- People with 1031 Exchange❖ needs

When you're calling on ads, you can increase your likelihood of finding a motivated seller by calling on the ads that have these hints in them. In fact, Robert Allen says that we should rate the ads, giving one point to each phrase that indicates motivation. You should call on the ads that rate a four or a five before you call on ads that rate only a one or a two. We don't want to waste any time.

By the way, do you think "For Sale by Owner" is an indication of motivation? Well, it can be or it can *not* be. It could just be a seller who's anxious to avoid paying Realtor fees❖ and isn't motivated at all.

I like to tell this story: Denise Michaels, the author of *Testosterone-free Marketing: The Yin and Yang of Marketing for Women,* was one of my first personal students. When she was doing her homework calling on FSBOs, she called a woman selling a condo who hadn't indicated any special motivation. Denise discovered that she was selling because her husband's transfer hadn't come through, and she wanted to move back to Texas quickly to be with her family shortly after 9/11. Denise asked the lady if she would consider letting her take over the mortgage payments and get a U-Haul trailer to take her stuff back to Texas. The lady said yes, and forty-eight hours later Denise and her fiancée owned a condo for $5,000 under market value, no money down.

The gal hadn't put any phrases in her ad, but she was sure motivated. I guess she just hadn't ever taken a real-estate class to learn about writing ads!

I always keep that story in mind, and I call all the FSBOs. I just don't get discouraged when they aren't motivated.

If you live in a very hot market with rapid appreciation in the double digits, you may not find as many of these keywords. If so, call on properties in another area so that you can get practice for when your market shifts. You could also consider buying in another area *if* you set up a team there (more on team building in another helping).

But when the sellers aren't motivated, I just remember my favorite four-letter word: next! If I know I'm going to get at least one yes out of every hundred calls, I get more and more excited with every no I hear, because I figure it's bringing me one step closer to the big yes!

> No *and* next *are my two favorite companion words. Every time I hear*
> *'no,' I say 'next,' and I know I'm that much closer to my* next *deal!*
> —KAREN NELSON BELL

Word Wizard

___ OWC	Short for "owner will carry."
___ Owner Will Carry	The seller will "carry" or "hold" the home loan, the down payment, or both, so that the buyer doesn't have to go to conventional financing resources.
___ Fixer-upper	A property that needs more than just a little cosmetic work; potential for deep discounts on a fixer-upper.
___ Repo	Short for *repossession.*
___ OBO	Or Best Offer; indicates the seller's willingness to negotiate.
___ As Is	The seller won't be doing any fixing up; all the responsibility for anything you find wrong will be yours.
___ Immediate Occupancy	Vacant property!
___ HUD	Short for U.S. Department of Housing and Urban Development; HUD's mission is to increase home ownership, support community development, and increase access to affordable housing free from discrimination.
___ Urban	Referring to city as opposed to suburbs (suburban) or countryside (rural).
___ HUD Foreclosure	A home that was covered by HUD, one that got foreclosed on and went back to ownership of the lender; available for

purchase by bid through a HUD-authorized Realtor.

___ 1031 Exchange — A real-estate tax strategy that allows a person to defer her taxes until later.

___ Realtor Fees — Typical fees that go to Realtors are 6 percent to 7 percent of the deal; if a $100,000 house is sold through Realtors, the fee would be $6,000 to $7,000; the buyer's agent and the seller's agent split the fee, usually in half; an agent representing both sides gets the whole fee; the agents must give a sizable percent to the broker who owns the agency they work for.

Quiz Wizard

1. How do you rate a real-estate ad?
    a. By how long it is
    b. By how short it is
    c. By the price listed
    d. By the number of motivated-sounding phrases in it
    e. By the area where the property is located

2. Does the abbreviation *FSBO* indicate motivation?
    a. Yes
    b. No

3. What's your favorite four-letter word (*my* favorite four-letter word)?
    a. Drat
    b. Heck
    c. Next
    d. Darn
    e. Rats

Turn to page 436 for the answers.

Whiz Wizard

1. Find ten FSBO ads in your newspaper (or another newspaper) that have motivated phrases in them and rate them. Use www.ReviewJournal.com if your own paper doesn't have enough.
Done _____

2. Call all ten ads, calling the highest rated first. Ask the Fave Five questions, take down the answers, and evaluate the degree of motivation. You don't need to worry about making a deal, just get used to finding some motivated people. If you just *have* to make a deal, call your mentor and have her walk you through the subsequent steps. But heavens to Betsy, don't feel pressured to do anything more than evaluate motivation! I want to keep this exercise as non-scary as possible! This is just for practice, so that when a real deal comes along, you'll be cool as a cucumber!
Done _____

3. Teach the concept of rating advertisements to someone else so that he or she understands it.
Done _____

HELPING 16

Easy Negotiating

(Comfortable Scripts to Get You Started)

Part of finding a deal is actually getting the deal to be *yours* and not some other investor's deal. You have to listen, listen, listen, and after that, feel the seller's pain, feel his problem. Then and only then can you begin to talk to him about solutions.

The first five questions you learned, "The Fave Five," are great for your initial conversations on the phone. You wouldn't go see a property unless you had already discovered a potential good deal. (A lot of Realtors have complained to me that they feel like glorified chauffeurs and salespersons. They spend all their time driving people around. We *never* spend time driving around unless we already know a good deal could come of it.)

Would-ja Take?

It's time for you to have a longer and more productive conversation with your sellers. OK, it's even getting to be time to pop the question. Yep, I'm referring to the "Would-ja take?❖" question. Once the seller has told you the figure he's *hoping* to get, you've done the

118

Money Pause, and you know you've got a flexible person on the other end of the conversation, it time to say "would-ja take?" Say it out loud with me! "Would-ja take?" Tom Painter taught me that one, and it will be ringing in my ears the rest of my life. "Would-ja take?" That's as in "Would-ja take $187,500?" Get it?

I'll bet you'd like some more nifty scripts, so that's what this helping is all about. It's about comfortable negotiating. It's about finding some phrases to get you going. After a while, you'll discover you're just listening and responding, and scripts will become a thing of the past. I don't use scripts now, but they sure came in handy for me when I was starting out. Are they a crutch? Yes, a very comfy, cozy crutch to get you over the fear of going further than the Fave Five with your motivated seller.

The Fave Five

The Favorite Five (a little reminder):
1. "Is this a good time to talk?"
2. "What can you tell me about the property?"
3. "Wow . . . that sounds so nice. How can you bear to part with it?"
4. "What are you hoping to get for it?" (*Pause.*) "Sczzschhhhh."
5. "How low could you go if I could close fast, and I give you all cash?"

Four for the Phone

The next four questions can happen on the phone, or they can happen when you visit the property for the first time.

1. "If you were going to move into the house tomorrow, what would you fix?" (*Helps get an honest answer about the condition of the property.*)
2. "Would you consider a rent-to-own❖ agreement?" (*Helps begin discussions on the concept of seller financing, even if the seller has never heard of seller financing. Everyone has heard of rent-to-own. If the seller shows any willingness at all to think*

119

*about it, you're opening up the subject of creative financing❖.
Just don't ever use the term "creative financing" or "seller financing" with your seller, unless the person is another investor.*)

3.   "When would you hope to close?" (*Lets you know if you need to close fast or slow.*)

4.   "If you don't mind my asking, what will you do with the proceeds❖?" (*This is such a cool question, I'm going to tell you a story about it now.*)

Whatcha Gonna Do with It?

I heard a story about a protégé who lived in the Midwest, and he found a seller who was highly motivated. Let's call him "Protégé Joe." Joe negotiated a deal with the seller, "Sam," to buy Sam's $100,000 house.

During the negotiations, Joe said, "Sam, if you don't mind my asking, what will you be doing with the proceeds❖?"

Sam told Joe that his wife had died recently, leaving $30,000 in medical bills. He intended to use the money from the sale of the house to pay off the medical expenses and also to pay off the $50,000 left on his mortgage.

Joe asked, "Sam, if I would take care of the medical bills, and if I could take over paying the payments on the mortgage, you could get on down to Florida right away. Would we have a deal?"

Sam happily agreed. Joe then went to the hospital and told them he was trying to help Sam pay off his wife's bill, since Sam was having trouble handling it. Joe negotiated the fees down to $13,000, which he put on a credit card!

So you see, Joe acquired the house for $63,000: $50K for the mortgage payments and $13K to the hospital. He acquired it with no money out of his own savings account and none of his own credit, since he didn't have to go get a bank loan; he just took over Sam's payments. (You'll learn how to do that in a later chapter!) Sam was thrilled, because he just wanted out from under the problems so he could go to Florida.

The reason I wanted you to hear that story is to drive home the importance of asking one little question. And when you phrase it the way Robert Allen teaches it, no one seems to mind:

"If you don't mind my asking, what will you do with the proceeds?"

Chain Yankers

The questions in this next set are the kind you might ask if you're already at the property. They're designed to help chip away at the seller's idea that the house is worth more than market value. Have a clipboard and jot down all the "deferred maintenance" you can observe.

- "Do those trucks make that much noise at night?"
- "Isn't that where the break-in occurred?"
- "How far will my kids have to walk to school?"
- "When was the roof last replaced? Air-conditioning?"
- "How long have you been trying to sell it?"
- "Have you tried anything to remove those stains? Odors?"

"Do We Have a Deal?"

These last seven questions are pure Robert Allen at his finest. They're useful when you're getting near the end of the negotiating process, and you just haven't quite come to any real agreement yet.

1. "If I can solve that one aspect, do we have a satisfactory deal then?" (If I can solve "that," do we have a deal?) (*This will tell you the seller will in fact do the deal. You just have to solve the one item!*)
2. "Can *you* help me figure out a way we can solve both our needs?" (*Involve the seller.*)
3. "Is there anything I need to clarify?" (*Use diagrams, illustrations. Don't ever ask, "Is there anything you don't understand?" Make it your fault something isn't clear, not the other person's!*)
4. "It *appears* we are still somewhat far apart in some aspects. May I suggest (*insert your suggestion here*)?" Then ask them, "What do *you* suggest?"
5. "Would you accept an offer that would provide you with $2,043.96 per month for the next fifteen years?" (*This question might be good when you're talking to a person who's retiring and might like to have a stream of income.*

> *You'll learn what to do and how to figure out the payments in a later chapter.*)

6. "How would you like it if I could show you how you could . . ." (whatever would be to the other person's benefit). (*Listen to your seller to figure out what's in it for him!*)

And last of all:

7. "Would-ja take?" (*As in "Would-ja take $149,500 for it?" In the final analysis, you have to make an offer the seller can accept or reject. You'll already have a great feel for it, because you'll have had enough communication to give you a notion of his or her flexibility.*)

Fear is expensive.
—ROBERT G. ALLEN

Word Wizard

___ "Would-ja Take?"	"Would you take?" A way of making an offer; "would-ja take $9,000?"
___ Rent to Own	An agreement between the renter/buyer and the seller that allows the renter to buy the property at some time in the future; sometimes a portion of the rent goes toward the eventual down payment.
___ Creative Financing	A phrase that has come to refer to all the wonderful strategies that Robert Allen offers to the world in his *Nothing Down* books.
___ Proceeds	The money that comes as a result of a sale.

Quiz Wizard

1. What could you say to get a true picture of a property's condition?
   a. What's the real deal here with all this mold?

    b. What would *you* fix if *you* were going to move in to-
       morrow?

    c. What's the condition of the property?

    d. How much fixing up is there to do?

    e. Why is the property boarded up?

2.   When would you ask, "Would-ja take?"
      a. On the phone on the second call.
      b. After getting in communication a little bit.
      c. After getting an idea of the seller's motivation.
      d. When you want to see just how low the seller might go.
      e. When nothing else works.

3.   Why would you want to know what the seller intends to do with
    the proceeds?
      a. To see if he has a problem you could solve creatively to
        make a win-win deal.
      b. To find out more about the seller's motivation.
      c. To get in better communication.
      d. To create a better deal.
      e. All the above.

Turn to page 436 for the answers.

Whiz Wizard

1.   Call motivated FSBOs until you find one that sounds like a potential deal. Have a conversation in which you really listen to the person's explanation of his situation. Use any of the questions above
that seem appropriate. Ask, "When would be a good time for me
to view the property?" Make a time to visit the property. This will
ideally be done in or near your own city.
Done _____

2.   OK, we've arrived at the time when you can actually go out and
see a house. You can even make an offer if you want to. Your
mentors can take a look at it afterward to see if you're on the
right track. But for now, all you have to do is go for a visit. Take
your clipboard with you and write down everything you see and

hear! If you don't feel like you're ready to do anything else, just tell the sellers you need to discuss everything with your partner and thank them for their time.

Done _____

3. Teach the concept of using handy scripts to someone else so that he or she understands it.

Done _____

5MM Time Capsule 3

5MM Module 3, Helpings 12–16

Here's what we covered in this chapter. These are the points you should feel very comfortable with, and by now, you should be able to explain these points to someone else. Check off every point you feel absolutely sure you understand.

If you're working with me as your 5-Minute Mentor at www.ND4W.com, be sure to clear up anything you feel a little foggy on. If there are points you don't feel good about, please don't go on until we can sort it out. Get on the phone calls and clear up whatever has you bugged, OK? Promise? Great!

Now here's a checklist of what you've learned. See how smart you are??? You're gonna be very surprised at how much you already know after just three modules of information:

Helping 12:

___ Your job description as a new real-estate investor.

___ The best tool an investor can have.

___ Ten really good reasons why sellers become motivated.

___ Five happy reasons why sellers become motivated.

Helping 13:

___ Twenty-one ways to find motivated sellers for free.

___ Twelve ways to find motivated sellers for very little.

___ Four more great ways to find motivated sellers that are definitely worth the high cost.

Helping 14:

___ Stuffy cards versus fluffy cards.

___ Templates for biz cards that really work in the real world.

___ A way to get free biz cards.

___ How to make sure no one throws away your biz card.

___ The most important secret there is about biz cards.

Helping 15:

___ How to rate classified ads so that you call the most motivated sellers first.

Helping 16:

___ Exactly what to say to find out the true condition of a property.

___ Exactly what to say to determine the level of your seller's motivation.

___ Exactly what to say to find out if seller financing might be possible.

___ Exactly what to say to see what the seller is going to do with the money from the sale.

___ Exactly what to say to actually make your first offer.

___ Six things to say to get your seller away from the idea that his house is worth top dollar.

___ Seven things to say to get over the hump when a deal isn't going your way.

___ How to grow more and more comfortable in negotiating.

___ I understand all the above points so well that I've taught them myself!

Wow, if you tell your friends you learned all that out of five bite-size helpings of information, they wouldn't believe you. When you've checked off every item, you can get started on module 4!

Bobservations

Fundamentally, good *Nothing Down* investing depends largely on communication. While there are styles of investing suited to people who are too shy to communicate, I urge you to develop a willingness to be in communication with your sellers. Because you, as a woman, have better language and communication skills than men (at least according to most of the experts in gender differences). Even if you are not outgoing and talkative, there are other people like yourself who would be relieved to negotiate with someone sympathetic.

In order to understand how to be the most effective, you might examine the parts of communication.

It starts with the *intention* to communicate. This resides within your own spirit. If you have no intention to communicate, you simply won't. I've seen people who've spent great time and energy to learn the tools of the trade, but their unwillingness to communicate causes them to fail.

Then you get someone's *attention.* Part of the challenge for beginning students is to learn how to find someone to communicate *with.* If you follow the steps in this module, you'll find so many people with problems, you'll wonder why you never saw them before. There are more people with problems who need our help than there are investors to help them. Many will end up with bad bankruptcies and crippling foreclosures. *They* are looking for *you.* When you find them, you now have their attention. Now the communication can begin.

Intention and *attention*—those are the two vital elements before communication can commence.

Intend it now. Resolve to communicate with someone today.

MODULE 4

FIGURING OUT
THE DEAL

HELPING 17

Analyzing

(It's Not Just Location, Location, Location)

Have you ever heard a Realtor say, "All you have to know about buying a home is location, location, location"? I agree 100 percent that location is very important, but boy howdy (that's a Kansas expression—I grew up in Kansas City), there's sure a whole lot more to it than that. No wonder hobby investors, amateurs, and one-time buyers get themselves into pickles from time to time.

I'd have to say that not analyzing a property accurately is the biggest downfall I see in newbies. Either they get all caught up in emotions, or they simply don't have a clue about what else they should be considering in the deal.

Remember the story about my first big mistake? When I bought the vacation property in Idaho during our first few months of investing, it was in a perfect, idyllic location. There it was on the best edge of a pristine lake in a thriving skiing community. It sat high on a hill, surrounded by lovely homes. There was just one problem. It was about to be condemned!

The appraiser❖ had falsified the appraisal❖ on behalf of the seller, and the whole property was more suitable for demolition than fix-up. It was a case of great location and highly motivated seller. We even got a great price, $300,000 for a house with a repaired value❖ of $700,000.

Pretty nice, huh? There was just a little matter of the fact that the house was falling down, and the cost to fix it up was astronomical, leaving no profit, only sorrow and regret and financial devastation.

Two years later, the same bank that repossessed the house through foreclosure called to ask if I'd like to buy it for even less. The bank was still sitting on this vacant house. If the bank could get the price down to the cost of the land, I would consider it!

You see, you have to juggle all the factors regarding any property and balance out location versus condition, price versus financing, weighing each element against the other. Now, to do that, you're going to have to gather data. This business is pretty paper intensive, so start getting organized right away.

Phone Fright

Early in my investing career, I was so nervous on the phone! No matter that I'd been onstage all my life, no matter that I'm not really shy, I was just nervous because I didn't think I knew enough. That's why I developed my three famous starter questions! If you feel nervous too, just remember that the (motivated) seller is much more desperate than you are. He absolutely *must* sell the house, but you have choices—like buy it or not buy it.

I started to get into the swing of things after I developed a little script for myself to remember what things were important to find out. I'd keep a legal pad beside the phone and scribble all over it during the conversation, then transfer the notes to the Robert Allen system I'm going to show you in the next section. It must be my theater background that makes me feel more comfortable when I have a script to follow.

Here's my little list of questions, but remember, you're going to be having a real conversation with a real person with real problems, not an actor in a play. The dialogue may not follow what you'd planned at all! Listening is much more important than talking, but if this list helps you remember certain points, then enjoy it.

You sure don't have to ask all these questions, and you don't have to follow *any* script at all; it's just there to help you get more comfortable in taking that first step: making the call.

"Is this a good time to talk?"
"What's your name?"

"Are you the owner?" or "Are you an agent?"
"Are you the listing agent?"
"What can you tell me about the property?"
>Where is it?
>What's the address?
>What's the zip code?
>When was it built?
>Square feet?
>Bedrooms? Baths?
>Stucco, brick, frame, siding?
>Condition of roof?
>How many stories?
>Garage, carport?
>What's the condition of the neighborhood?
>What's nearby? Schools, shops, churches, freeways?
>What's the condition of the property?
>Are there any things that need repairing?

This next batch of questions may not come up in the first or second call, and if you feel uncomfortable talking to someone about his or her financial life, I'll help you find ways to make it graceful and compassionate.

By all means, don't grill the seller like a suspect. This list is just to remind you of some information you're eventually going to need.

>"Tell me about the financial aspects:"
>Asking price? How much down?
>Do you know the comparable sales price?
>Has it been appraised recently?
>Do you know the true market value?
>Wow . . . that sounds so nice. How can you bear to
>>part with it?
>Do you have plans if it doesn't sell?
>Have you had any offers? What prices?
>How long has it been on the market?
>How much equity do you have in the property?
>Are there mortgages on the property? First?
>>Second? Third?
>Are the loans assumable❖?
>Are there any balloon payments❖?
>Are there any liens❖ on the property?

Do you think you could take payments over time
 for the down payment?
Would you consider a rent-to-own arrangement?
 (Could I lease-option ❖ this property?)
What do you feel would be the best price and terms
 you would accept for a quick sale?
How low could you go if I could close fast, and I
 give you all cash?
Do you know what it could rent for?
Would-ja take _____ ?
Would you accept my offer as a backup offer ❖?
"If you don't mind my asking, what will you do
 with the proceeds?
"Do you know anyone else who might need our
 help?"
"Do you have any other properties for sale?"

You'll probably think up some more questions to add to the list. Just remember, it's only to get you to the point where you feel comfortable talking to someone about his house and his problems. You may never need this list at all, but it's there for you as a little safety net!

I'd rather fix people than houses.
     —ROBERT G. ALLEN

Word Wizard

___ Appraiser   A professional observer and analyst of the values of homes.

___ Appraisal   An opinion report created by an appraiser describing the value of a property.

___ Repaired Value The amount of money a buyer is likely to pay for a house once the fix-up is done, based on what similar homes in similar condition have sold for.

___ Assumable   A loan that the lender will allow you to take over and make payments on; can be qualifying or non-qualifying, meaning that you might have to prove your credit worthiness if it's "qualifying."

___ Balloon Payment   A lump sum due at some specified time on a loan; usually at the end.

___ Lien   A debt owed that has to be paid before the property can be sold; it could be a mortgage or loan, it could be an obligation to pay back taxes, it could be a legal judgment, or it could be an old bill due to a pool builder.

___ Lease-Option   In this usage, *lease* is another word for "rent," and *option* means "privilege." In a lease-option, a person can rent for a while, and after some time, he has the privilege to buy the house if he chooses (or not).

___ Backup Offer   An offer made if the first offer is rejected, which the seller can hold onto and say yes to if he doesn't get any better offers.

Quiz Wizard

1. What's the best criterion to use to evaluate a property?
   a. Location.
   b. Condition.
   c. Price.
   d. Financing.
   e. Motivation of seller.
   f. All of the above.

2. Which of these questions is absolutely vital on your first call?
   a. Do you have plans if it doesn't sell?
   b. Have you had any offers? What prices?
   c. How long has it been on the market?
   d. How much equity do you have in the property?
   e. Are there mortgages on the property? First? Second? Third?
   f. Are the loans assumable?
   g. None of the above.

3. What is the definition of "repaired value"?
   a. The amount of repairs plus the cost of the home.
   b. The perceived value of the home after it's fixed up.

c. The asking price suggested by your Realtor.

d. The amount people are willing to pay for houses just like it in the same condition.

Turn to page 436 for the answers.

Whiz Wizard

1. Make a copy of the questions in the script to keep near your phone.
    Done _____

2. Call a FSBO seller and, just for the heck of it, see how many questions on the list you can get answered. No pressure, just have fun with it. Write up how many you got: _____.
    Done _____

3. Teach the concept of "It's not just location, location, location" to someone else so that he or she understands it.
    Done _____

The Beautiful Bargain Finder

It's time to show you the very best gift that Robert Allen gave to the world of *Nothing Down* real-estate investing. It's the tool that will minimize your risks better than any other strategy. It's laser precise, it's creative, it's beee-yoooo-tee-full!

Can you tell I'm a fan? I don't leave home without it! The "Bargain Finder"❖, otherwise called a "Property Profile"❖, is the rating system that will help you sort out the balances among the five areas of important facts you're going to uncover with all those questions from the last chapter.

> Location
> Condition
> Price
> Financing
> Flexibility

Let me repeat: *Location, Condition, Price, Financing,* and *Flexibility* should become so natural to you that you'll be saying it in your sleep. This strategy is pure gold, classic RGA.

What you're going to do is give a score to each of the five factors, from 0 points to 3 points, with 0 points being the worst and 3 points being the best. If the property was incredible, and you gave it 3 points for each factor, it would rate 15 points (3 points x 5 factors, 3 x 5 = 15).

OK, I'm going to show you a simplified version of the Bargain Finder:

Factor:	Rating 0–3
Location	_____
Condition	_____
Price	_____
Financing	_____
Flexibility	_____
Total:	_____

If you put down the number of points for each area and add them up, you'll have a number somewhere between 0 and 15. If the property doesn't rate at least a 12, you probably shouldn't buy it! Robert Allen says it's no go.

Wasn't that pretty simple? Of course, in the next chapters we'll see just exactly how to grade each factor, because Bob is pretty specific about how we decide what number to give each one.

If you find a property that rates an 8, 9, 10, or 11, you could try to "massage" it up to a 12 by getting in better *communication* with the motivated seller to reduce the price or improve the financing.

Let me tell you a story about a deal my husband was doing. We were buying an office building on Sahara Avenue, and it was owned by an elderly lady named Betty who had retired down to Baja, California. (I confess it gave me the idea that if I had this apartment building, I too could could retire in Baja!) She had an old friend, Joe, who acted as her property manager, and when Duncan and Joe met, Joe told Duncan that Betty wasn't going to sell the property unless she *liked* the person who was buying it. Of course, what Joe really meant was that she wasn't going to sell it to anybody that *Joe* didn't like!

But that drives home a point that's important for the Bargain Finder and for your overall success as well. People sell to people they like and trust. It's true in every single deal, not just our deal with Joe and Betty. So how can you massage a "9-pointer" up to a "12-pointer"? By establishing *communication* and an *affinity* (liking) with the sellers! They can't change the Location, and they probably

138

aren't going to change the Condition, but if they like you and trust you, they might change the Price and the Financing. Your communication would have helped them to have better Flexibility.

Just rating the property isn't the end of the Bargain Finder. There's another huge step: You have to figure out if it's going to make any money. You have to figure out if it's going to make any money. *You have to figure out if it's going to make any money.* At the bottom of the Bargain Finder are some questions to help you remember *to figure out if it's going to make any money somehow!* Can you sell it for more money than you paid for it? Can you rent it or lease it for a profit? Can you refinance it to get some cash out of it?

Even if it rates a 12, if you do some simple math and discover you can't sell it because the price is already at the market value, or you can't rent it because your mortgage payments are higher than what it will rent for, then it's not a good deal. Yes, sometimes even a 12 turns out to be a bad financial risk. That's why you use all of the areas of the Bargain Finder together with one another.

If you ever ask me to help you analyze a deal, I'm gonna ask you, "Is it a twelve?" and "What are you going to do with it (to make a profit)?"

In the next helping, we'll take a look at the real Bargain Finder itself. What a fabulous precision tool it is. Don't *you* leave home without it!

Money is a symbol . . . a symbol of energy . . . human energy, to be precise.

—KAREN NELSON BELL

Word Wizard

___ Bargain Finder   Robert Allen's amazing rating system for analyzing whether a deal is a good one or not; giving scores to Location, Condition, Price, Financing, and Flexibility, and then analyzing how the deal will make a profit.

___ Property Profile   A more formal synonym for the Bargain Finder.

___ A 12   A house that rates well enough on the Bargain Finder to make it eligible for consideration as a potential deal.

Quiz Wizard

1. What's the best criterion to use to evaluate a property? (Same question as last lesson!)
    a. Location
    b. Condition
    c. Price
    d. Financing
    e. Motivation of seller
    f. All of the above

2. Which aspects of the Bargain Finder are things about which the seller could be flexible? (This is a trick question!)
    a. Location
    b. Condition
    c. Price
    d. Financing
    e. Flexibility (increased as a result of your communication)

3. What things could help you improve a seller's flexibility? (This is a trick question too!)
    a. Communication
    b. Explaining the Bargain Finder
    c. Affinity and friendliness
    d. Going over the seller's loan documents
    e. Trust
    f. Showing the seller your credit score

Turn to page 436 for the answers.

Whiz Wizard

1. Call a FSBO seller and get enough information to fill out the score on the simplified form of Bargain Finder I included above. Give your best guess at what the scores should be.
    Done _____

2. Ask yourself two of the questions that would tell you if you could make a profit, and write down the answers.
   a. Can I sell it for more than I paid for it?
   b. Can I rent or lease it for more than my mortgage payments would be?
   Done _____

3. Teach the concept of rating with the Bargain Finder to someone else so that he or she understands it.
   Done _____

The Bargain Finder Form

Here it is!

Robert Allen doesn't mind if you copy this into your own computer and print it out freely. It's a gift he gave us to *use*. Use it when you first call the seller. Use it when you first visit the property. Use it when you're in the middle of negotiations, to see where you need to head. Use it when you've shaken hands, to make sure it's still a good deal. Use it after you've figured out your financing, to make sure it's still a good deal. Use it all the way up to closing, just in case something goes wrong at the last minute that would make you walk away. Use it, use it, use it!

My partners and I rate a property separately, then we get together to see if we agree. I recommend you do the same with your partners.

Your Risk Minimizer

Read over the Bargain Finder line by line and make sure you understand every little square inch of it. It's going to be your best

THE BARGAIN FINDER™

Name _____ ☐ owner ☐ agent   Sq. Ft. _____ Age _____

Address _____ Bedrms _____ Baths _____

City, State, Zip _____ ☐ Carport ☐ Garage ☐ None

Neighborhood _____ ☐ Brick   ☐ Frame

Phone _____ Other: _____

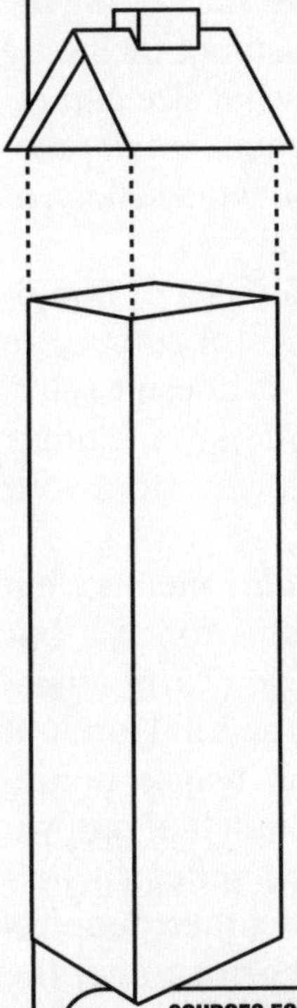

Why are you selling? _____

Plans if it does not sell: _____

Any offers? _____ How long on mkt? _____

Value _____

Price _____

(-) loans _____

(=) equity _____

Down _____

Balance _____

_____

RENT

(-)
Payment

(-)
1/12 taxes

(-)
1/12 insurance

(-)
Utilities

(-)
Misc.

(=)
CASH FLOW positive or negative

FUND IT   What do you feel would be the best price and terms you would accept for a quick sale? _____

_____

Loan	Amount	%	Payment	Terms	Holder	Assum	Balloons
1st						Y/N	Y/N
2nd						Y/N	Y/N

SOURCES FOR DOWN PAYMENT

10 Areas of Flexibility

Seller	Short-term loans
Buyer	Long-term loans
Realtor	Partners
Property splits	Investors
Renters	Options

TOTAL SCORE _____

The BOTTOM LINE:
(How can I profit from this property?)

Sell	Keep	Refinance	Trade

Could I sell for a quick profit?	Can it be fixed up for long-term equity profit? Will it enhance long-term cash flow?	What benefits could come from financing the property?	Is there enough built-in equity profit to trade for something else of value?

Right margin (vertical):
LOCATION 2 0 3
CONDITION 2 1 3
PRICE 2 1 3
FINANCING 2 1 3
FLEXIBILITY 2 1 3

friend. It's going to keep you from being like the hobby investors who get in over their heads. It's your risk minimizer.

Do you see the words written down the right hand side? Location, Condition, Price, Financing, and Flexibility. There's a place for the total score just to the left of them, near the bottom.

At the top, you see a place for the seller's name, and whether he's the owner, the agent, or both. Then you see a place for the seller's contact data and the name of the neighborhood. Just personally knowing the neighborhood may be enough for you to start rating the location. To the right of the seller's data are the data about the house itself: square feet, number of bedrooms and baths, what size garage, what style roof, and what kind of construction. Of course, you'll probably get a lot more data from some of your very motivated sellers, as they try to sweet-talk you into buying their sweet deal.

The next section has four questions to give you an idea of how to score the seller's motivation: "Why are you selling?" (of course, we won't ask it that bluntly), "What are your plans if it doesn't sell?" "How long has it been on the market?" and "Any offers?" meaning, what am I competing with? All familiar concepts to you from your scripts in module 1.

The section in the middle talks about money. *Value* means what the property is actually worth; what could you sell it for at a fair price? *Price* means what the seller is asking, and as you carry on negotiations, that number can change. *Loans* means the total amount due to lenders, including first mortgages, second mortgages, home-equity lines of credit, and liens. *Down* means how much of a down payment you'll be expected to make by either the seller (if he's going to help finance it) or the lender you use for other people's money. Subtract the loans and the down from the price to get the balance. That number will reflect your potential profit if you decide to sell it.

The little box with *Rent* at the top is a worksheet for figuring out if you're going to have a positive cash flow from the rent or lease. *Payment* means your monthly mortgage. *Taxes* means monthly taxes due if they're not included in the mortgage. *Insurance* means the monthly insurance due if it's not included in the mortgage. *Utilities* means the monthly fees if you pay the utilities instead of the renters. *Miscellaneous* might mean lawn care, pool care, fixing up, cost of possible vacancies, marketing costs, property managers, bookkeeping, and so on.

Deduct all those items from Rent to see what kind of cash flow you'll have on the next line, whether it's positive or negative, a plus number or a minus number. That'll sure tell you a lot about whether you should move forward with the deal! Stay away from those minus numbers!

Take Your Time!

Go slow, take your time, and review each little section so you really get it, OK?

Right in the middle of the page is another question to test the seller's motivation and find out what your lowest price could be. "What do you feel would be the best price and terms you would accept for a quick sale?" Doesn't that sound a lot like "How low could you go, if I could close fast, and I give you all cash?"

The next little box is a place for you to put in the data about the seller's loans. You probably won't be getting that data on the very first call. Be patient. You're developing a relationship. Don't worry for now that you're going to have to talk to the person about his private affairs. When you're ready for that discussion, it'll come easy to both of you. The data the box is asking for are the amount of the whole loan, the interest rate, the monthly payment, the terms (meaning how long in years, for example), who holds the loan (what lender), and whether the loan is assumable and whether it has a balloon. You've already come across all those terms, so nothing new there!

In the little box called "Sources for Down Payment," RGA reminds us where we can find some OPM. You'll be studying a lot more about that in the chapter on funding the *Nothing Down* way, but for now, enjoy the list as a hint of things to come: seller, buyer, Realtor, property splits❖, renters, short-term loans, long-term loans, partners, investors, and options (meaning lease-options). I promise we'll go over every one of those and many more, but for now, just know that the box is to remind you of some techniques you'll be learning soon.

The Real Bottom Line—A Line at the Bottom!

The box near the bottom, called "the Bottom Line," takes us all the way down to the last section and demands that we analyze how this property could make money.

- Could I sell it for a quick profit?
- Can it be fixed up for long-term equity profit?
- What benefits could come from financing the property?
- Is there enough built-in equity profit to trade for something else of value?

For now, until you've read the lessons on funding, we're going to stick with just two questions: "Could I sell it for a quick profit?" and "Could I rent it for a positive cash flow?"

Whew! We made it through the whole form. Are you wondering about the cute house on the left-hand side? That's where you can draw a graphic representation of the mortgage(s). If the house is worth $100,000, put that figure on the roof. If there's a first mortgage for $60,000, draw a line about two-thirds up from the bottom and write that figure in the bottom. If there's a second mortgage for $10,000, put that figure in the next section up. If you deduct $60,000 and $10,000 ($70,000 combined) from $100,000, you end up with $30,000. You put that figure in the little open area. That represents the amount of equity that's potentially there for you to possess, depending on how well you negotiate. You could also draw a line to show the seller's profit. You keep working them back and forth.

Remember, take it slow and easy.

If you're not good at math, don't worry, neither am I. I have to use calculators and double-check myself all the time. Go through this section slowly and carefully, looking for words that might trip you up. You've learned all the words before, but here they are on this new form. Remember, you can always revert to the simplified form from the last helping:

Simple Bargain-finder Form

Factor:	Rating 0–3
Location	_____
Condition	_____
Price	_____
Financing	_____
Flexibility	_____
Total:	_____

"Could I sell it for a quick profit?" _____

and "Could I rent it for a positive cash flow?" _____

Wish for it, but work for it.
—STACEY KEEBLER, PRO WRESTLER, DANCER

Word Wizard

___ Property Split   Dividing up a larger property into smaller separate identifying units, such as making a six-bedroom home into three separate condos, or dividing two acres into ten parcels.

Quiz Wizard

1. What's the best criterion to use to evaluate a property? (Same question as in the last helping!)
   a. Location
   b. Condition
   c. Price
   d. Financing
   e. Motivation of seller
   f. All of the above

2. At what times should you use the Bargain Finder?
   a. Before you call the seller
   b. The first time you talk to the seller
   c. During negotiations
   d. While you're having lunch
   e. After you've shaken hands, and your offer has been accepted
   f. As you do your homework and diligently check out all the facts of the deal (called "due diligence" period).
   g. At closing
   h. At dinner to celebrate with your partner or friends

3. Which of these items would not help you compute cash flow on a rental?
   a. Mortgage total
   b. Monthly mortgage payment

    c. Taxes

    d. Insurance

    e. Lawn care

    f. Mortgage interest

Turn to page 436 for the answers.

Whiz Wizard

1. Go to www.ND4W.com/bargainfinder, then click on the Bargain Finder. Download it to your computer and print out multiple copies.
Done _____

2. Call a FSBO seller and get enough information to fill out the score on the simple-form Bargain Finder. Add that data into the real Bargain Finder. Leave anything you don't have information on blank. Give your best guess of what the scores should be. You'll be learning guidelines for the scores next.
Done _____

3. Ask yourself two of the questions that would tell you if you could make a profit, and write down the answers.
    a. Can I sell it for more than I paid for it?
    b. Can I rent or lease it for more than my mortgage payments would be?
Done _____

4. Teach the concept of Robert Allen's Bargain Finder form to someone else so that he or she understands it. Show the person the form and explain each little area.
Done _____

Location

In the next five helpings, we're going to take a look at Robert Allen's original writing. It's so beautiful because he's very, very precise about how you score a property.

Here's what he has to say about Location:

Point Number One: <u>Location</u>

<u>0 Points:</u>

Never! There is no pride of ownership. Junk and debris line the streets. High crime area. There's no appealing shopping nearby. The neighborhood is clearly in a decline. There are nearby abandoned buildings and boarded-up properties. It's close to major streets, industrial areas, or commercial zones. It's far from employment centers or commuter accessibility.

<u>2 Points:</u>

Might be clean older neighborhoods. Close to shopping, churches, schools, but not very appealing. There are working-class tenants, neat, and established. It might be a poor location on the upswing with brave fixer-uppers, nicer inner-city neighborhoods.

3 Points:

There's easy accessibility to all necessary amenities and transportation. Middle-class suburban neighborhoods are ideal. Not on a busy street. Cul-de-sacs are ideal. Properties nearby are very similar in price and condition. There's good foliage and landscaping unless it's a very new subdivision. Only high-class inner-city locations.

Notice that the points go from 0 to 2! Somewhere in between there, you'll find a 1-pointer, a house that's not good enough to be a 2 and not bad enough to be a 0. On the subject of 0-pointers, I'll say there actually is money to be made from them. However, these properties are outside the bell curve, and I personally don't like the small number of people who want to live there. I also know that I'll have to have some big guy named Bubba❖ go get the rents, and I don't want to do that. Give me a nice family in a middle-class neighborhood any time. No being a slumlord for me, and not for you either.

Also notice that the 2-pointer doesn't have to be anything fancy. You may not want to live there yourself, but most of America looks like a 2-pointer.

On the 3-pointer, observe that it doesn't have to be in a luxury gated community or extra ritzy. I have some houses that are almost thirty years old, and they still rate a 3 on location because they're near shopping, freeway access, churches, schools, and entertainment.

I do love those cul-de-sacs, by the way, and so do many families buying with the safety of their kids in mind!

Location, location, location, yes, but be sure to score it from 0 to 3!

"Location, location, location" as a mantra leaves out 80 percent of the proper decision-making process.

—KAREN NELSON BELL

Word Wizard

___ Bubba   Name for a caricature of a man who's big, burly, and kinda dumb.

Quiz Wizard

1. How many points would you give to a house that had bullet holes in the front door?
    a. Zero
    b. One
    c. Two
    d. Three

2. How many points would you give a house that looked pretty humble, even shabby, but was close to the center of town, near all the action, and close to shopping, churches, schools, and transportation?
    a. Zero
    b. One
    c. Two
    d. Three

3. How many points would you give a house that was forty years old on a classic tree-lined street near a university and all its satellite businesses?
    a. Zero
    b. One
    c. Two
    d. Three

Turn to page 436 for the answers.

Whiz Wizard

1. Call a FSBO seller and get enough information to fill out the score on the simple-form Bargain Finder in the prior helping. Give your best guess at what the scores should be. This exercise is just for practice, so don't worry about forcing it into a deal! Just talk! Done _____

2. Ask yourself two of the questions that would tell you if you could make a profit, and write down the answers.
    a. Can I sell it for more than I paid for it?

           b. Can I rent or lease it for more than my mortgage payments would be?

Done _____

3. Teach the concept of scoring locations to someone else so that he or she understands it.

Done _____

Condition

Here's what Robert Allen has to say about Condition:

Point Number Two: <u>Condition</u>

<u>1 Point</u>:
 <u>Consider only if *price* is *excellent*.</u>
 It needs major cosmetic and *structural* improvements. <u>At least 10 percent of the purchase price will have to be spent in order to make the house rentable</u>. The improvements do not significantly increase the rent, because of the income strata of the tenants and the location. Improvements wouldn't increase the value more than 10 percent over the purchase price. This rating is usually associated with poor locations. It's possible to find this property in locations where prices are so high that improvements don't increase the value but just make units acceptable to renters. Look at it as making a much larger down payment (the $$$ for the improvements) and getting an average-priced property.

<u>2 Points</u>:
 This is a true fixer-upper. Cosmetic improvements would be nice but

are not absolutely necessary. <u>Cost of upgrades should not exceed 5 percent of the purchase price</u>. The cosmetic improvements immediately boost the value higher and make the property more attractive, saleable, and rentable. It hardly needs any structural work, only paint, landscaping, drapes, and other inexpensive improvements. It should *not* be bought if buyer doesn't have the confidence to do the upgrades or have access to a crew who can do the work at wholesale prices. It can prove to be the most profitable in the short run. Choose the worst house in the best neighborhood!

3 Points:

A newer property or else an older property that has been recently renovated. No problems inside or outside; clean, good landscaping. New components have replaced major items. It might have been a recent fixer-upper project that is being sold by the fixer for an excellent price. There is extremely little or no work before a renter moves in. It's a solid property with a hassle factor of zero! (Zero GPD, or Grief per Dollar, says KNB!)

Take a look at the 1-pointer and notice that I've italicized the word *structural.* If the roof is leaking or the plumbing is backed up, you *must* give it a 1 on Condition. Simple as that. Then take a look at the price of the house and the cost of repairs, and figure out the percentage (divide the repairs by the price of the house). If it's more than 10 percent, you're going to give the house a 1. Simple, right?

Now check out the 2-pointer. I love these houses. Stinky houses. Cluttered houses. Houses that need carpet and paint. Piece o' cake! In the early days, we did all the fixing up ourselves. It was a ton of fun! Plus I learned a lot. Now I hire crews at wholesale prices. I wouldn't mind personally doing one myself again for the fun of it—I do love to paint!

When you read the 3-pointer, go to the last sentence and relish the phrase "hassle factor of zero." I call it zero "GPD," or "Grief Per Dollar." By the way, even people in terrible financial trouble can have their houses in great shape. We bought a foreclosure in the first year that was perfect in every way. We cleaned the carpets, and the new renters moved in. That's my favorite kind of deal!

Stinky Houses are potential gold mines to me!

—KAREN NELSON BELL

Quiz Wizard

1. How many points would you give to a house that had a crack in
    the foundation?
    > a. Zero
    > b. One
    > c. Two
    > d. Three

2. How many points would you give a house that needed a lot of
    painting, carpet, drapes, landscaping, and cleaning?
    > a. Zero
    > b. One
    > c. Two
    > d. Three

3. How many points would you give a house that had zero GPD?
    > a. Zero
    > b. One
    > c. Two
    > d. Three

Turn to page 436 for the answers.

Whiz Wizard

1. Call a FSBO seller and get enough information to fill out the
    score on your simple-form Bargain Finder. Give your best guess
    at what the scores should be.
    Done _____

2. Ask yourself two of the questions that would tell you if you could
    make a profit, and write down the answers.
    > a. Can I sell it for more than I paid for it?
    > b. Can I rent or lease it for more than my mortgage pay-
    >   ments would be?
    Done _____

3. Teach the concept of scoring condition to someone else so that he
    or she understands it.
    Done _____

HELPING 22

Price

Here's what Robert Allen has to say about Price:

Point Number Three: Price

1 Point:
>   Market value or 5 percent or more *above* the reasonable market price. You should consider this only if the terms of financing are outstanding.

2 Points:
>   Within 10 percent off of the market price.

3 Points:
>   At least 15 percent or more below market price.

This is just as straightforward as it can get. I personally up each item by 5 percent to be even more conservative, but just follow these guidelines, and you're going to be light-years ahead of all your hobby investor pals. This tool will keep you sharp.

One other thing to remember is that in order to know what percentage your discount is, you're going to have to have an accurate, true accounting of what the property is really worth. You won't want to take the seller's last re-fi appraisal as the true value, by the way, because in general, re-fi appraisals are higher than independent appraisals.

You'll get a lesson on finding comparable market value before we leave this module.

A house is only worth what someone is willing to pay for it, not what the comp is, not what the appraisal is, but exactly what someone is willing to pay for it!

—KAREN NELSON BELL

Quiz Wizard

1. How many points would you give to a house that you could buy for $96,000 if it were worth $100,000?
   a. Zero
   b. One
   c. Two
   d. Three

2. How many points would you give to a house that you could buy for $91,000 if it were worth $100,000?
   a. Zero
   b. One
   c. Two
   d. Three

3. How many points would you give to a house that you could buy for $84,000 if it were worth $100,000?
   a. Zero
   b. One
   c. Two
   d. Three

Turn to page 436 for the answers.

Whiz Wizard

1. Call a FSBO seller and get enough information to fill out the score on the simple-form Bargain Finder. Give your best guess at what the scores should be.
    Done _____

2. Ask yourself two of the questions that would tell you if you could make a profit, and write down the answers.
    a. Can I sell it for more than I paid for it?
    b. Can I rent or lease it for more than my mortgage payments would be?
    Done _____

3. Teach the concept of scoring price to someone else so that he or she understands it.
    Done _____

HELPING 23

Financing

Here's what Robert Allen has to say about Financing:

Point Number Four: Financing

1 Point:
> You have to put more than 15 percent down, Seller needs lots of cash and wants all of his equity. Or property will have large negative cash flow for more than two years. Or there will be a large balloon payment due in less than three years from the date of purchase. Consider only if the price is outstanding.

2 Points:
> Financing is required from a commercial lender with up to 15 percent down of buyer's money. You must have credit checks. Institutional loans must be secured for part of the down payment, with high interest and high monthly payments. Cash is required from buyer. A balloon payment is due in less than five years.

3 Points:
> There is less than 5 percent of the buyer's cash involved in the deal.

The seller is willing to carry most of the financing at lower than market rates. There are no balloons due earlier than seven years. There are no negative cash flows projected beyond the first year. The deal is done as a contract sale, and there are no credit checks.

Once again, this is pretty straightforward. You've already learned all the words used in this section, but if you need to review them, go to the glossary in the back of the manual.

One point I'd like to make is that loans available from your broker are so different today than they were even ten or twenty years ago that I think a little extra clarification might be valuable as to what could constitute a 3-pointer.

It's my opinion (I asked Bob recently, and he agreed with me) that if you have decent credit and can get one of the creative mortgage programs that brokers have these days, you could call that a 3-pointer on financing. Do you remember when I said that credit is going to be an important tool for you? Just having great credit could mean that you could always rate every property you're looking at as a 3-pointer on financing. We'll talk about some of these creative programs in the module on funding.

> *The best problem one could have is finding wise ways to distribute one's money and its energy.*
>
> —KAREN NELSON BELL

Quiz Wizard

1. How many points would you give to a $100,000 house that you could buy with a down payment of $20,000?
    a. Zero
    b. One
    c. Two
    d. Three

2. How many points would you give to a $100,000 house that you could buy with a down payment of $14,000?
    a. Zero
    b. One

   c. Two

   d. Three

3. How many points would you give to a $100,000 house that you could buy with a down payment of $4,500?

   a. Zero

   b. One

   c. Two

   d. Three

Turn to page 436 for the answers.

Whiz Wizard

1. Call a FSBO seller and get enough information to fill out the score on the simple-form Bargain Finder. Give your best guess at what the scores should be.

 Done _____

2. Ask yourself two of the questions that would tell you if you could make a profit, and write down the answers.

   a. Can I sell it for more than I paid for it?

   b. Can I rent or lease it for more than my mortgage payments would be?

 Done _____

3. Teach the concept of scoring financing to someone else so that he or she understands it.

 Done _____

HELPING 24

Flexibility

Here's what Robert Allen has to say about Flexibility:

Point Number Five: Flexibility

<u>1 Point:</u>
<u>Seller</u> won't budge on price or on terms. His motto is "Take it or leave it." He doesn't need to sell. He is not anxious at all and feels he is in the driver's seat.

<u>2 Points:</u>
<u>Seller</u> might consider a small discount in price. He needs cash for his next property. He needs cash for other reasons, bills, and so forth. He might carry a small second but is leery of "creative financing."

<u>3 Points:</u>
<u>Seller</u> is flexible in *price* or *terms.* He needs cash urgently; for example, he's behind in payments. *Or:* He doesn't need cash but has other problems such as transfer, divorce, tax problems, management problems. Possibly an investor looking for a solution without much need for cash.

This is my favorite topic to discuss, because it's so open to improvement through communication.

On the 1-pointer, you'll instinctively feel it through the seller's coldness, haughtiness, or lack of desire to give much data. Just thank the person for his time, and use our favorite four letter word: next!

With a 2-pointer, see if you can build more trust through communication.

The 3-pointer seller is a lot of joy to encounter. It makes negotiating *fun,* like a game. Take a close look at the first sentence under the 3-pointer: Seller is flexible in PRICE OR TERMS. Go back and underline or. A lot of people miss it.

Price OR terms.

You see, the seller only has to be flexible in one OR the other to get 3 points! When you find a rare seller who's flexible on both, maybe you should give him an extra half point!

By the way, if you can't decide on a point, choose the lower one. Don't get yourself caught up in wishful-thinking ratings. You'll just be cheating yourself out of good judgment. You can also use half points. Heck, you can use decimal points and call it 2.6 if that communicates the true rating in your best opinion.

I have a really cool secret to tell you now. Guess what? You actually know enough to make an offer. You know how to find deals, and you know how to tell if they're any good. All you have to do is ask "Would-ja take?" and see if anybody says yes. OK, I know you don't know what to do next, but the nice thing is, you can get access to mentors. Call up your mentor and say, "Help! I think I've got a live one! Now what the heck do I do?" You see, as long as you have a good mentor, you've already learned all you need to get started! Take a deep breath and enjoy it!

If you don't have a mentor yet, visit www.ND4W.com/5MM and let me introduce you to some wonderful multimillionaire women who are ready to help me help you!

I have another secret: Some of you will have already found a deal by now. You've been making calls to motivated FSBOs, and there's a chance you might have already talked to somebody you felt you could actually help. All right! Congrats to those of you who've already found someone you'd like to make an offer to, and here's a shout of encouragement to everyone else, because the deals could be right there in your next five calls!

Am I worried about a real-estate bubble? No. If you work it right, a downturn in prices can be bubblelicious. When they're all cryin', I'll be buyin'.

—KAREN NELSON BELL

Quiz Wizard

1. How many points would you give to a seller who says, "I just put the ad in to see if there were any takers"?
    - a. Zero
    - b. One
    - c. Two
    - d. Three

2. How many points would you give to a seller who says, "I really need to sell this house because we're building a new one, and I need to get this one off my credit report. However, I need cash for the new one, and I'm only willing to let you pay me the down payment in three monthly installments"?
    - a. Zero
    - b. One
    - c. Two
    - d. Three

3. How many points would you give to a seller who says, "I'm in foreclosure, and I'm under so much stress that I can't bear it anymore. I just need some help getting into an apartment I can afford, and you can just take over my payments"?
    - a. Zero
    - b. One
    - c. Two
    - d. Three

Turn to page 436 for the answers.

Whiz Wizard

1. Call a FSBO seller and get enough information to fill out the score on the simple-form Bargain Finder. Give your best guess at what the scores should be.
   Done _____

2. Ask yourself two of the questions that would tell you if you could make a profit, and write down the answers.
   a. Can I sell it for more than I paid for it?
   b. Can I rent or lease it for more than my mortgage payments would be?
   Done _____

3. Teach the concept of scoring flexibility to someone else so that he or she understands it.
   Done _____

HELPING 25

What's It Worth?

When you're rating your property for the Bargain Finder on the subject of Price, you have to have accurate evaluations of its true worth, or your whole formula will turn out catawampus❖. Part of your game, from now on, will be to discover the real true value of the property you're rating. You're going to have to have comps❖ (reports on comparable homes and what they've sold for).

Comps I Hope You Never Use

Here are some ways to find comps that I hope you never use:

1. What the seller's Realtor tells you
2. What the seller tells you
3. What the seller's recent appraisal tells you, if it was a re-fi.

Here's why: the Realtor can go into the Multiple Listing Service (MLS) on her computer and select only the properties in a high range to compare it to. She can deselect any properties that aren't high enough to keep her comp where she wants it to be. In addition, she typically will include properties that are on the market but haven't been sold yet.

What a neighbor's asking price is has no business being included in *your* comps. The neighbor's wishful thinking doesn't necessarily represent what buyers are actually paying. The only comps you want to look at are *sold* comps. If a buyer was willing to plunk down good money for a house just like yours, then that's a comparable sale. That's a good comp.

Don't get me wrong, I'm not trying to paint all real-estate agents as naughty boys and girls, but you should trust *your* real-estate agent for comps, not the seller's. You say you don't have a real-estate agent yet? Well, should I give you some homework to make it easy to get one? Yep, that's what I'm going to do.

Do you have the idea that a Realtor might not want to waste her time giving you comps? Do you feel like you don't want to bother her, you don't want to intrude? A lot of people, especially women, are sensitive about not asking for something without giving anything in return. Well, here's the way to solve that problem: You're going to give your Realtor a lot of business.

You're going to buy houses from her, and you're going to let her sell some of your houses. You're going to take her along when you buy properties directly from the bank (remember those REOs?). You're going to take her along when you buy new construction from a builder in a development. You're going to refer all your friends to her! Yes indeed, she's going to make a lot of money from your relationship! We'll talk more in another chapter about wonderful ways to utilize your Realtor's resources, but for now, just know that she's going to be ever so glad to help you out!

If you still don't feel comfortable, ask your prospective real-estate agent if he requires a small fee in order to furnish comps. He should say no. I really mean it; he *should* say no. If he says yes, find someone else. It takes only two to five minutes to do a search on the MLS. Now, don't load the person down with twenty properties a day. In fact, only ask for comps on properties you've already rated and suspect you're very interested in.

Comps in Your Jammies

Here's what I suggest: Use some of the consumer methods to get a ballpark figure on the value before you ever call up the local real-estate office. You can use these methods while you're in your jammies in the middle of the night, when you can't reach your Realtor.

Here are a few websites people have used over the last few years, but remember, websites change. The last time I used these, they weren't up to the standards from a year ago. Either they now cost money, or they now make you go through a real-estate agent to get the report. Anyway, I want you to see what tools are out there. Here they are: www.HomeGain.com, www.HomeRadar.com, and www.HomeValues.com. When I went to these sites tonight, Home Radar.com was the only one that didn't require you to be contacted by a real-estate agent.

Once you have the comp list of similar properties, add up all the prices of the houses and divide that number by the amount of houses on the list. The resulting figure will give you an average of all those houses sold that were similar to yours. If you want to be even more accurate and do it the way many experts do, throw out the highest figure and the lowest figure before you add them all up and average out.

A Secret between You and Me

OK, now that I've given you some consumer places to check out, how would you like a professional resource? It's a resource you can get for free, but there'll be a little social interaction required before you can get it. It's called www.FidelityPassport.com, and it's furnished to real-estate agents by Fidelity National Title Insurance Company. In fact, almost every title company has a similar online tool these days. You don't have to use this company, but if you don't already have a friend at a title firm, you can make a new friend at Fidelity Title!

First, you go to www.fntic.com and click on "Branch Directory." When you find a branch near you, call and ask to speak to the marketing director. When you get her on the phone, say, "Mrs. Jones, I know you have resources for the professional Realtor. Do you also make those tools available for professional investors? I'd be interested in using your services. What do you have for a person like me?"

Mrs. Jones will make an appointment to meet you (my rep came to my home bearing a bag of goodies). If she doesn't bring up Fidelity Passport, tell her, "You know, my friend Karen, the author of *ND4W,* swears by Fidelity Passport. Can I get that here in my area? I can? And what does it cost? Oh, it's free? Well, how nice is that!"

The thing you're going to love about Fidelity Passport or any similar tool from another company is that you can get customized comps! That's right, you can research properties like a pro in the comfort of your own home!

You'll be signing on to Fidelity Passport and clicking on the "Property Profile" tool. Now, this is a different property profile than the one I referred to as the formal name for the Bargain Finder. About halfway down Fidelity Passport's property profile, you'll find a section regarding comps, where you can customize it to suit the needs of the property you're researching. For a short video on how to use *this* property profile, go to www.ND4W.com/ppdemo.

My last recommendation to you is that you use multiple resources for checking out your comps. The quality of results you get from any company will depend on your ability to choose the settings on what they call the Property Profile for the search. Fidelity Passport does include all sales, whereas the MLS doesn't include sales of FSBOs, so sometimes Fidelity Passport gives you more useful information. Here's what I always do: check with my favorite Realtor after I've checked on HomeRadar.com and Fidelity Passport. Sometimes I'll even ask my favorite appraiser to give me a thumbnail appraisal (a quick check of the comps by the appraiser can be even more accurate than by a Realtor). When all three sources agree with one another, I know I've got a pretty good idea of what someone will be willing to pay for the property.

A Wonderful Resource

In February 2006, a new resource for comps popped onto the internet. It's so powerful that it will likely change how real-estate transactions are done both in our *Nothing Down* world and in the regular retail world. To see this super intelligent analyzer, go to www.Zillow.com. Take your time and look into every nook and cranny, because there are all kinds of helpful statistics on this wonderful website. Another version can be found at www.realestateabc.com. By the time this book gets into your hands, I believe these sites will be famous. Everyone will have a much clearer picture of home values all over America.

What's It *Really* Worth?

Remember, the value of any property is measured only by what someone is willing to pay for it now. It won't matter if the last appraisal said it was worth $300,000, and the Realtor says it's worth $300,000. If it's been sitting on the market for two years going nowhere, it's not worth $300,000. It's that simple. I repeat, the value of any property is measured by what someone is willing to pay for it now. Today.

If you come on the 5-Minute Mentor Power Hour calls with a great deal, one of the first things I'm going to ask you is "What does it rate on the Bargain Finder?" and "What's it worth?" As a wealthy investor, you're going to start looking at everything by asking "What's it worth?"

> *If the house has been on the market for six months at $300,000, and the seller says it appraised for $300,000, I'm telling you it's not worth $300,000, because no one is willing to pay it.* It's only worth what someone is willing to pay.
>
> —KAREN NELSON BELL

Word Wizard

___ Catawampus   All lopsided and out of whack. In a diagonal position or arrangement.

___ Comps   Short for "comparable," as in the price of comparable houses nearby.

Quiz Wizard

1. What are the best ways to find comps?
   a. What the seller's Realtor tells you.

    b. What the seller tells you.

    c. What your own Realtor tells you the lady down the street is asking for a similar house.

    d. An online research service like Fidelity Passport.

    e. An online research service like www.HomeRadar.com.

    f. Your own Realtor selecting sold comps only off the MLS.

2.   Is Fidelity Passport free?

    a. Yes, but you have to make a friend at the title company first.

    b. No, it has a monthly fee.

3.   What really tells the *true* fair market value of a property?

    a. The comps from a Realtor.

    b. The comps from an online research resource.

    c. What a buyer is actually willing to pay for it.

Turn to page 436 for the answers.

Whiz Wizard

1.   Call around to your friends and associates to find out if they have a real-estate agent they like. Call the agent and make an appointment to see her in her office or take her to lunch. The homework is done when you have the appointment, but you must also follow through with it! (You're on the honor system, but of course you'll follow through; why wouldn't you?)
Done _____

2.   Go to www.fntic.com and find a branch near you. (Or call up any title company near you.) Call up the branch and ask to speak to the marketing director. Ask if you can meet to go over what resources he has for you as a professional investor. When you've made the appointment, the homework is done!
Done _____

3.   Teach the concept of why accurate comps are so important to someone else so that he or she understands it.
Done _____

Getting Organized

(Before It's Too Late!)

There's so much to tell you, so much to share, that I want to give you some ways to tap into all the resources that will get you moving in the right direction right now!

This is a very, very short section, as you'll see!

Your lesson is waiting for you on the internet, at www.ND4W.com/organize. I created a little video for you to see on a resource you don't want to miss. It's called *Organize*, and it's going to save you a whole lot of aggravation in your real-estate investing.

This business is a lot easier when you keep yourself organized. That's where PaperPort❖ comes in. I use it, along with MS Outlook❖, MS Excel❖, and MS Money❖ or QuickBooks❖. If you start *now* instead of *later* in organizing, you'll be miles ahead of all your competitors. In fact, you'll be miles ahead of where *I* was at your stage. (I've explained each one for you in the Word Wizard.)

Of course, you don't have to use these specific brands. I'm not connected with these companies in any way, I'm just a fan. If you can find a similar or better tool, email me and let me know; I'm always on the lookout for ways to streamline my organization. Remember, everything changes on the internet and in the computer world just about every Friday, but these recommendations were "cool and groovy" at the time I wrote this.

You don't have to go out and buy PaperPort or QuickBooks today, but why wouldn't you want to keep yourself organized right from the start? You're going to be a real-estate millionaire, right? You're going to need a way to conveniently access all the documents your real estate is going to generate. Especially when you're getting loans, you're going to love being able to give lenders everything they need in five minutes. And they will love you!

Well, I had fun preparing the little video. Enjoy!

Your net worth is equal to your network. Your team is everything.
—SUZAN HUDSON, DIRECTOR OF THE 5MM ACTION WEEKEND

Word Wizard

___ PaperPort

An organizing software developed by ScanSoft; great for keeping all your documents generated by your real estate, plus all the documents you need often for the lending process. Many uses, business and personal; I can't live without it.

___ MS Outlook

A personal productivity software developed by Microsoft; calendars, contact files, notes, email. I use it to keep records of all my houses, along with their directions and maps, names of lenders, names of renters, and so on; I can't live without it.

___ MS Excel

A spreadsheet that can contain financial data or any other data; used by most lenders, easy to learn, and great for tracking all aspects of your properties and your net worth.

___ MS Money

A financial software program developed by Microsoft; the version called MS Money for Home Office compares to QuickBooks. I use it because it syncs nicely with my little handheld computer; I can't live without it.

___ QuickBooks

A financial software program developed by Intuit, similar to its consumer product called Quicken; the most popular bookkeeping software for small businesses.

Quiz Wizard

You won't be able to answer the quiz until you've seen the video. (Hint: Keep the questions by your side while you're watching, so you don't have to go back again if you forget.)

1. Which of these folders were not on the video demonstration of PaperPort?
   a. Finance
   b. Houses
   c. Tax returns for 2003
   d. House on Willow Street
   e. Landscapers
   f. HUD-1s

2. What are four ways mentioned on the video to track properties?
   a. Outlook
   b. Excel
   c. PaperPort
   d. QuickBooks or MS Money

Turn to page 436 for the answers.

Whiz Wizard

1. Go to www.paperport.com/paperport/standard and take a look around. Go "window shopping" if you're not ready to make a purchase! Search for other similar tools and other brands.
   Done _____

2. Teach the concept of why every investor needs to get organized with a PaperPort type of software and other organizational tools to someone else so that he or she understands it.
   Done _____

5MM Time Capsule 4

5MM Module 4, Helpings 7–26

Here's what we covered in this chapter. You've actually assimilated a ton of data already, and you know more about investing than 98 percent of America (including real-estate agents)! Check off each item that you know you can easily explain to someone else.

Now here's a checklist of what you've learned. (There's no turning back now, is there?!)

Helping 17
___ Why "Location, location, location!" just won't do the trick.
___ The most common mistake of investor newbies.

Helping 18:
___ How to use a Bargain Finder to minimize investor risk.
___ How to massage a lower-rated property into a higher-rated property.
___ How to figure out if there's really any profit in the deal.
___ How to improve a seller's flexibility.

Helping 19:
___ How to use the actual Bargain Finder form.

Helping 20:
___ Exactly how to rate for Location.

Helping 21:
___ Exactly how to rate for Condition.

Helping 22:
___ Exactly how to rate for Price.

Helping 23:
___ Exactly how to rate for Financing.

Helping 24:
___ Exactly how to rate for Flexibility.

Helping 25:
___ Three ways other people find comps that we *never* use.
___ The coolest layman's way in the world to find comps!
___ What the truest measure of a property's value is.

Helping 26:
___ How to get organized better than you've ever been before.
___ How to make lenders love you.
___ I understand all the above points so well that I've taught them myself!

When you've checked off every item, you can get started on module 5 and the amazing world of foreclosures!

Bobservations

When I created the Bargain Finder, the purpose was to try to force investors to be more conservative. I want you to get out and buy properties, but I don't want to see you getting burned on bad deals. It's a lazy man's way to force you to think about things that will help you analyze intelligently.

One afternoon, Karen was grilling me about questions of applications using the Bargain Finder. I replied with a quote from the movie *Pirates of the Caribbean:* When asked about the code of a pirate, the captain says, "It's not exactly a rule, it's more of a guideline."

Karen's first question revolved around the fact that unlike in the past, today you can get *Nothing Down* financing on every street corner from your local mortgage broker. If you have a high enough credit score, you can rest assured that you can do *Nothing Down* deals. She wanted to know if you could rate a 3 on financing if you knew you personally could get a *Nothing Down* loan. My consideration is that if you do deals only with your personal loans, you'll miss out on all the other great opportunities for deals. However, if you can get a property with no hassles on the finance lines, I do indeed think you could rate it a 3.

Her second question was how to rate a rare moderately priced house in a high-priced city. Students were encountering a few properties in the $200K price range in a city where the prices were all over $400K. My instinctive response was this: If you're smart enough to ask that kind of a question, you're smart enough to break the rules. If you've thought that deeply on it, you're way beyond the Bargain Finder. Congratulations.

So you see, the Bargain Finder is there to help you think. Once you've learned the principles, it will keep you steady as she goes. I want to see you winning, and the Bargain Finder is one way. Complete, careful, conservative analysis will always stand you in good stead.

MODULE 5

FORECLOSURES

How to Really, Truly Help People in Need

Help and Hope

One successful investor I know refuses to invest in foreclosures. He says that he doesn't want to take advantage of people. I say invest in foreclosures *and don't* take advantage of people!

The most satisfying deals I've done have been the ones where I helped folks who were in such desperate need that they were nearly done in. When I helped them, sometimes you could see the relief pouring over them. Remember Janie, the lady who wanted to keep her refrigerator? Her relief was physically visible. I've received letters from the people I've helped, claiming that I was their guardian angel. They had nowhere else to turn. Believe me, you don't get that kind of reward with ordinary business relationships; helping people out of foreclosure can be *spiritually* satisfying!

Maybe my investor friend doesn't "get it," because he's, well, a man. Maybe women do have kinder ways of approaching life in general. I'm no statistician, but I think women are much more able to help people in distress. *You* can use your intuitive abilities to help you in foreclosure investing. I urge you to trust your instincts in this arena.

What Is Foreclosure?

Let's define *foreclosure* again, just in case you've forgotten from your earlier lessons. A foreclosure takes place when a home owner can't pay the mortgage for a number of months, and the lender (the bank) says, Either you pay your back-due mortgage payments and all the fines and penalties, or we're going to kick you out and take back the house.

Then if the home owner still doesn't pay up, the bank says, OK, we gave you every chance. Now we're going to sell your house in a public auction unless you pay the whole amount of the loan in full. And then the lender does sell it. If nobody buys it at the auction, the bank is stuck with it, and it goes into its inventory.

There are four major stages in the progress of a foreclosure:

1. Predefault
2. Preforeclosure
3. Foreclosure (auction)
4. Bank REO (Real Estate Owned)

Let's take a look at these four stages one by one:

Predefault❖

That's when the bank hasn't yet sent the home owner a notice that it intends to foreclose. The bank is probably sending letters requesting payment but haven't used the "F word" yet (*foreclosure*). In many states, a person can go ninety days before the foreclosure process begins. When the bank sends the notice that it indeed plans to start the foreclosure procedure, that notice is called a Notice of Default (NOD). Default means the home owner didn't pay up.

I like to go to www.Dictionary.com a lot; it defines default this way: "failure to perform a task or fulfill an obligation, especially failure to meet a financial obligation, as in default on a loan. To fail to do what is required. To fail to pay money when it is due."

The stage of foreclosure we're examining right now is predefault, so it means that the bank hasn't sent the Notice of Default yet. The homeowner knows he's behind, and the bank knows he's behind, but nobody else knows. No other investors know either! I like that, because at this point I'm not competing with ten other investors for the opportunity to help the owner.

Preforeclosure❖

Preforeclosure refers to all of the time between the arrival of the Notice of Default and the time the bank sells the property on the courthouse steps (literally). The NOD must be made public, usually by publishing it in the legal section of a newspaper and by notifying the home owner by mail. Each state has its own rules and regulations on the foreclosure process, and the length of time between the NOD and the actual sale varies. The most common time frame is ninety days. So in general, after ninety days of nonpayment, the owner gets a notice. Then there could be ninety more days before the sale. That means the process could take as much as six months! More in some states.

Preforeclosure is the best time to get in and help people out. This is the time when you can create hope for them, hope for a better future where they can afford their housing. You create help in many forms, depending on their situation. But I truly believe that your product in the business of real-estate investing, especially in the foreclosure market, is hope and help❖.

Foreclosure auction❖

OK, the bank is *really* not happy by now! It's so unhappy that it is selling the owner's property on the steps of the courthouse. Some investors specialize in buying at these auctions, and you can too if you live in a town where there are still bargains to be found. In hot markets, like where I live, the auction gets into an eBay kind of frenzy, and the bids go up over market value. I recommend you do what Robert Allen says. Go to the auction and just watch for a few times. Keep your hands in your pockets and your lips zipped. Talk to the other investors there and find out what they're looking for. You may be able to network with them when you've got a great deal for sale, or you might be able to call them when you need some other people's money.

By the way, in most counties you have to come to the auction with cash or a cash equivalent like a cashier's check and pay for the property in full that morning. If you don't have the cash yourself, you'll need to use OPM. (You'll learn how to get that in the module on funding, don't worry!)

Bank REO (Real Estate Owned) ❖

What if nobody buys the property at the auction? Then the bank owns it. The bank doesn't really want to own real estate, though, so it would like to get it off its books before the next time the bank examiner comes around. (If a mortgage lender's books contain too many nonperforming loans, it looks bad, and the bank can't get the new bunch of money it needs to operate with.)

What does the lender do? It might sell it to you if you find the right person to talk to at the bank. The people at the bank usually assign it to a Realtor who specializes in REO properties. They'd *like* to get the amount that was left on the loan or even market value, but they'll often take less, because, frankly, they made their money in the early days of the loan. Sometimes though, they'll be sticklers and want full retail price. Donna Fox says it depends on how good their cup of coffee was that morning. I agree!

Anyway, if you can find a banker or a Realtor who knows these ropes, you'll be able to get some wonderful deep discounts on properties that other people (who aren't willing to take the trouble to develop those relationships) won't ever find.

All in all, the thing I want you to remember from this helping is that we're going out there to dispense hope and to give real help. If we do it right, it's not just a regular win-win. If we do it right, the *bank* wins, the *home owner* wins, and *we* win in a very rewarding and enlightened way. Win-win-win. Triple win! ❖

Our minds and imaginations can help us to ride out, to rise above—and even prosper in—times of both recession and inflation.

—MARK VICTOR HANSEN

Word Wizard

___ Predefault   The time during which a homeowner falls behind in payments, but before the bank sends a Notice of Default.

___ Preforeclosure   The period of time between the arrival of a Notice of Default and the actual auction.

___ Hope and Help   The real true product of the enlightened real-estate investor.

___ Foreclosure Auction   The day the property gets auctioned off to the public.

___ Bank REO   A property that didn't sell at the foreclosure auction; it goes back to being owned by the bank (Real Estate Owned).

___ Win-win-win   Triple win; better than win-win. The bank wins, the seller wins, the buyer wins.

Quiz Wizard

1. What are the four stages of foreclosure?
   - a. Predefault
   - b. Prefault
   - c. Preforeclosure
   - d. Preforbearance
   - e. Foreclosure
   - f. Enclosure
   - g. REO
   - h. REO Speedwagon

2. What is the true product of an enlightened real-estate investor?
   - a. Hope and Hype
   - b. Hip and Hop
   - c. Hope and Help

3. What is an NOD?
   - a. Notice that the property is scheduled for auction

    b. Notice that the mortgage payments haven't been made and must be paid in a certain time frame

    c. Notice that due diligence must be performed

    d. Notice of Defamation

    e. Notice of Divorce

Turn to page 436 for the answers.

Whiz Wizard

1.   Call your county office and ask when and where it holds foreclosure auctions. Ask where you can get the rules and regulations for purchasing properties at the auction. If your county has a website, visit it to see if the rules and regulations are posted there. Go to www.netronline.com for portals to different city and county websites. (It's a great all-around investor resource.)
Done _____

2.   Call your Realtor (the one you met in a previous lesson!) and ask if she has any connections for finding preforeclosures or REOs. You don't have to make any offers now, but in upcoming lessons you'll refer to the leads you get in this step.
Done _____

3.   Teach the concept of the four stages of foreclosure to someone else so that he or she understands it.
Done _____

How Can They Find You?

Usually when you think of finding great deals in real estate, you wonder how *you* can find *them*. I suggest you let *them* find *you*. That's even truer when you specialize in predefault and preforeclosure investing. It's much more fun to get a call from someone who already wants to do business with you!

The ways I've found people I can help have all been by putting out some communication and then letting the home owner call me for help. This lesson is about the different forms of communication you can use.

Let me list them in the order I used them:

1. Word of mouth and business cards
2. Writing letters to people whose names appeared on the NOD list
3. Putting an ad in the newspaper's Homes Wanted section
4. Bird dogs❖
5. Real-estate agents

A Half-million Dollars from a Dime

Remember, our first Robert Allen–style deal, a preforeclosure, started with a ten-cent business card, and we earned $75,000 in equity and $18,000 in cash when we closed (cash at closing❖ comes from borrowing some of the existing equity).

Now the house is worth triple what we paid for it, and the renters are giving us an $800-per-month positive cash flow. Wow! From one conversation and one business card, we acquired a house that now has more than $500,000 in equity in it. Do I like word of mouth? You bet. Business cards? Indeed!

The next house we bought was through a real-estate agent. It wasn't a foreclosure deal, but you can find preforeclosures from your agent (we found a great one that we still have today through an agent).

Then the next house we found was when a sweet single-mom nurse with five children called us in response to a letter we had sent her when we saw her name on the NOD list. She said she thought our letter sounded more sincere than all the others she had received, and she felt God had led her to us. I think she was right. The whole next lesson will show you how to write a letter that will allow people to be magnetized to you for the right reasons.

We bought a lot of houses through the letters-out, calls-in strategy. Then, just for the heck of it, we switched and started running an ad in the paper. It worked equally well. If we'd been sharper, we should have done *both* techniques at the same time. The ad went like this:

"0" Stress, "0" Cost to You!

> 0 Stress, 0 Cost to You! Sell your house to us in 72 hours for cash! Foreclosure OK. We can even help you move. Husband/wife team in LV since '67. Extensive references available. Call Karen now, 999-9999.

Let's analyze the ad. The zero up front placed the ad at the top of all the other ads. The fact that callers could speak to either a man or a woman was important. The fact that we'd been around town for all those years meant we weren't fly-by-night scam artists. No one has ever asked us for our references, but adding it to the ad meant a much better response rate. We had references, yes, and so do you: your banker, your attorney, your CPA, your affiliation with the Better Business Bureau and the Chamber of Commerce, and so forth.

To be completely candid, ads like these all sound a little unbelievable, don't they? People don't understand how you can do what's promised, so they can't believe it, really. You have to establish trust better than all the other ads surrounding yours. Write it from your heart, not from a template. Don't use the ad that I wrote verbatim, because it needs to come from your personal core values and experience. The best way to get someone to call you because they believe you are sincere is to *sincerely be sincere*.

Are you thinking right now, "I can't publish an ad that says I'll pay cash for their house; I don't *have* any cash"? Remember, you're going to use other people's cash, and you're going to learn how to do that in another lesson. Be patient with yourself! It's a layering process, OK?

Word of Mouth

When I use the word "bird dogs" I'm referring to people who go out looking for properties and let *us* know about them in exchange for some part of the deal. I guess it's the same as word of mouth, but it's based on your telling people you'll compensate them if they help you do the detective work to find people who need your help. Remember to tell them they're not looking for houses, they're looking for people with problems.

The least expensive ways to find preforeclosures are through the word of mouth and bird dog strategies. To find predefault, you won't be sending letters, because there's no list of people who are simply in trouble. One time we got a call on our ad from a gentleman who wasn't behind in his payments, but he knew (and *only he* knew) that he couldn't make the next month's payment. It sure was nice getting a call out of the blue one morning that ended up making us more than $100,000 in equity. And the seller is back home in Tennessee with his family, enjoying life in a place he can afford.

There is little true joy in relaxing; true joy lies in being valuable to someone else.

—KAREN NELSON BELL

Word Wizard

___ Bird Dogs   People who keep a look out for good deals for you in exchange for some compensation.

___ Cash at Closing   Money you get back if you finance or refinance a property for more than the original loan amount it had on it.

Quiz Wizard

1. What are five ways to help distressed preforeclosure home owners find you?
   - a. Word of mouth and business cards
   - b. Faxing
   - c. Writing letters to the names on the Notice of Default at the county records
   - d. Hiring a clown to stand on the sidewalk and hold a sign
   - e. Placing a good ad in the "Homes Wanted" section of the newspaper
   - f. The Goodyear blimp
   - g. Bird dogs
   - h. Real-estate agents

2. What is the most important quality of an advertisement you place in the "Homes Wanted" section?
   - a. Trust
   - b. Sincerity
   - c. Both

3. Whom can you use for references if you haven't ever done any deals? (This is a trick question.)
   - a. Attorney
   - b. Mom and dad
   - c. CPA
   - d. Karen Nelson Bell
   - e. Better Business Bureau
   - f. Your tax preparer

Turn to page 436 for the answers.

Whiz Wizard

1. Look in your newspaper to see if any investors are advertising in the "Homes Wanted" section. Rate the ads according to their believability.
    Done _____

2. Call on one of the ads and ask, "How can you do what you've advertised? I don't quite understand."
    Done _____

3. Teach the concept of how to help people in foreclosure find you to someone else so that he or she understands it.
    Done _____

HELPING 29

Letters to Get
Them Calling *You*

The first time we ever got a call in response to a letter we sent to a name on the Notice of Default list, it was pretty exciting. The woman told us that she picked us to call out of all the people who had written to her, because she felt our letter was the only one that was sincere. I was really glad she said that, because the letter was indeed sincere; it was from deep in my heart.

A few years later, after I'd been teaching for a while, a student asked if she could borrow the letter. I said she could if she promised to use it only in her city, not in mine. I knew if she wrote it to the same list I was writing to, it would instantly wipe out the sincerity, and the recipients would know it was a template or form letter. All investors are writing to the same list, so each person can end up getting ten to one hundred letters or postcards from investors, Realtors, mortgage brokers, and loan sharks.

Well, I gave her the letter to use. She knew we were getting a 10 to 14 percent response rate, which is unheard of in the direct-mail industry (1 to 2 percent is considered awesome). What kind of response do you think she got? Zero, zilch, nada❖. She thought it was because her city was different from my city. I don't think so, because I have other friends in her city who do get responses. I personally think it was because it didn't come from her core desire to help them; it didn't express her personal intent.

That's why I'm going to ask you to *not* use this letter as is. You need to write it from your heart. Period. All I'm doing here is showing you some principles that I learned from reading *The Ultimate Sales Letter* by Dan Kennedy. (Bob introduced us students to him in the Protégé Program.) You could write your own letter from your heart, then comb through that book chapter by chapter and implement the ideas in your letter. You'll come up with an even better letter than mine, I'm sure of it!

OK, here it is:

Your Company, Inc.

101 Success Boulevard
Your Home Town, YS 99999
Phone: 555-555-5555   Cell: 555-555-5555
E-Fax: 555-555-5555 or Fax: 555-555-5555
Email: YourEmail@yourserver.com

Información Importante con Respecto a Su Hogar
(if you speak another language)

Are You in Trouble?

What Do You Need?

How Can We Help You?

(Use the words you and your as opposed to I, me, my)

Dear {Title} {Last Name}, *(Don't use "Dear Neighbor")*
     (Tell them how you found them:)
Anytime a bank or mortgage company records a notice on your property, it becomes a matter of public record. We hope this letter helps you to understand that your lender has begun foreclosure proceedings on your property. Therefore, your name has appeared on the county records, and you'll probably find a lot of letters in your mailbox from various companies who check every day to see who's on the Default list.

(Tell them who you are and who you are not!)
We're not real-estate agents or mortgage brokers;
we're a husband-and-wife couple, living in Las Vegas
since 1967, who buy houses privately for cash.

We can stop the pending foreclosure on your property right now.

We specialize in helping people who are having difficulty keeping up payments, for whatever reason. We can stop the pending foreclosure on your property right now. Even if you've listed your home with a real-estate agent, we can help.

(Have a section that has bullets, preferably an uneven number.)
Do you need to sell your home for cash today?

There are many reasons why a person finds themselves the *victim* of foreclosure proceedings:

- Loss of job
- Reduction of salary
- Downsizing
- Transfer
- Divorce
- Gambling debt
- Illness
- Death in the family
- Paying on two homes
- Landlord with bad tenants or no tenants
- You may have run into some other financial troubles and now risk losing your home.

Whatever your personal situation, we understand and would be very happy to talk with you about solving your problem by buying your home right away.

(Tell them the bad stuff:)
You probably already know what happens after a foreclosure: you don't get a dime for the sale (the only winner is the bank), and your credit is ruined for seven to ten years. It's *embarrassing* and *stressful.* You may even be bombarded by harassing calls and letters. But there is a way to turn this negative experience into a positive one. You can discover HOPE for the future, especially if you can get HELP from someone who specializes in solving foreclosure problems.

We're private investors with a sincere desire to assist people who deserve help. We buy properties in all price ranges, in all conditions, and we can even help you move into a place you *can* afford. Some of the people we've helped have even come back to us later to help them find out how to buy another home after they've gotten their situations under control.

We may be able to help you create a *win-win-win* situation, so that you *and* your mortgage lender can both get your problems solved.

(Summarize your best benefits!)

That's what our main job is: solving problems. Call now and ask us to *custom-design* some solutions for you. There's *no cost* and *no obligation,* just call to talk to either of us in *complete confidence.* If you're in trouble, you can call to tell us what your needs are. Let us find out if we can help you today.

Call to Action:

Call us at 999-999-9999 right away!

Very Sincerely,

Duncan and Karen Guertin

> *(Describe your references. Better Business Bureau, Chamber of Commerce, your attorney, your CPA. This is critical to your success. No one has ever asked me to see my credentials or my references, but knowing they can makes them feel a lot better. I really do think joining the Better Business Bureau is a great idea.)*

Extensive references available.

Información Importante con Respecto a Su Hogar

Si tiene preguntas acerca de su hipoteca o se le hace difícil mandar los pagos mensuales de su casa, por favor llame y deje su nombre y la manera más efectiva para podernos comunicar con usted. Se habla español, y es nuestro placer ayudarle.

P.S.: Here's what just one of our many former clients wrote to us:

October 12, 2001

Dearest Karen & Duncan,

Just a brief note to thank you for all of the help you have extended to us in our recent troubles. Not only did you save our credit rating, we made two new friends. Now, how many businesses can say that?

We wish you continued good luck in your real-estate dealings. If there is anything we can do for you, do not hesitate to ask. Your caring made our troubles seem less painful.

Once again, thank you for all of your help and valuable information.

Sincerely,

(Testimonials are vital. Gather them as you do your deals. Ask for them!)

All achievements, all earned riches, have their beginning in an idea.
　　　　　　　　　　　　　　　　—NAPOLEON HILL

Word Wizard

___ Zilch, Nada　　　　　Nothing

Quiz Wizard

1. What is the single most important element of your NOD letter?
    a. Be brief.
    b. Address the letters by hand.
    c. Be sincere from your heart.
    d. Use empathy.

2. Which elements would you include in your NOD letter?
    a. References.

    b. Testimonials.

    c. Use of foreign language if fluent.

    d. First name for greeting.

    e. Explanation of how you found them.

    f. *You* words.

    g. Confidentiality.

    h. All of the above.

3. Would you be successful if you sent out the letter in this chapter as is?

    a. Probably.

    b. Probably not.

Turn to page 436 for the answers.

Whiz Wizard

1. In a previous lesson, you called the county courthouse to find out where the NODs are posted. I want you to find an NOD list and just take a look at it. It will seem like a lot of gobbledygook, but just look for the name of the owner and the owner's address (as opposed to the property address). Just look at it. Don't do anything else but look at it! If you haven't found a free resource for the list yet, call your marketing rep at Fidelity National Title or your favorite title company and ask to have it sent to your in-box every day. (That's the rep you've already become friendly with; the rep who is already on your team!)
Done _____

2. Try your hand at writing a letter based on the ideas in the sample letter you read in this helping. Show it to someone to see if he or she understands it. Remember, the people in trouble may not have a clue what's going on; it's up to you to make it clear and simple.
Done _____

3. Teach the concept of how to write a great NOD letter to someone else so that he or she understands it. Have the person read your own NOD letter to see if it has the principles embedded in it.
Done _____

Help! They're Actually Calling! Now What?!

Let's say you actually sent out one hundred letters like the one in the last lesson. Let's say maybe five people call you up and say something like, "Um, I was wondering if you could help me with my house even though I'm four months behind, and it's scheduled for sale in five weeks." Let's say out of those five people, *one* of them actually has a situation where you know you could help the person. *Eek!* Now what?

Would it help if you had another one of my handy-dandy scripts? I'll bet it would. Let me whip one up for you. Of course, in this situation, a script won't really work, because there are as many different problems as there are people, and you'll have to actually L.I.S.T.E.N. and respond! However, here are some of the points you'll very likely be discussing:

- Well, Mrs. Smith, I'm glad you read my letter and didn't throw it away. Sometimes I can help people out very fast; what I'll do is, I'll get some information from you so I can do a little research, and if it looks like I can help you out, I'll explain everything in very simple terms. Basically what I do is buy your property and help you move to a place you

can afford. Then I usually rent out the house, but sometimes I sell it. It just depends on my research. I want to let
you know I'm in this business to make a profit too, just so
that's not left unsaid. Hopefully, I'll be able to make it
work out for both of us.

- Why don't you tell me a little bit about the situation you're
in, so I'll be able to get the general picture?

- Well, I might be able to help. I never know until I've done
some preliminary research. Would it be OK if I ask you
some questions that might seem personal? I'll need to
know certain things about the property and about your
loans in order to do my research.

- First, what's the address and the zip code? What's your full
name, and what's your phone number? Are you living in
the house now?

- Do you know how much you owe on the loan that's behind? Do you know how much it would take to catch you
back up with all the interest and penalties? When is the
auction?

- Do you have any other loans on the property? Are there
any liens, like IRS liens or other tax liens? How about contractor liens❖, like a pool builder? You might have forgotten, in all this stress.

- Who all lives in the house? Spouse? In-laws? Children?
Common-law spouse❖?

- What condition is the property in? (Do all the normal
steps of a Bargain Finder.)

- What would be your own personal best-case scenario? Are
you trying to move to another state? Are you looking for
an apartment? How do you hope I can help you? What
would that help look like?

- I really understand the situation you're in, and I'm going to
do everything I can to help. If I can't personally help out,
I'll try to find some other solutions for you. I can't promise
I can fix the problem, but I can promise to try. I also
promise I'll call you back within forty-eight hours to let you
know what I find out. (And by the way, never, *never* break
that promise!)

In good times and bad times, ideas make millionaires.
—MARK VICTOR HANSEN

Word Wizard

___ Contractor Liens

When a person makes a contract to build a pool or a room addition, for example, if they don't pay for it, the builder (contractor) goes down to the county courthouse and records a lien against the property so that the owner can't sell it until the contractor gets paid off.

___ Common-law Spouse

A husband or wife that doesn't have a marriage certificate but lives as if there were a legal marriage.

Quiz Wizard

1. Can you use the script in this lesson for every call?
    a. Yes
    b. No

2. What promise should you never break, according to this lesson?
    a. The promise to help the owner move
    b. The promise to call back in forty-eight hours
    c. The promise to give the owner 10 percent of his or her equity
    d. The promise to refer the owner to a good Realtor

3. What skill do you need the most when you're talking to the owner in preforeclosure?
    a. The ability to read if they're lying
    b. The ability to rate the property on the Bargain Finder
    c. The ability to listen

Turn to page 436 for the answers.

Whiz Wizard

1. If you think you would like to help people in foreclosure, it's time to start writing to them. Send out one hundred of the letters you wrote in the last lesson and see if you get any calls during the next four weeks. Send the letters to houses in the median price range for your area. Be sure to write to the owner's mailing address and not the property address (if they're different). On the outside of the envelope, write "Urgent, re: Your Home" in red ink.
    Done _____

2. Practice using this helping's script by doing a little role-playing. Have a family member or friend (perhaps someone you've been "teaching" the various lessons in this book) pretend to be the home owner. Have him or her make up different stories, and try your hand at responding to the moment. It'll be awkward at first, but you'll get smoother as you practice. Would you rather be awkward with your first seller or in a nice, safe conversation with a friend?
    Done _____

3. Teach someone else the concept of what to say when a person in preforeclosure calls so that he or she understands it.
    Done _____

HELPING 31

How to Avoid
Doing a Bad Deal

You've been called in response to your NOD letter, and you've talked to the distressed home owner. You know she's motivated because she's not only about to lose her house but is headed for a stain on her credit that will haunt her forever—foreclosure.

You told the caller that you'd get back to her after you do some research, but what research might that be? There are some basic things you're going to have to find out. I don't know when you're going to get that call, but you need to have all these tools at your disposal for when it comes. Not only will this research help you with preforeclosures, but you can use the same routines and thought processes on other kinds of deals.

Here's a list of questions to ask yourself about the deal; check them off as you go about searching the county records for details about the property. If you live in a medium-sized city, you'll probably be able to do all of your research on the internet. If not, you may have to go to the courthouse or send someone (perhaps a hungry college student) to do it for you.

1. Who is the legal owner? In other words, who is on the title❖? I've been in two situations where the person seeking

my help wasn't the legal owner! One of these sellers was a renter trying to defraud me. The other was a renter who had a deal with the owner, and he ended up putting us in touch with the real seller for a finder's fee. If the title doesn't show the same owner as the person you've spoken with, ask bluntly, "Whose name is that on the records as the owner?"

2.   Do the records show the same amount of bedrooms and bathrooms you've been told the property has? If they don't, you may be looking at a property where additions were made without permits. It isn't always a problem, but it could be.

3.   Get some comps from your internet resources. If it looks like the property is in a good price range, then call your real-estate-agent friend for accurate comps.

4.   Ask your friend at the title company to do a preliminary title search❖, called a "prelim❖." This is where you'll find out if the owner has four more liens than what he told you! You'll also find out how much money is owed on the loan(s).

5.   Now you have enough data to see if there is any equity in the house. If there is a lot of equity, there are a lot of ways to do the deal. If there is very little or no equity, the only way to do the deal is if you can rent the house for any profit. If another investor tells you that you should try a "short sale" when there isn't enough equity, tell him or her that you prefer to deal with basic strategies at the moment, until you've mastered them. However, later on you can even do houses where people owe more than the house is worth, by using the short-sale❖ strategy, where you negotiate with the lender to reduce the amount owed.

You'll have to do a little math at this point. If you're bad with numbers like I am, don't worry. Get out your calculator, and I'll walk you through it.

Don't Read This Next Section!

Don't just read this next section. Really! Take out your calculator and go through the sample here. It's gonna make it seem a lot easier, trust me. Promise me you'll take out your calculator. You're *practicing* for your first preforeclosure!

6. Here are the steps:
    a. Enter the amount of the house's value (like $100,000).
    b. Now subtract the amount of the first mortgage ($100,000 – $55,000 = $45,000).
    c. Now subtract the other loans and liens ($45,000 – $10,000 = $35,000).
    d. Now subtract the amount necessary to bring the loan current, taken from the owner's mortgage coupons or letters from the bank ($35,000 – $5,000 = $30,000).
    e. Now subtract what you think the owner might need in order to be able to move on with his new life ($30,000 – $3,000 = $27,000).
    f. Now subtract some money for a buffer to cover the potential cost of fixing up and marketing ($27,000 – $2,000 = $25,000).
    g. Hmmmmmmm, $25,000 is a good deal. It would even be a good deal at $20,000, if we use the percentages on the Bargain Finder's property selection grid.

7. Now's the time to do your Bargain Finder, as well as you can without having seen the property. Remember, motivation will most likely be a 3 because the owner is going to lose the house and get a foreclosure on her credit report. If the house can't be sold for a profit, check out what houses are renting for in that area to see if the rents are higher than the mortgage payment on the property. (My *favorite* way to get rental comps is just to look in the newspaper's rental ads and see what everyone is charging.)

8. Now it's time to call back the owner and say, "Look, I think I might be able to save you from having a foreclosure on your records. Plus, I may be able to help you with moving costs, get you into a place you can afford, and put some cash in your pocket. Would you like me to come over this afternoon, or would this evening be better?"

Now you're going to finally go see the property. That's where you continue doing your research, because what you were told the condition is and reality might not be exactly the same. One Realtor I know told me, "If their lips are moving, they're lying." I don't have that jaded a view, but owners have been known to "exaggerate."

That's about all there is to the basics. Just see if there's any chance for you to *sell* the property for a profit or *rent* it for a profit. I'll bet you thought it was going to be a lot more complicated, right? Between the Bargain Finder and some simple math, it's pretty easy to tell if there's a deal percolating.

Let's be the "other" investors. Let's really, truly help people avoid fore-closure. Let's not just give lip service to helping others, let's help from the deepest part of our hearts.

—KAREN NELSON BELL

Word Wizard

___ Title	The piece of paper that tells who the legal owner is to a thing—like the title to your car. It's usually (but not always) recorded on the county records.
___ Title Search	Looking around to see what data are connected to the title; for example, are there any mortgages? Are there any liens? The search can be done by a private party, but it's usually done by professionals at a title company.
___ Preliminary Title Search	The title search that gets you going during your due diligence period; it helps you decide whether you want to proceed with the deal.
___ Prelim	Short for Preliminary Title Search ("Can you do a quick prelim for me?").
___ Short Sale	When the lender is willing to sell the property for less money than is owed on it.

Quiz Wizard

1. What should you do first if the seller isn't on the title as the legal owner?
    a. Pass on the deal.
    b. Hire a private detective.
    c. Ask the seller why his or her name isn't on the title.
    d. Contact the person on the title first.
    e. Call the county recorder's office.

2. If you find a house with a first mortgage of $114,000 and a second mortgage of $12,500, and you find out that the property is worth $205,000 fixed up, and the wholesale fix-up cost is $7,500, *and* the sellers need $2,000 to move to Texas, how much potential profit do you have? (Use your calculator to find the answer.)
    a. $96,000.
    b. $69,000.
    c. $24,500.
    d. $7,500.
    e. None of the above.

3. What are some of the tools you will use to decide whether or not to do the deal?
    a. Simple math
    b. Bargain Finder
    c. Prelim
    d. Comps
    e. Communication

Turn to page 436 for the answers.

Whiz Wizard

1. If you think you would like to help people in foreclosure, you need to help them find you. Send out another one hundred copies of the letter you wrote in the last lesson and see if you get any calls during the next four weeks. Send the letters to houses in the median price range for your area. (How does one find median price range? Ask the Realtor on your team. In some cities it

changes every three months!) Be sure to write to the owner's mailing address and not the property address (if they're different). On the outside of the envelope, write "Urgent, re: Your Home" in red ink (same as last lesson).
Done _____

2. Find three properties that are in the preforeclosure stage (use any of the resources discussed in prior lessons) and analyze whether they would be good deals, using all the tools we've discussed. If there is a potential good deal among them, communicate with the seller; then let your phone mentor help you create your next set of steps to take.
Done _____

3. Teach the concept of what to research on a preforeclosure property to someone else so that he or she understands it.
Done _____

HELPING 32

What to Bring to the Kitchen Table

You've been talking on the phone with a preforeclosure lead, "Maggie," and you already know there is a potential deal. You've done your research on the property and you've rated it. There is also a potential for you to help Maggie by keeping her from having a foreclosure on her records and by possibly helping her move to a place she can afford. And, yes, you see that there's even some potential for you to have a profit too. You're pretty sure you can give her help and hope, and you're pretty sure that you'll have some benefit as well.

Now it's time to go to the property. Or is it? Have you forgotten anything? Here's what I like to have before I take the time, trouble, and gasoline to go to the seller: I want to have some agreement with the seller that there is a deal going on here. I say, "Well, if I come see the house, and everything checks out the way you've described, I can get you the truck so you can move your things to Houston to be with your daughter by the time the baby's born. I can also give you enough money for travel expenses and the first and last months' deposits on your apartment in Texas. Would you like for me to come by in the afternoon or the evening?"

When Maggie tells me yes, I know I'm going there to do a deal. I like to know there's a deal in the air before I ever get in the car.

When I get to Maggie's house, we end up sitting in the kitchen. That's where the best deals are done. Not in the living room, not on the dining room table, not in the office. In the kitchen. It's friendly and warm. It's where trusted friends hang out. I've got a yellow pad with me, with some papers stuck in the back, not a briefcase. I'm just another person, not a big hoity-toity real-estate investor. I could be a neighbor or an acquaintance from church.

Yellow Pads and Smiley Faces

While we're talking, I make notes on the pad, and when it's something we agree on, like, "OK, I'm sure you don't want the trouble of having to mess with unplugging the washer and dryer—I'll save you the aggravation and give you an extra hundred dollars, too, just to help you out"—I draw a nice smiley face.

If the subject goes a little less to my liking—for example if Maggie says, "Well, I have to stay in the property; I can't move out"—I'll put a little frown-y face and say something like, "Look at it this way: I know you aren't able to make the payments on the current amount, and when I buy the house, I'm going to have to charge even more to cover my expenses plus the existing mortgage. If you can't manage it now, it will be even more difficult for you to manage a higher amount. I think you're going to have to face the fact that you need to find a place that you can really afford. You don't want to end up in this same jam again, right?"

I've been working on the pad all along and writing down things we're going to agree on. Finally, I can put down a list of what the owner is going to get and what she's going to do, as well as a list of what I'm going to get and what I'm going to do. I say, "Look, I'll take what we've agreed on here and put it into a simple contract, and I'll walk you through the steps of it in plain English. Do you have a lawyer you can take it to?"

That means we've got a big yes. We're doing this deal, and it just feels natural. Now, the paperwork is just to memorialize what we've been chatting about. What we've been chatting about was just what we'd already talked about in simple ways on the telephone. It went step by step as natural as can be.

So what are all the things we're going to take care of to make it legal and binding? What are the different papers we need, and where do we get them? Let me list what you're going to want to have, and I'll go into detail on each item:

1. Contract for sale (purchase agreement)❖. This is the written expression of what you've both agreed upon. We'll go over contracts in a separate helping.
2. Permission letter❖ from the home owner for you to speak to the lender, includes the home owner's Social Security number. You can't talk to the bank or mortgage company without it.
3. Letter of duress❖ stating that the home owner understood you intend to make a profit, and he or she was not under duress or coercion by you. This is important, so that the seller won't claim you ripped him/her off, just because you made a profit.
4. All loan documents in possession of the home owner. You'll need these in order to know who to contact.
5. All insurance documents in possession of the home owner. You'll send them to your own insurance agent right away. Insurance policies have to be in the name of the person on the title.
6. Grant, bargain, sale deed❖ or warranty deed❖ (called by different names in different states). This is the document that actually gets recorded to show you're the new owner.
7. Quitclaim deed❖ from any other occupants, quitclaim deed from spouses, ex-spouses, common-law spouses, relatives living in the house. This is important. You don't want a relative coming to you a year later saying that he or she still owns an interest in the property. Some states require a "grant, bargain, sale deed" even for the transfer from spouse to spouse. I recommend it for foreclosures.
8. Keys, garage door openers, appliance manuals.
9. Forwarding address, telephone number, cell phone number, email address.
10. Contact information for close relatives.

As you're going to find out in detail in the next chapter, you're most likely going to be catching up the past-due payments and then taking over the future payments yourself. It's a little bit like "assuming" a loan, but you don't really assume it, you just start making the payments. More on that in helping 33.

The cash you're going to be paying for the house will be the cash you give to the lender to catch up any back payments and the cash you give to the seller. That's going to be OPC, of course, right? (Other people's *cash*!) More on that in module 7. Remember, this is a layering effect. I know you want to know everything right this minute. Hang in there with me.

Let's learn two very important rules right now:

1. Never give the seller the cash until she moves out, and
2. Never let the seller stay in the property. In addition to the financial no-no of letting the person stay, there are legal ramifications that will place you at great risk down the road. Just don't let a seller stay in the property.

So you've signed your first preforeclosure deal, you've got all the paperwork, you've shaken hands, you've probably hugged, too, and I want you to notice the mood of the seller. She's gone from being stressed to the max to being relieved beyond belief. She may call you her guardian angel. You may actually become friends in a way. You've helped the person make a big change, from feeling like hiding from the world to imagining a better future. If you've done the real job of providing hope and help, whether your profit is $5,000 or $50,000, you're going to feel like a million dollars!

One can judge a life by its problems. The highest order of problem would be to find wise ways to distribute one's wealth and its energy for noble results.

—KAREN NELSON BELL

Word Wizard

___ Contract for Sale	An agreement between the parties saying that the seller wishes to sell and the buyer wishes to buy, and here's what they've agreed upon.
___ Purchase Agreement	Another way of saying "contract for sale" (see above).
___ Permission Letter	A letter signed by the seller that grants you permission to speak on his behalf to

the lender. Without the letter, the lender is not allowed by law to speak to you.

___ Letter of Duress — A letter signed by the seller that confirms that you didn't force him into selling his property. It usually states that the seller understands clearly that you expect to make a profit on the house.

___ Grant, Bargain, Sale Deed — A deed resulting from a bargain between a buyer and a seller of real property, resulting in a sale.

___ Warranty Deed — A deed in which the seller warrants or guarantees that a good title is being transferred to the buyer.

___ Quitclaim Deed — A deed releasing whatever interest one may hold in a property but making no warranty whatsoever. It quits whatever claim one has to the property. The least powerful deed, since it doesn't make any guarantees.

Quiz Wizard

1. What should you do before you visit the seller at the property?
    a. Get a prelim from the title company, so that you know if the title is clear.
    b. Get a good yes from the seller that a deal is in the works.
    c. Call the lender to find out what the late fees and legal fees come to.

2. Which of these documents are *not* necessary for you to get during this visit?
    a. Contract for sale.
    b. Grant, bargain, sale deed or warranty deed.
    c. Quitclaim deed from spouses.
    d. Letter of duress.
    e. Permission letter.
    f. Credit application.

        g. Loan documents.

        h. Insurance documents.

3. What rules are you always going to follow when investing in pre-foreclosures?

        a. Give the seller their money *after* he moves out.

        b. Make sure the seller moves into one of your other properties.

        c. Make sure the seller moves out of the property.

        d. All of the above.

Turn to page 436 for the answers.

Whiz Wizard

1. Go to www.ND4W.com/docs to read samples of the various documents discussed in this chapter.
   Done _____

2. Go to the www.ND4W.com/MP3s to listen to Live PreForeclosure calls and Preforeclosure role-playing.
   Done _____

3. Teach the concept of what to do at the kitchen table to someone else so that he or she understands it.
   Done _____

The Subject of "Subject To"

If you ask a Realtor if she understands "subject to," she will surely say yes, because there are all kinds of clauses that you can use to protect the buyer, like "subject to pest inspection" or "subject to my attorney's approval." However, there's one use of the phrase that is so powerful, the term has become an adjective or adverb. You might hear someone say, "I bought the house *subject to*," Or you might hear, "It was a *subject-to* deal." This is where your Realtor may or may not know what the concept is.

The term comes from a simple clause that goes like this: "subject to✢ existing financing."

Here's the simplest essence of what it means: "leaving the existing financing in place and taking over the existing payments."

Now, a lot of folks will tell you that you can't assume a loan that isn't an assumable loan. But we're not going to assume anything. There are very few assumable loans left out there in the world, and if you run across one, you still wouldn't necessarily want to assume it unless it was a nonqualifying assumable loan✢—meaning that you didn't have to run your credit and go through the whole qualifying process. Even if it was a nonqualifying assumable loan, you still might not want to take it on, because it might have very high interest rates, or you might not want another loan on your credit report right now.

The main thing to remember is that we're not talking about assuming a loan, so scratch that phrase from your vocabulary for a while until you really get the distinction.

"Subject To"

Once again, the subject of "subject to" means this: The buyer takes over the payments on the seller's existing mortgage. The phrase really means that the buyer is buying the property "subject to the existing financing." So the term *subject to* is used one way when you're talking about contingency clauses and another way when you're talking about taking over someone's loan.

How is it different from assuming? The huge difference is that your name is not going on the loan. It stays in the seller's name. It stays on the seller's credit. The lender probably doesn't even know that you made a contract with the seller to do so. In fact, we'd most often rather not bother the lender with the news (more about why down below).

Is it legal? You can read all kinds of opinions on the answer to that question, but the answer lies in this truth: Anyone can make a private contract to sell a property.

You're walking away with the deed, and the seller still has the loan. You may be asking yourself why a person would let you do that. This technique is often used in conjunction with the acquisition of a property that is facing immediate foreclosure. In those times, you are more likely and more able to pay the mortgage than the seller. You actually are going to make the payments on time, so his or her credit is going to get a boost from the fact that the payments won't be late anymore.

Here are the things you need to do when you're getting ready to buy a property subject to:

1. Tell the seller about the due-on-sale clause❖. There is a clause in most mortgage contracts that says the lender has the right to call the whole loan due if it's sold. (It's not a law that says they *must,* just a clause that says they *can.*) The seller needs to know it exists. Here's my personal opinion

on the subject of the due-on-sale clause. It's basically something that almost never happens as long as the payments are being made on time. It may tend to happen more during times of a high rise in interest rates.

2. Get insurance on the property. Make sure that the insurance is in the same name that is on the title. (The seller's name is still on the loan, but his or her name is off the title, got it?)

3. Get a permission letter❖ to speak to the lender that has the seller's Social Security number on it.

4. Put the mortgage coupons in your address (after you have the permission letter).

5. Get a declaration page❖ or distress letter❖, a document that shows there was no stress or duress on the part of the seller.

6. Don't put any money into the deal, yours or anyone else's, until you have the deed in hand and the sellers have moved out.

7. *Never be late on the payments.*

8. Never allow the seller to rent the property from you. I know that sounds harsh, but even if there are reasons why you should trust that she could miraculously make the payments, there are *legal* reasons why you mustn't rent it to her. If the person lives in the property, there is a chance that sometime in the future, she could choose to contest your ownership. If you must rent to the seller, rent her another property, something that she *can* afford. Remember, there may be reasons that aren't visible to you for her late payments: sometimes alcoholism, gambling addiction, criminal activities, and so forth. Help the person move on to a better life, but protect yourself at the same time.

"Subject to" is the best way for people who have poor credit to be able to get into a property. After six to twelve months of paying on time, you'll have a credit record that will allow you to refinance the property in your own name. Most people keep it "subject to" for only a year or two. However, it could go for the whole term of the mortgage.

So you say to the seller, "How about I just take over your payments so that you can walk away and be free of the stress and strain of these bills you can't pay?" Sometimes you can even use this strategy when there is no foreclosure pending! Sometimes people just want to get out from under debt, and they are happy to have you relieve them of a burden they don't want, for whatever reason.

Here are the ways you can help the seller to understand why it's a win-win situation:

1. Explain that you're going to pay on time, which will improve her currently nasty credit.
2. You're even going to pay a month (or two months) in advance to make her feel comfortable. (And by the way, did you know that paying early improves your credit?)
3. You can even use a title company to run the payments through.
4. You can have an attorney draw up everything to make everyone safe.
5. You can show the owner your credit report, if you have no late pays yourself.

Here is a list of all the items you need to get from the seller:

1. Permission letter from the home owner to speak to the lender, includes the home owner's Social Security number.
2. Distress letter (also called a declaration page) stating the home owner understood you intend to make a profit, and they were not under duress.
3. All loan documents in possession of home owner.
4. All insurance documents in possession of home owner.
5. Grant, bargain, sale deed or warranty deed transferring the title.
6. Quitclaim deed from any other occupants, quitclaim deed from spouses, ex-spouses, common-law spouses, relatives living in house.
7. Keys, garage door openers, appliance manuals.
8. Forwarding address, telephone number, cell phone number, email address.
9. Contact information for close relative.
10. Contract for sale.

Just don't give up trying to do what you really want to do. Where there is love and inspiration, I don't think you can go wrong.

—ELLA FITZGERALD

Word Wizard

___ Subject To	An escape clause that a buyer can put in a contract, such as "subject to my attorney's approval" or "subject to suitable financing."
___ "Subject To"	An investing strategy based on the clause "subject to existing financing," meaning that the buyer will take over the payments of the existing loan.
___ Nonqualifying Assumable Loan	An assumable loan where the buyer puts her name on it, but she doesn't have to qualify for it through the loan application process.
___ Due-on-Sale Clause	A clause in almost all loans that says if the property is transferred to another owner, the lender can request that the loan be paid in full.
___ Permission Letter	A letter from the seller to the buyer that says the buyer can talk to the lender on his behalf.
___ Distress Letter	A letter from the seller "to whom it may concern" that says he wasn't pressured, forced, or coerced into selling his property.
___ Declaration page	See *Distress Letter.*

Quiz Wizard:

1. What are some aspects of an investor's subject-to deal?
   a. It's subject to the existing financing.
   b. It always means the seller is in foreclosure.
   c. The buyer takes over the payments of the seller's loan, even though the seller's name still stays on the loan.

      d. The deal is subject to a pest inspection.

      e. The deal could possibly trigger a due-on-sale clause.

2. Which of these items are not necessary for you to get during this visit?

      a. Permission letter from the home owner to speak to the lender (includes the homeowner's Social Security number).

      b. A pest inspection.

      c. All loan documents in possession of home owner.

      d. All insurance documents in possession of home owner.

      e. Quitclaim deed from any other occupants, quitclaim deed from spouses, ex-spouses, common-law spouses, relatives living in house.

3. What rules are you always going to follow when doing a subject-to deal?

      a. Never be late on the payments.

      b. Make sure the seller moves into one of your other properties.

      c. If you rent the property back to the seller, make sure you get a declaration page.

      d. *Never* rent the property back to the seller.

Turn to page 436 for the answers.

Whiz Wizard

1. Go to www.ND4W.com/foreclosure to see samples of the various documents discussed in this chapter.
Done _____

2. Go to www.ND4W.com/pre4 to listen to an audio lecture on pre-foreclosures.
Done _____

3. Teach the concept of the subject of "subject to" to someone else so that he or she understands it.
Done _____

HELPING 34

You Can't Invest in a Vacuum

You're at the point now where deals may be starting to pop into your life. Whether it's from a regular motivated seller or from a person in preforeclosure, now you may begin to attract deals to yourself. You're going to begin to think, "Hey, I can't do this alone."

You couldn't be more right!

No one, not one single successful real estate investor, can invest in a vacuum. It simply can't be done. If you only had yourself and the seller, you'd still need to involve a third person, your buyer or your renter. Well, believe me, you're going to want to have a whole lot more than that on your team.

When my husband passed away suddenly, my incredible team, led by my business partners, Suzan Hudson and Frank Woodbeck, completely carried on all our operations until I could find a way to return to active duty. I rely on my stellar team every single day. It's Suzan's favorite mantra: "The TEAM is EVERYTHING."

Who are the essential team members?

The Fab Five
___ Real-estate agent or broker
___ Real-estate attorney

___ Escrow agent (title closing person)
___ Mortgage broker at correspondent lender❖
___ Personal banker

More
___ Insurance agent who knows real-estate investing
___ Accountant who knows real-estate investing
___ Handyman
___ Inspector
___ Appraiser
___ Other investors
___ Bird dogs
___ Rental management assistant or property manager❖
___ Suppliers of materials, carpet, tile, appliances
___ Painter

Here's your script for talking with any of these potential team members: "Hi. I'm calling to find out what, if any, services you offer to the professional investor. I'd be interested to meet with you to find out if we might be able to work together, and I'd be glad to refer you to the rest of my team." Then you hush up and let them pitch you on their services.

My underlying concept is that I want everyone on my team to make money from just knowing me! I want to be a rushing river of referrals for them, because I think it makes me teacher's pet in their customer service department!

By the way, I'm sure there will be other people on your team besides the ones above. This is a starter list, just like this is a starter course! I now have county officials, well diggers, trust specialists, and publicists as a part of my team, but you won't need them for a while. If you surround yourself with the Fab Five, you're off to a great start.

If we do our investing in an enlightened way, we'll be bringing benefit to everyone in our sphere of influence. What a wonderful way to live our lives!

You are the only human being on this planet who is truly powerful enough to stop yourself.

—KAREN NELSON BELL

Word Wizard

___ Correspondent Lender   A mortgage brokerage company that already has developed lines of credit with big money lenders, so it doesn't have to go outside its own company to find the loans for you.

___ Property Manager   A real-estate agent who has taken a special course in order to become a licensed property manager; he also works for a broker (not out in the field by himself).

Quiz Wizard

1. Can you invest in a vacuum; alone, with no help from anyone else?
   a. Yes
   b. No

2. Which of the Fab Five should you put on your team immediately?
   a. Real-estate agent
   b. Real-estate attorney
   c. Title expert (closing expert)
   d. Mortgage broker
   e. Personal banker

3. What's the best way to construct a great team? (One answer isn't in the text.)
   a. Go to a lot of cocktail parties for schmoozing.
   b. Refer all of your good team members to your other good team members.
   c. Refer all of your good team members to everyone who might desire their services.
   d. Put an ad in the paper in the help wanted section.
   e. If you need a good mortgage broker, ask one of your other good team members, like your real-estate agent, to recommend one.

Turn to page 436 for the answers.

Whiz Wizard

1. You know what's coming in this homework, don't you? I want you to make appointments to meet every one of the Fab Five team players this coming week. You can sign off on the homework when you have the appointment, but don't cheat yourself by not going to meet them. Enjoy letting them tell you what they can do for you!
    Done _____

2. Practice saying the little introductory speech out loud. You know from past lessons that I really mean it, right? I expect you to *do* this! No cheating! Say it out loud to your dog, your cat, your mom, your sister, your next-door neighbor. I want you to feel confident when you call on your Fab Five. You're not begging for help, you're a successful real-estate investor with whom they should be eager to do business!
    Done _____

3. Teach the concept of building a team to someone else so that he or she understands it.
    Done _____

5MM Time Capsule 5

5MM Module 5, Helpings 27–34

Here's your familiar checklist of what your lessons included in module 5. You've come a long distance—doesn't it seem like light years since you began? Check off each item that you know you can easily explain to someone else! Just honestly put a checkmark by each concept you really know you know. If you don't, look back through the materials.

Helping 27:
___ The four major stages of foreclosure.
___ Why hope and help are your true product.

Helping 28:
___ How to get people to call you instead of the other way around.

Helping 29:
___ How to write a truly compelling letter to people in foreclosure so they'll call you.

Helping 30:
___ What to say when you're negotiating a deal with people who are in preforeclosure.

Helping 31:
___ Exactly what research to do on a preforeclosure.
___ How to do the simple math to discover if the deal is a potential winner.

Helping 32:
___ What to bring to the kitchen table.
___ What paperwork you need to protect the seller about to be foreclosed on and you, the buyer who's saving the day.
___ The two most important tools for deciding if the deal is good.

Helping 33:
___ What the amazing subject of "subject to" is all about.
___ Why you don't need to worry if a loan is assumable or not.
___ How to purchase a house no matter how stinky your own credit might be.
___ How to purchase a house without getting a loan at all.
___ How to create confidence between the seller and you so you can help him the best.
___ Two absolute no-no's for preforeclosure buying.
___ Exactly what you need to get from the seller who's in preforeclosure.

Helping 34:
___ How to create your power team.
___ Exactly what to say to a new team member to get the ball rolling.
___ A list of the Fab Five team members you can't do without, plus a dozen more.

___ I understand all the above points so well that I've taught them to someone else myself!

When you've checked off every item, you can get started on module 6 all about contracts! I promise to make it much more interesting than you might imagine!

Bobservations

At this point in my career, I find myself vastly more fascinated by people than by houses. In addition, I'm at a juncture of life where real-estate investing interests me only if it is *enlightened* investing. If you will permit me to speak to some stereotypes, I can demonstrate why women investors will change the entire paradigm for foreclosure acquisitions.

Many experts agree that women are hardwired to be better listeners. They are better communicators and better nurturers. We've even seen science to prove that these qualities are built right into the makeup from birth, and that they require no socialization to emerge.

If that is true, then women can assist in matters of foreclosure more than men. Women, you'll be listening for the clues to let you know exactly how to proceed. You'll be able to read the people sitting in front of you and empathize with them. And even though I wish it were different, you'll be much better able to engender trust. There is no factor more important than trust in negotiations with people in foreclosure.

They have trust issues, because they themselves, at least for the moment, can't be trusted. (They aren't acting in trust with the agreements they made with the lender.) And people who don't feel that they themselves can be trusted (even if it's subconscious) do not trust others. So you see, your womanly ways of kindness and understanding will win over a slick salesman coming into their home to rip them off. Never mind that the man might have been just as kind and understanding as you. He will not be so easily perceived in that light, because of eons of programming.

I can envision a whole new army of women investors invading the land with a new set of weapons: intuition, gentle persuasion, tender concern. Look at that sentence! I see an army, an invasion, and weapons. Oh, my, I really am a "guy," aren't I? Intuition and concern aren't *weapons*—they're aesthetic characteristics and advantages.

So use your beautiful skills, and go help as many people who need you as you can!

MODULE 6

RISK-FREE CONTRACTS

Contracts, the Easiest Lesson of All

During this lesson, you'll be doing your actual action step while you read this page. We're going to do something that we'll call "immersive❖" learning! I want you to go get a piece of blank paper and a pen right now.

OK, stop reading, and get yourself a blank piece of paper and a pen. Really! I want you to *feel* this lesson. If you do the action step right now, you'll be immersed in the feeling of what you're going to learn here. You'll remember it from now forward.

Do you have your paper and pen ready? Good!

1. First, I want you to write this sentence at the top of the page: "I'll take it . . ." Yes, put the dot, dot, dot after "I'll take it."
2. Second, after the dot, dot, dot, I want you to finish the sentence this way: ". . . unless I change my mind."
3. Third, go down to the bottom of the paper and sign your name. Really. Sign your name at the bottom!

Now, let's talk about what you just did. You wrote a contract and signed it. You wrote a risk-free contract and signed it, didn't you?

Yes, you did! Did it give you a laugh? I hope so; it was supposed to!

How did signing it make you feel? Did it make you nervous? I'll bet it did *not* make you nervous. It was easy to sign because you knew it was *risk free,* right?

Trouble is, you might have a hard time getting someone else to sign it, because it isn't written in legalese❖, the way everyone expects a contract to be written. OK, how about if we rewrite the contract, and we say the same thing, but we put it in language that lawyers would respect? If it says, "I'll take it . . . unless I change my mind," translated into legalese, wouldn't you still feel comfortable signing it?

Well, then, that's what we're going to do. Before the lessons in this helping are finished, you'll know how to write a contract that says, "I'll take it . . . unless I change my mind."

Just to get you started, here are some things I try to get into every contract. I don't always get them all in, but I always try. What we're going for is *assignability* and *escapability.* We want to be able to assign the contract to someone else in case we decide not to go the distance on the deal, and we want to be able to escape via a "lifeboat" clause❖ (an escape clause that allows you to row away from a sinking ship).

Your New Last Name

Here's your new "last name❖" that you'll put on every contract you write (other than contracts for new construction or REO properties):

"And/or Assigns❖."

You'll write your own name, followed by the phrase "and/or Assigns," and it'll look like this:

"Jane Dough, and/or Assigns."

It means that you have the right to assign the contract to someone else. If anyone wants to know why you're putting it there, you simply say that you don't know how you're going to take the title❖; whether it'll be in your name or a company name. You could even say that you might decide to sell it to someone else right away.

Lifeboat Clauses

Here are a few of my very favorite lifeboat clauses:

1. This contract subject to the approval of my attorney.
2. This contract subject to inspection by _____.
3. This contract subject to suitable financing.

By the way, clause one can't be rejected, because everyone has the right to have an attorney review a contract. Clauses two and three are standard language even in the approved contracts used by real-estate agents state to state. You'll see a lot more addendums in another lesson, but this is a beautiful starter set.

One more note: On clause three, to whom does the financing have to be suitable? You! Does that give you a hint that we've written a clause that basically says, "This contract is subject to me, myself, and I changing my mind"? Another hint: If you can't get your attorney to disapprove the contract if desired, then I'd disapprove of that attorney!

John Childers taught me this exercise, and he really wants you to feel it. So: Now you know how to write a "risk-free" contract. Is anything at all in life truly risk free? I think the answer is no. However, you've learned how to write a contract that gives you multiple opportunities to back out. You should feel your confidence rising, just like you did when you signed "I'll take it . . . unless I change my mind."

Make the decision, then *find the provision.*

—MARK VICTOR HANSEN

This is a delicious way of saying, "I'll take it . . . if I can work out the details, and, of course, unless I change my mind!" It's also a way of making things go right in the physical universe: The decision comes first; the provisions are merely the physical universe catching up!

Word Wizard

____ Immersive

To immerse: to cover completely in a liquid; submerge. To baptize by submerging in water. To engage wholly or deeply, absorb (*"scholars who immerse themselves in their subjects"*). So an immersive style of training engages you completely, almost surrounding you in the experience.

___ Legalese — Fancy legal language that lawyers use.

___ Lifeboat Clause — A clause in a contract that allows the buyer to row away if the ship starts to sink; a clause that allows the buyer to change her mind and not do the deal.

___ Your New Last Name — A phrase that you put after your name on a contract. See "and/or assigns."

___ And/or Assigns — A phrase that you put after your name on a contract to indicate that you have the right to assign the contract to someone else, whether it be a person, a company, or any other entity.

___ Take Title — A phrase that means how the title will be when it's recorded: will it be in a personal name, several names like husband and wife, or a business name? *"How will you take title?"*

Quiz Wizard

1. What one thing do you want a contract to say at the fundamental level?
    a. I'll take it, if the price is right.
    b. I'll take it, if the terms are right.
    c. I'll take it, unless I change my mind.
    d. I'll take it, if my mother lets me.
    e. I'll take it, unless I find something I like better.

2. What is your new last name?
    a. Dough.
    b. And/or Assigns.
    c. And/or a Sign.
    d. Jones.
    e. Home Owner.

3.　What would be some good lifeboat clauses?
　　　　a.　Subject to women and children first.
　　　　b.　Subject to approval of my attorney.
　　　　c.　Subject to termite inspection.
　　　　d.　Subject to the average rainfall.
　　　　e.　Subject to suitable financing.

4.　Wasn't this lesson kind of fun after all?
　　　　a.　Yes.
　　　　b.　Yes.

Turn to page 436 for the answers.

Whiz Wizard

1.　You already did the immersive training of writing your first risk-free contract. Sign off here that you really did do the physical doing-ness of it! You're under oath!
　　Done _____

2.　Take the contract you already wrote and write in two lifeboat clauses. Then put your new last name after your signature. Now it's really, really your first really, really risk-free contract!
　　Done _____

3.　Teach the concept of writing a risk-free contract to someone else so that he or she understands it.
　　Done _____

Elements of a Legal Contract

Let's get a good list of things you will want in your contracts; things that make them legal and things that make them beneficial to you, the buyer. By the way, as we discuss contracts, we will be discussing buyers' contracts, not sellers' contracts. The basic contract used by Realtors has been tweaked through the years to protect sellers and does it very well. Sometimes, when you're buying through your real-estate agent, you'll actually use the standard contract, but you'll be adding your own addendums❖.

Although we're going to focus on buyers' contracts, *this* lesson is going to cover the elements of what makes *any* contract legal. I'll give you a list, and then we'll talk about each item.

Elements of a Legal Contract
1. Competent❖ parties of legal age and sound mind.
2. Legal in nature, legitimate (can't sell the Golden Gate Bridge).
3. Legal description❖ of the property being transacted ("legal description to be supplied by title company") or ("legal description to follow"). An address is not a legal description.
4. Purchase price.

5. Terms of the sale (down payment, payments, earnest money❖, interest rate, all details of monetary aspects of purchase, when it's due, and so on).
6. Some form of consideration❖. (Check written to escrow company❖—not the seller—barter❖ of goods, barter of services, fixing up property, one dollar.)
7. Signatures, dates, and times.

Additional Desirable Elements
8. Addendums or stipulations❖ (subject to's, lifeboat clauses, escape clauses).
9. Put in an acknowledgment that the other party has read the contract and understands it (and has had the chance to meet with his attorney). "This document is a legal and binding contract. If not fully understood, seek the advice of an attorney prior to signing."
10. A clause that limits the time for the response.

All right, let's dive into these ten elements individually.

1. **Competent parties of legal age and sound mind:** Basically, you can't do contracts with people who aren't old enough (eighteen or over in most states); you can't do a contract with someone who's drunk; and you can't do a contract with someone who's mentally challenged (Alzheimer's, dementia, learning disabled, and so on).
2. **Legal in nature, legitimate (can't sell the Golden Gate Bridge):** You could legally buy a house of ill repute in Nye County, Nevada, but you couldn't legally buy one in Clark County, Nevada. You couldn't make a legal contract to buy a crack house. You couldn't legally sell something you didn't really own, like the Golden Gate Bridge.
3. **Legal description of the property being transacted:** Just having the address of the property may or may not be enough for the contract to be legal, but to be on safe ground, you can reference that you'll get the legal description from some resource like the title company. Remember the Property Profile you can get from Fidelity National Title (or any title company)? When you use www.FidelityPassport.com, you can cut and paste the legal description from the report. You can also use the legal description from the seller's existing deed.

I have found that many county websites only give you the identifying parcel number.

One thing that you'll find efficient about Fidelity Passport or any similiar tool from another company is that you can get a lot of the legal data you need for your contract. You can research properties via the internet to obtain the data you require to fill out your contracts.

4. **Purchase price:** Don't forget to include the agreed-upon price. Or if you're making an offer that hasn't been agreed upon yet, don't forget to include the price you're offering.

5. **Terms of the sale** (down payment, payments, earnest money, interest rate, all details of monetary aspects of purchase, when it's due, and so on): When you look at a regular Realtor's contract, you'll see all these items. There will be a space for them on your contract too.

6. **Some form of consideration** (check written to escrow company—never the seller—barter of goods, barter of services, fixing up of property, one dollar): Never write the check to the seller. If that's all you learn in this lesson, so be it. OK, you can write a check to the seller when it's someone in a foreclosure, and he's moved out, and you're giving him a leg up on his next life. Some investors always close with private sellers through an escrow. But other than that, no checks to sellers.

7. **Signatures, dates, and times:** Don't forget to include the signatures, the dates, and include the time to protect yourself even further.

Those elements are all vital parts of a legal contract. Now here are three more points that will be important to you:

8. **Addendums or stipulations** (subject to's, lifeboat clauses): There may already be some of these clauses in your contract, but you can also add them in a separate document (called schedule A, for example). You can even add more clauses and stipulations to a regular Realtor's contract; they even have a special form for you to do so.

9. **Put in an acknowledgment**❖ that the other party has read the contract and understands it (and has had the chance to meet with his attorney): "This document is a legal and binding contract. If not fully understood, seek the advice of an

attorney prior to signing." This clause is a way to make sure someone doesn't come back and say that he signed it without knowing what was in it. I even have the person initial this phrase at the bottom of every page.

10.   **A clause that limits the time for the response:** If you're sending an offer that hasn't been agreed upon yet, then limit the amount of time the seller has to respond to you. I've used anything from one day to three days, but you could use longer as well. Use your instincts, and also be guided by the specifics of the situation.

The Good News and the Bad News

The good news is you know a whole lot more about contracts than you did yesterday. The bad news is that you can't always use the exact escapeability and assignability clauses we've talked about every time.

1.   When you're working with a real-estate agent as your buyer's broker, he'll want to use his own contracts. Let him. Then work with him to get in as much escapeability and assignability as possible through his company-approved addendums.

2.   When you're working with builders and purchasing new construction, it's usually their way or not at all. Read their contract and understand it, but most of the time there's no negotiating. Ask your Realtor to help you wade through everything, so you aren't surprised by any trick clauses that might change if you sell during the first year.

Your First Real Contract

Now that you know what a legal contract should contain, I'll bet you'd like to get your hands on one, right? OK, I've put one on the training website, and your homework will direct you to it. Here's my warning: Don't just copy it and start using it. First of all, it wasn't written for your state. Remember in helping 25 when your homework involved getting an attorney? Guess what?

Let your attorney look at this contract and tweak it for your home state! Once he does that for you, you'll have a contract you can have complete confidence in. *I'm not an attorney, and I don't know the laws of your state.* Here's where you have to do some research on your own.

Please, please, please, don't be penny-wise and pound-foolish. Don't try to save money on the legal fees at the beginning of your career, because it could take you down in the end. Spend enough for an hour of review and get yourself a document that you can use as a template. Then when a contract requires additional elements, your attorney will take only a few minutes to look it over, because he's already familiar with the overall document.

You'll never regret having someone on your team who can protect you from legal woes.

Every man is guilty of the good things he didn't do.
—SIGN ON THE DAILY-SPECIAL CHALKBOARD
AT TC'S RIB CRIB, LAS VEGAS

Word Wizard

___ Addendums	Additional stuff; pages added on after the body of the contract.
___ Competent	Able to make sound decisions.
___ Legal Description	The way the property is described in the actual book at the county recorder's office; sample: *APN: 139-20-716-363, District: LV Subdivision: CORTE MADERA AMD Map Ref: PB B0087 P0047 Sec/Twnship/Range: PART OF N2 SE9 S20 T20S R61D Abbreviated Description: PLAT BOOK 92 PAGE 32 UNIT 155 BLDG 7 City/Muni/Twp: LAS VEGAS*
___ Earnest Money	The amount of money a buyer gives up front toward the purchase of a property to prove that she's sincere and "earnest" about doing the deal.
___ Consideration	The exchange paid for the thing— whether in money or something else, some other form.

___ Escrow/Escrow Company	Escrow is money, property, a deed, or a bond placed in the custody of an impartial third party for delivery to the proper parties only after the specified conditions have been met. An escrow company is an impartial company that helps the buyer and the seller close their deal.
___ Barter	Trading; exchanging services or goods for another person's services or goods.
___ Stipulations	Things that have to occur before something else occurs ("I stipulate that you clean the carpets after you move out or before I move in").
___ Acknowledgment	A written authentication that the signer understands what she's signing.

Quiz Wizard

1. Which of the following are not elements of a legal contract?
    a. Competent parties of legal age and sound mind.
    b. Legal in nature, legitimate (can't sell the Golden Gate Bridge).
    c. Legal description of the property being transacted.
    d. Asking price.
    e. Terms of the sale (down payment, payments, earnest money, interest rate, all details of monetary aspects of purchase, when it's due, and so on).
    f. Some form of courtesy.
    g. Signatures, dates, and times.

2. Why would you put in an acknowledgment that the other party has read the contract and understands it?
    a. Because he might have Alzheimer's.
    b. Because he might be too young to understand all the legalese.
    c. Because he might come back at a later date and say the contract was null and void because he didn't understand it.
    d. Because he may have language barriers.

3. When you get the sample contract, what's the first thing you're going to do?
   a. Send it to the seller you're working with on a deal.
   b. Have it translated.
   c. Frame it.
   d. Ask your attorney to evaluate it and make it appropriate for your state's laws.
   e. Highlight the parts that are elements of an illegal contract.

Turn to page 436 for the answers.

Whiz Wizard

1. Go to www.ND4W.com/docs and download a copy of "Sample Contract." First read it out loud. Then copy it and highlight the parts of it that are elements of a legal contract.
   Done _____

2. Take the contract to your attorney and ask him to review it. Ask if he has a standard contract for purchase of real estate that he would prefer you to use. If he does, get it and use it! This step may take you a few days, so you may go on to the next lesson even before you've done this step. *But:* Only sign off on this if you promise you're going to do this step within one week!
   Done _____

3. Teach the concept of elements of a legal contract to someone else so that he or she understands it.
   Done _____

But Wait! There's More! (Addendums)

In this lesson, you'll have the chance to look at some typical addendums that may be useful to you. Not every one will be useful on every contract, and you won't want to intimidate the seller with a huge list of addendums that look like you're throwing in the kitchen sink.

Remember, you want to provide yourself *assignability* and *escapeability.* First let's review the addendums you already know and expand on them:

1. "Subject to my attorney's approval." (This could also read "subject to the approval of my partner, my husband, my board of directors," and so forth.)

2. "Subject to inspection." (This often reads "subject to satisfactory inspection by termite inspector, pest inspector, roof inspector, mold inspector," and so forth.)

3. "Subject to suitable financing." (This phrase is very common and raises no eyebrows. In a Realtor's contract, it would typically spell out the amount of time the buyer has to apply for a loan.)

These various addendums are applicable in various situations. You don't have to memorize them!

1. This offer is subject to the following terms: _____.
2. This transaction is subject to an inspection by Buyer or any partner within three days of the Seller's acceptance of the offer (or up to three days before closing).
3. The Buyer has the right to personally inspect and give his written approval of the described property within seven days after the acceptance of this contract by the Seller.
4. This transaction is subject to the acquisition of suitable financing satisfactory to Buyer and any partner.
5. Earnest money deposit shall be held in escrow by closing agent.
6. Seller warrants that the information attached hereto as addendum A is true and correct.
7. This contract is contingent upon an independent appraisal of the property in an amount not less than the purchase price.
8. The Buyer has the right to assign this contract.
9. Any escrow account held by the mortgagee or trust company shall be conveyed❖ with the property and is included in the purchase price.
10. The closing date shall be extended for any and all time necessary to cure title defects❖.
11. Seller's right to retain deposit money in the event of default by Buyer shall be in full settlement of any claims and shall be the Seller's sole remedy❖. Seller shall not be entitled to specific performance. If Seller defaults, Seller shall return Buyer's deposit plus an equal amount of his own money.
12. This transaction is subject to complete inspection of the property for compliance with the building, health, and fire codes, and Buyer's written acceptance of the condition of the premises. Seller shall correct all code violations.
13. All closing costs❖, including prepaid items, are to be paid by Seller.
14. Seller warrants that all personal property, building structure, wiring, appliances, electrical fixtures, plumbing, heating, and air conditioning devices are in good operational condition and that the roof is in good repair and free of

leaks, and all will be so at closing and for one year after the date of closing. These warranties shall survive and extend past delivery of deed.

15. Seller shall deliver to Buyer at closing a complete set of keys to the property, all insurance policies being assumed by the Buyer, copies of all mortgages if assumed or taken over by the Buyer, all warranties and instructions on fixtures and personal property being sold, all leases and tenants applications, all service contracts on property being sold, payment books on mortgages if being assumed, and any blueprints or surveys❖ regarding the property.

16. If property is vacant, Buyer has the right to immediate possession of the property for purposes of making improvements and/or showing said property.

17. All mortgage payments shall be paid in equal *annual* payments, with all principal and interest due.

18. Each party acknowledges that he/she has read, understands, and hereby agrees to each and every provision of this page unless a particular section or paragraph is modified by an addendum or counteroffer.

Buyer's Initials: _____ Date:_____
Sellers' Initials: _____ Date:_____

19. Purchaser shall have the right at the termination of this agreement to renew, for a like period, under the terms contained herein.

Each one of these clauses protects you, the buyer, or gives you an advantage of some sort in the deal. I don't think you have to memorize all these phrases, but when you're offering a contract, you can read through them and see if there's something that applies to the situation at hand.

Wiggle Room

Remember this: Don't lose a deal because you are stubbornly clinging to one point. In fact, some savvy negotiators put in clauses they know they're willing to give up ("wiggle room"), so the seller will feel as though he was able to win some concessions.

Let me tell you what happened to me recently: I was working with a seller through a real-estate agent to buy some land upon which I intended to build several "green-built❖" custom homes❖. I had offered "Mrs. Jones" $500,000 for five acres with the contingency that I be allowed forty-five days for due diligence and forty-five days after that to arrange financing, so it would be a ninety-day closing. I wanted ample time to research the problems inherent in buying raw land, since I'd done this only twice before. I also asked Mrs. Jones to do some seller financing.

She turned down my offer, and she apparently accepted a better offer that went into escrow. A month later, Brid'Jette Whaley, my real-estate agent, called me to say that the property had fallen out of escrow; was I still interested? Yes! Especially since Mrs. Jones had lowered her asking price to $365,000 for the same five acres. Yippeee!

However, Brid'Jette told me that Mrs. Jones was insisting on a thirty-day close and all cash. No terms, no financing, just all cash, thirty days, take it or leave it. Well, I didn't think I could close in thirty days. I made the offer for $400,000 all cash, with a closing that added up to about sixty days. Mrs. Jones turned me down again.

I decided to make the offer exactly the way she was wishing for it; no contingencies, no lifeboat clauses, because her asking price was $135,000 under the price I had just paid for the two identical parcels next door to hers. I could sell it for at least that much in a flash.

How amazing it was to receive Brid'Jette's call saying, "Yes! We did it!" It just confounds me that I offered $500,000 and was turned down, I offered $400,000 and was turned down, and I offered $365,000 and was accepted! I made an instant $135,000 in equity by *not* insisting on my terms! What is the point of this story? Every deal is unique and requires you to look at it cleverly. Don't get stuck on an addendum if you know the deal is a great one. Don't lose an opportunity by being stuck on a certain point. Be flexible in your thinking, and let that flexibility be reflected in your contracts.

My prayer or vision every morning says this: "Something wonderful is going to happen." That way, the universe can engage me in delightful surprises I would have never thought to ask for.

—KAREN NELSON BELL

Word Wizard

___ Conveyed	Transferred.
___ Title Defects	Any circumstances that prevent the title company from ensuring that the title really is free and clear.
___ Sole Remedy	The only way for a conflict to be resolved.
___ Closing Costs	The costs incurred to get a deal closed: loan fees, document fees, transfer taxes, arbitrary fees snuck in by the title company and/or the lender, anything extra added on to the price of the property itself.
___ Surveys	When experts look at a piece of land and report what they see; usually done by *surveyors* or engineers.
___ Green built	Designed and built to be energy-efficient as well as creating as little damaging impact on the environment as possible; environmentally conscientious.
___ Custom home	A home built specifically to the preferences of one owner, not a part of a housing tract.

Quiz Wizard

1. What are the two fundamental elements that create a beneficial buyer's contract?
    a. closeability.
    b. believeability.
    c. assignability.
    d. understandability.
    e. escapeability.

2. Why don't you have to memorize the addendums listed above? (Trick question.)
    a. Because they don't *all* apply *all* the time.
    b. Because writing contracts isn't mechanical and robotic.
    c. Because they're a list of resources; a list of potential solutions.
    d. Because one needs to be flexible and creative in using them.

3. Why might you put in some clauses that you don't care about losing?

      a. To make the contract longer in order to confuse the seller.

      b. To give the seller the feeling of satisfaction at getting some concessions.

      c. To give your attorney something to do.

      d. To make the clauses you do care about seem more important.

      e. To demonstrate your superior knowledge of contracts.

Turn to page 437 for the answers.

Whiz Wizard

1. Use the person you've been teaching to help you with this action step. Read each one of the addendums listed above out loud and discuss what its intended uses might accomplish.
Done _____

2. Using the sample contract you obtained in the last lesson, make a pretend offer to someone, and fill out all the blanks. Have your "student" sign as the seller. Now you've done an offer and had it accepted; it won't be nearly as scary when you do it with a real seller.
Done _____

3. Teach the concept of addendums to someone else so that he or she understands it.
Done _____

5MM Time Capsule 6

5MM Module 6, Helpings 35–37

Here's your familiar checklist of what your three helpings included in module 6. Check off each item that you know you can easily explain to someone else! If you can't, then look back through the text. Use this list as an opportunity to review! Only 23 more helpings left, you're almost two-thirds done:

Helping 35:
___ How to write a risk-free contract.
___ How to write a contract that basically says, "I'll take it . . . unless I change my mind."
___ What your new last name is.
___ The two most fundamental elements that create a desirable buyer's contract.
___ How to increase your confidence regarding the offering and signing of buyers' contracts.

Helping 36:
___ The seven elements of a legal contract.
___ Three things to decrease your risk in a buyer's contract.

___ How to make sure your contract conforms to your own state laws by having your attorney review it.

Helping 37
___ Nineteen more cool clauses to mix and match.
___ How to negotiate better by the use of clauses you're willing to concede on.

Now it's time to send you headlong into the world you've been waiting for: how to do all this without using your own money!

Bobservations

Remember that a contract should be a reflection of something you've already agreed upon, and you're just finalizing and memorializing it on paper in legal language. If you already know what you agreed on before you write the contract, the process will be much less intimidating. The contract is a written communication that represents your verbal communication.

The best way to take the fear out of writing contracts is to give the job to a trusted team member whose deep knowledge removes the fear. New students often want to write the contracts themselves, and I applaud their courage. However, the best advice I can give you is to show your contract templates to your attorney and let her be the one who tweaks it to make it perfect. You want your legal team to think your contracts are appropriate and sound, so that when they represent you in a dispute, they know they're on solid ground.

If you have to start with prepaid legal counseling, that's fine. Just get real legal advice. (Parents, siblings, and uncles don't count unless they have their law degree!)

If you end up in front of a judge, you don't want to have to say, "Well, my home study course said it would work that way."

MODULE 7

FUNDING
NOTHING DOWN

HELPING 38

Your Partner in a Pocket

You're already one of the insiders, because you already know the truth behind *Nothing Down* investing, the truth that it's just not *your* money! You also have a pretty good idea that the system works, so you're not a naysayer trying to prove that we've got something goofy going on! OK, we've been saying it for the last umpteen helpings, that *Nothing Down* means OPM—other people's money—and now it's finally time to tell you how to get your hands on some of that OPM!

Most people think you should get funding and *then* go out looking for properties, but that's completely backward. Here's why:

Good money flows to good deals. Great money flows to great deals. What kind of money do you think flows to mediocre deals? Mediocre money? No! *No* money flows to mediocre deals! That's why we've spent time learning how to find and get great deals under contract before we ever begin to learn how to get OPM. If you've got a great deal, then OPM will flow to it. You wait and see—it's amazing.

In any g iven year, there will be investors who yank billions of dollars out of the stock market, and those investors want to put their money someplace better than a jumbo CD❖ that gets them 2 percent ROI or less. These same investors need to place their money, and you happen to have the great deals they'd love to fund. I know that doesn't seem logical to you yet, but call me up a year from now and let me know if you agree that great money flows to great deals.

Your whole job now is to find good/great deals, and then these sources of OPM will be much easier to access!

Fifty-Fifty Partners

The first thing that crosses a lot of new investors' minds is that maybe they could have a partner who would put up the money. The partner brings the dough, you do the work. You split it fifty-fifty. This is a pretty commonplace arrangement, and I'll bet you've already got friends and relatives who don't have the energy you do to read this book. They'd be mighty happy if you did all the work, and they put up some money for their 50 percent share of the deal! If you don't have friends already rarin' to go, you will once you've made a bundle on your first property.

Think about someone you know who has a 401(k)❖ or an Individual Retirement Account (IRA❖) that's earning less than 5 percent interest right now. The person might even be losing money in his retirement fund. What if he had the chance to make a *ton* more money by splitting the profits with you—the person with all the knowledge, skill, and energy? For example, if he put up the money for a down payment of $5,000, and you ended up making a $40,000 profit on the property, his share would be $20,000. That would mean he had quadrupled his investment, for an astonishing ROI of 400 percent. Wouldn't anyone want to do that over and over again? Of course!

Think about asking your mom and dad, son and daughter, aunt and uncle, brother and sister, grandma and grandpa, next-door neighbor, best friend, next best friend, doctor, dentist, chiropractor, attorney, CPA—all busy people with no time to learn what you've taken the trouble to learn—if they'd be interested in being partners with you.

Now, remember, you're not begging for a handout here. You're not like little Oliver Twist asking, "Please, sir, may I have some more?" in the porridge line at the orphanage. You're able to offer them vastly better returns on their savings than they could get in a bank or mutual fund. They can hardly wait to give you their investment dollars, because it's great business. You're going to put a lot more money in their pockets.

By the way, be sure to put all your agreements in writing, even with friends and family. Don't you dare ignore me on this one, OK? It's just good business for both of you.

Which Is Better?

In terms of interest paid, how much did that money you borrowed from your fifty-fifty partner cost you? It cost you 50 percent of your profits, so it was a pretty high-interest rate. Fifty percent is higher than any nasty credit card you can find. In fact, the highest credit cards are around 24 percent per year. Well, what if you did need $5,000 to get a house under contract, and maybe you needed another $5,000 to fix it up before you could sell it? What if you put all that $10,000 on your worst credit card at 24 percent per annum❖, and then you went lickety-split to fix the house, and in three months you sold it for a $20,000 profit?

Think this through with me: A 24 percent per year credit card means you're paying 2 percent per month. If you borrowed the money for only three months, that would be only 6 percent interest on the $10,000. That means you spent $600 for that money, and you made $20,000. Actually, you paid back the credit card with the profits, so really, you made $19,400. Well, is $19,400 better than what you would have made with a fifty-fifty partner? You'd have had to pay your partner $10,000. Wow, you just made an extra $9,400 by using your credit card instead of a fifty-fifty partner. Is the lightbulb glowing? You've got a partner right there in your pocket!

I Hate Bad Debt! I Love Good Debt! Join Me!

Am I saying that I think everybody should go out and get in debt? Let me be really, *really* clear: I hate consumer debt. I hate *bad* debt. What's the difference? Consumer debt is spent on things that go down in value: big-screen TV, vacation, shoes, automobile, Starbucks, and now you can even use your credit card at Jack in the Box. That's bad debt because you'll still be paying when that thing you bought is worthless. The coffee is worthless twenty minutes later. Pay cash!

Two Rules for Using Credit Cards

However, if you will follow two simple rules, the use of a credit card to acquire things that go *up* in value is definitely good debt. If, by putting $10,000 on a credit card and incurring $600 of charges you could make $19,400 profit, that's *good debt*. Let me tell you the rules now:

Rule 1: Use your credit cards and credit lines (like home equity lines of credit) only for things that go up in value or things that make things go up in value.

Rule 2: Make sure the deal (or another deal of yours) pays off the credit you used. That's called your "exit strategy❖."

On rule 1, you could use your credit to buy the drywall❖ and paint you need for a fixer-upper. You could use your credit to bring a pre-foreclosure property current on its back payments. You could use credit to buy a manual on how to repair a window. But you would *not* use your credit to take a vacation when you celebrate finishing a deal. That gets paid by debit card or cash!

On rule 2, you want to make sure that the money you'll make when you sell the house, or the money you'll get as deposits from the renters or the lease-option tenants, will cover what you used on credit. If the money from the deal itself won't quite cover it, make sure money from some other deal will. The main thing to remember is not to get stuck with a lot of debt that you have no way to pay off. Your exit strategy is your escape route, your plan to get out. Make sure the exit strategy isn't based on wishful thinking!

I was debt free in 1999, and now I have millions of dollars of debt. I'm very happy about it, but I wasn't at first, until I really understood the power of leverage. I still don't have any consumer debt, only real-estate debt, and thank goodness, someone else is paying it all off!!! Don't ya love it?

These two rules work just as well for a home equity line of credit (HELOC—pronounced "Hee-Lock"). Remember back to the first chapter when you discovered how much real estate you could buy with $100,000 of money from a HELOC? Well, make sure the deal will pay it down so that you can use it again and again and again. I'm still using a line of credit I got in 2000. It goes up and down and up and down! It's like having a partner who always does what I ask. And no begging!

Of course, if you read Donna Fox's book way back in module 3, you know that you'll be working on improving your business credit, so that someday all this borrowing will go on in the business name instead of your personal name. Be sure to keep your borrowing levels at 49 percent or less of your credit limit. Some experts even recommend staying at 30 percent of the limit to protect your credit score.

Yes, we're going to go get ourselves in debt, but it's not going to be just good debt, let's go get into *great* debt! Ready, set, get debt!

Use credit only for things that go up in value.
— KAREN NELSON BELL

Word Wizard

___ Jumbo CD	A certificate of deposit in a bank that is quite large, usually $500,000.
___ 401(k)	A form of retirement plan in the workplace where the employer can match your contributions if it chooses.
___ IRA	Investment Retirement Account, a form of retirement plan that allows for some tax advantages. There are several different kinds, each with different tax strategies.
___ 24 percent Per Annum	24 percent per year, or 2 percent per month, interest rate on a credit card.
___ Exit Strategy	Your plan for getting out of something, in this case, out of the debt you incurred.
___ Drywall	Material used to build walls in houses.

Quiz Wizard

1. Which *Nothing Down* strategy would give you a better financial advantage?
   a. Fifty-fifty partnership.
   b. Twenty-four percent per annum credit card.

2. What are the two rules you should always follow when using a credit card or credit line?

     a.   Use it only for things that go up in value.

     b.   Use it only for things that go down in value.

     c.   Be sure you have a great exit strategy.

     d.   Be sure you have a great entrance strategy.

     e.   Never get into consumer debt unless it's for a vacation, and you can pay it back in three months.

3.   Which comes first, according to this lesson?

     a.   The money.

     b.   The deal.

     c.   The credit card.

     d.   The partners.

     e.   The HELOC.

Turn to page 437 for the answers.

Whiz Wizard

1.   Speak to three people you know about your real-estate investing, and ask them if you found a great deal, would they be interested in partnering in it for a great return on investment?
Done _____

2.   Take out all your credit card bills and find out what your interest rates are. Also find out what your limits are. Add up all your limits and divide it in half, and that's how much you could safely borrow without impacting your credit.
Done _____

3.   Call up at least one of your credit card companies and request a raise in your credit limit. Do it with as many as you please. Write down how much OPM you have from cards and credit lines. If you're in the process of getting a mortgage, don't do this step until you've closed on the loan.
Done _____

4.   If you own your own home, I would recommend that you begin the process of finding out if you can get a HELOC so that you can use your "dead equity." I personally believe in using the equity

during the building phase of your investment career and then paying it down in the later stages of your wealth. This is not something you have to do as an action step; it's just a suggestion.
Done _____

5. Teach the concept of fifty-fifty partnering versus the partner in a pocket to someone else so that he or she understands it.
    Done _____

P.S.: I know there is more action to this homework, so I won't nag you if you take a few days. It's *great* homework, because you could end up with a whole lot of OPM as a result!

Places to Get OPM

There are so many ways to get OPM, there isn't room in one module for all of them. But let's look at a list of ways for you to get started. Then we'll go into detail on some of my favorite juicy ways in the next few helpings.

Here are the ways we discussed in the last chapter:

1. Partner who gets a fifty-fifty split; he puts up the money, you put up the knowledge and the work.
2. Credit cards (partner in a pocket): only 2 percent per month, better than 50 percent to partner, but only use if you follow the two rules:
    a. Only use credit for things that go *up* in value.
    b. Always know your exact exit strategy; the deal or another deal must pay back the credit.
3. Equity line (same rules as credit cards—never use for things that go down in value).

Here are some more ways, and you'll get details on them in the next few helpings:

1. True *Nothing Down,* where seller walks away.
2. Lease-option.
3. Your seller.
4. Your buyer, your renter, or your lease-option tenant.
5. Develop your relationships with multiple lenders, particularly mortgage brokers as opposed to bankers.
6. Get your credit up over 700.
7. When interest rates are relatively low, you can actually find attractive *Nothing Down* deals by going to almost any lender and asking for a 100 percent loan-to-value program. There are programs that even have 100 percent financing for investors. One day, I think *Nothing Down* investing will be thought of as perfectly commonplace. Perhaps it already is. In recent years, as many as 35 percent of all homes bought were purchased with *nothing down.*

Here Are Some Ways That Will Seem Amazingly Easy:

1. Hard-money lender who gets a hard-money interest rate

A hard-money lender is a person or company that will lend to you quickly and without a lot of fuss, as long as there's enough equity in the property, and you have a fairly decent credit score. Believe it or not, a hard-money lender isn't too unhappy if you default on your loan, because unlike a bank, the company would really love to get its hands on your property. Insiders call it "loan to own" lending. The rates are high (12 percent to 50 percent), it charges you "points❖" (each equaling 1 percent of the loan amount), and you usually pay interest-only payments with a balloon payment at the end of a fairly short period, like a year.

2. Auto title loans❖—definitely the highest cost for borrowing

Use only when you absolutely know the deal will pay it back quickly. I may be the only person teaching auto title loans as a source of quick OPM, and that's because it's very, *very* costly and therefore somewhat dangerous. The rates are outrageous, and if you let it go very long, you'll have paid more than the value of the vehicle! (This is exactly what they'd like you to do!) The nice thing is, if you own your car free and clear, you can get money in an hour, and it won't go on your credit report. One time, I had a deal that was going to evaporate if I didn't act immediately. So I took the big red truck over to the best lender from the Yellow Pages, which gave me $18,000 in less than an hour, and I still kept the vehicle to drive. *And* it didn't go on my credit. The warnings I gave you for credit cards *triple* if you use this strategy.

3.   Equity in another property

If you do own a property other than your home, and you're having a hard time getting a HELOC because it isn't your primary residence, consider using that equity to secure money from a private lender. You can give the lender a deed to collateralize❖ his investment, which makes him feel very safe. Because if you don't pay back your loan, the lender can claim the property! I have quite a few investors who want me to use their money, pay them 12 percent interest, and when we do the contract, I give them a deed to a property that has enough equity to cover the loan if I default.

4.   Advertise for money ("Tired of seedy [CD] rates of return? Receive 8 percent to 12 percent interest secured by prime real estate. Call . . .")

When Duncan and I needed money for the mansion (the one written up in *The One Minute Millionaire*), we put an ad in the paper. We were able to borrow $100,000 for fixing up and holding costs, and we didn't even have to secure it with collateral. The investor just trusted us, for some reason. You can also look in your local paper to see if there are investors advertising money to lend. In many cities, there are dozens of people looking for ways to make better interest than in their savings account at the bank. Show the ad to your attorney to make sure you're not violating any SEC rules or any other legal restrictions. WARNING! CAUTION! You have to make sure it's LEGAL!

5.   Swap boats, cars, personal services, do fixing up, barter (list what you have)

What do you have that could possibly be valuable to someone else? Do you have a truck or a trailer? Do you have skills? Barter or trade can be a wonderful way for both parties to get what they want without any money changing hands. Value gets exchanged, but not money per se.

6.   IRAs and 401(k)s

Do you or an acquaintance have an IRA or a 401(k) that is underperforming, getting little or no interest? There are ways to roll those over into a self-directed IRA❖, with which you can invest in real estate. There are a lot of ins and outs to it, so read up on it at www.equitytrust.com before you decide if it's for you. If so, there are a handful of banks that know how to be custodians of a self-directed IRA. Contact Equity Trust or another firm and ask the folks there how to do it. I'm not a licensed financial planner, so I can't give you that advice, but wouldn't you rather be getting a 100 percent ROI on your retirement plan?

7.   Borrow it from your own corporation

If you own a business that has resources, borrow money from your business.

8.   Private lenders

This is just about my favorite form of OPM, because it's such a win-win for both my investors and myself. They don't charge outrageous interest rates, they don't charge points (like the hard-money lenders), and sometimes I don't even have to make payments until the end of the loan period! Sweet! Often, they can loan as fast as or faster than any other resources. Who is a potential private lender? Everyone you know, and everyone you don't know. Remember the ad for the newspaper above? You might meet a private lender that way. I find that my professional associates don't have time to learn how to invest in real estate, so they ask me to do it for them. I don't ask them, they ask me! Doesn't that blow your mind? It did mine until I found out it was commonplace! Try your family—you'll be surprised! Try your friends and coworkers. Remember, you're not begging, you're offering them a chance to make much greater interest than they can in their savings or mutual funds. Just be sure to put it all on paper.

9.   Read *Nothing Down for the 2000s* by Robert G. Allen!

This is really the bible for *Nothing Down* strategies. Never mind that my picture is on the back cover, that's not why I love it. It's just chock-full of Robert Allen's investing wisdom. You can wait until you finish this course, but do yourself a favor and read the greatest book ever written on *Nothing Down* investing by the original granddaddy who first brought it to the general public.

When things reach their limit, they are forced to bounce back.
                                                     —CHINESE PROVERB

Word Wizard

___ Points   A percentage point charged as a fee on a loan; equal to 1 percent.

___ Auto Title Loans   Loans made on a free-and-clear car; very expensive and dangerous, but quick and confidential.

___ Collateralize   To put up something tangible of value to be held by a lender, so that if the borrower defaults, the lender gets to keep the actual thing.

___ Self-directed IRA   An IRA that you can use to invest in a lot of financial instruments; real estate, in particular. You can't use it for your own home.

Quiz Wizard

1. What are some differences between a hard-money lender and a private lender?
   - a. A private money lender won't likely charge you points like a hard-money lender.
   - b. A private lender is nicer than a hard-money lender.
   - c. You shouldn't give a recorded trust deed to a private-money lender, but a hard-money lender will require it.
   - d. A private lender is harder to find.
   - e. There aren't any differences; it's all OPM.

2. What's so risky about an auto title loan?
   - a. The loan sharks could come after you.
   - b. They're usually found in a bad part of town.
   - c. They can cost more money than even a fifty-fifty partner.
   - d. You could lose your car if you don't pay it back.
   - e. It's often illegal.

3. What are some sources of private lending (even if you don't have any relatives, you can still answer as if you did)?
   - a. Mom and dad
   - b. Aunt Effie and Uncle Ade
   - c. Dr. Brown, DDS
   - d. John Dough, your attorney

    e. Jane and Robert from your church group

    f. All the above

Turn to page 437 for the answers.

Whiz Wizard

1. Call an auto title loan company and ask what it would lend on your own car. You'll receive a quote in just a few minutes. If you don't own your car outright, the answer might give you some incentive to pay it off! Your car can become your bank under the right circumstances! Don't use this type of OPM unless you follow the credit rules very strictly!
   Done _____

2. Look in your newspaper to see if anyone is advertising money to lend. Call the person and ask him to tell you about it. Just be very inquiring, and let him fill you in. If there aren't any ads in your own paper, look in ads at www.ReviewJournal.com under Classified and under Money to Loan.
   Done _____

3. Teach the concept of how to get OPM to someone else so that he or she understands it.
   Done _____

HELPING 40

Don't Own It!

J. Paul Getty❖, the billionaire, said, "Own nothing, control everything."

How would you like to learn a strategy that lets you do exactly that? You can make money with real estate you don't even own!

It's a great secret weapon in the world of *Nothing Down* financing, and it's called the lease-option.

How to Work a Lease-option

Let's redefine it, even though you've learned the definitions before. *Lease* means almost the same thing as *rent,* but it usually involves a specific time period of longer length than rent. *Option* means a privilege or opportunity, in this case, to buy the property after a span of time has passed with the buyer just renting as a tenant. You could say that rent to own is a synonym for lease-option.

Here's how it will work for you as a *Nothing Down* strategy:

1. Find a property that's being advertised as either lease-option or rent to own. If you don't see any, call some phone numbers in the For Rent section, and ask them if they would consider renting to own.
2. Ask the seller some questions:
   a. How much is the option payment?
   b. How much are the lease payments?
   c. How much of my lease payment goes toward my down payment?
   d. Can I lock in the price today?
   e. If not, how will you compute the future price?
   f. Does all of my option payment go toward the down payment?
   g. Can I lease it for five years? Two years? One year?
   h. Will you let me take the interest deduction on the mortgage payment?
   i. Will you allow me to sublease❖?
3. If the questions get satisfactory answers (we'll talk about that below), then whip out your check book and write a check for the option payment and the first lease payment.
4. Now, where is the OPM coming from? Well, remember you asked if you could sublease? Guess who's going to reimburse your check? *Your* lease-option customer is going to give you an even higher amount of option payment, and an even higher amount for the lease payment, so you're going to make money on the "spread❖," or the difference between your payment and his!

Here are some things you need to know: The option payment is an amount of money that locks in your privilege to buy the house at a later date if you wish. You are not obligated to buy it, of course. The lease payments are like the rent payments. The down payment will only come into play if you decide to exercise your option❖, or say yes to the privilege of buying the house at some future time.

Ideally, as the buyer you want at least a couple of hundred dollars of the lease payment going toward the down payment as a credit. You want all of the option payment to go toward the down payment. You want to lock in the price today if you can, at today's prices. If you're in a wildly appreciating market, you probably won't get that concession, but see if you can lock in a modest appreciation rate. Try to get a long lease period, so that you'll have flexibility with *your* tenants.

By the way, if the owner won't let you sublease, the only way you'll want the deal is if you really are looking for a place to live. If you currently rent, consider shifting right away to a rent-to-own contract, and you'll have your own home in no time, even if you have credit issues.

By now you can see that *buying* with a lease-option is very different from *selling* with a lease-option. Here are some guidelines:

Lease to Buy	Lease to Sell
Try to get a long-term lease, five to seven years. Get permission to sublet❖	Try to get a short-term lease, one to two years
Get small option payment	Get larger option payment
Get payments as low as possible	Get payments as high as possible
Get the price locked in at today's rate	Get the price locked in at future rate

I want to share a fascinating statistic with you: Only 5 percent of all lease-option contracts result in the option being exercised. That means that 95 percent of the time, the tenant chooses not to exercise his or her option.

By the way, the option payment is nonrefundable. So if the tenant decides to move on, you actually will be just fine, because you'll now take a new tenant's option payment. Wow, does that mean that you don't actually want the person to buy the property? Nod your head up and down. Yes! That's exactly what it means! Of course, if he does take the option, you're happy to have done an enlightened deal.

This is a way to have a great "rental," with the rents being higher than normal, and with tenants who treat the house like their own. But at the end of the day, I personally hope that each tenant will decide he doesn't want the house; or maybe I even wish he'll be a little late and violate the terms of the option agreement (payments have to be made on time in order for the option to remain valid). And if he ends up taking the house, I'm *still* happy! You could even specialize in helping people who can't get their dream home any other way.

Lease/Option with a Twist

Sometimes I like to do a lease-option "with a twist," which I learned from famous mentor John Childers. I tell the tenant that if he doesn't want to pick up the option, I'll return the $200 per month he's been credited for the past two years. However, there are two requirements: (1) he has to always pay on or before the first of the month, and (2) he must take care of the property and never call me for any "fixings."

Don't be scared of having to refund $2,400, because you're getting yourself a renter who pays on time and takes great care of the property! On top of that, you can always offer to move the person to another one of your properties (maybe he wants to move across town or to a different-sized home). If he's been a great tenant, I'd go out and buy whatever house he wants to lease next! In the "worst-case" scenario, and he really qualifies for the refund, you've had use of his money as an interest-free loan for two years!

What you've just learned is sometimes called "the lease-option sandwich❖," because you're the delicious connection between two different lease-option deals: one to buy and one to sell. How would you like to walk through a sample demonstration, just to make sure it's completely clear?

Sample Sandwich (Mmmmm-Mmmmmm, Good!)

You find that "Seller Sam" wants to lease-option his house for $800 per month. His own mortgage payments are $500, and he wants to make that positive cash flow of $300 per month. He wants a $3,000 option payment, and he's willing to let you sublease if you'll get a renter's insurance policy. He has owned the house a long time, and in two years he'll sell it to you for 10 percent over its current market value of $100,000—that is, for $110,000. You'll have to go get qualified for a loan at that time.

You find that "Buyer Becky" wants to lease-option this house from you, and because she's been a victim of identity theft, her credit is really bad right now. She has a good job, but she can't get a loan for a house. She thinks she'll be able to get it cleaned up in the next year. You ask her if she'd prefer to do a straight rent for $900 per month, or would she rather have a kind of enforced savings account and pay $1,100 per month, and you'll credit $200 per month toward her eventual down payment? You'll let her have the house for $120,000 if she can get a loan in a year, and if it takes two years, she'll have to pay $140,000. Her option payment will have to be pretty high, since her credit is so bad, so she gives you $8,000. That locks in her privilege to buy the house if she can get her credit good enough to qualify for a loan.

You gave Sam $3,000, but Becky gave you $8,000, so you made $5,000 on the difference, also called the spread. Every month when you give Sam $800, Becky gave you $1,100, so you made $300 on that spread. This sandwich is starting to taste pretty good, isn't it? You will make $8,600 in the first year of leasing this property, and you don't even own it yet! You do control it, though, and your $8,600 spends just as good as if you owned it. I think of that as a "sandwich spread"!

No tenants, no toilets, no trash, no trouble for me—the lease-option buyer gets to take care of everything!

—KAREN NELSON BELL

Word Wizard

___ J. Paul Getty	Fabulously wealthy U.S. oil industrialist (1892–1976).
___ Sublease	When a lease tenant leases to someone else.
___ Spread	The amount of money between two different amounts.
___ Exercise Your Option	To say yes, you want to buy the property.
___ Sublet	To sublease.
___ Lease-Option Sandwich	To buy a property on a lease-option and then sell it on a lease-option.

Quiz Wizard

1. Where does the money come from for you to use OPM to pay for a lease-option on a property that you'd like to acquire?
   a. Your checking account.
   b. Becky's checking account.
   c. Sam's checking account.
   d. J. Paul Getty's checking account.
   e. A 100 percent loan from a mortgage broker.

2. What's the difference between an option payment and a down payment?

     a. A down payment comes when you actually buy the house.

     b. An option payment gets you the privilege to lease the house.

     c. An option payment gets you the privilege to buy the house at a future date.

     d. A down payment doesn't have to be as much money as an option payment.

     e. An option payment doesn't have to be as much money as a down payment.

3. What's a lease-option sandwich?

     a. Two lease-option properties side by side on the same street.

     b. When you buy through a lease-option and turn around and sell through a lease-option to someone else.

     c. When the property is located next door to a delicatessen.

     d. When you do the deal with the seller over lunch.

     e. When you sell a property through a lease-option, and your buyer takes a hike, and you have to find another buyer.

Turn to page 437 for the answers.

Whiz Wizard

1. Look in your newspaper for any lease-option or rent-to-own properties. Call up the seller and ask the questions on page 265. Done _____

2. Go to www.ND4W.com/lease-option and download the MP3 about lease-options so you can listen to it. Done _____

3. Teach the concepts of "Don't Own It" and lease-options to someone else so that he or she understands it. Done _____

Partners: The Buyer, the Seller, the Realtor

Today I heard a speaker say that the best OPM you can have in real estate is seller financing. That was kind of amazing, because the speaker was a professional lender (as well as a very experienced multimillionaire investor), and I would have thought he'd be trying to sell loans to the audience. He said, "Anytime you can get seller financing, take it. It's the best money out there."

Seller financing. What is it? How do you get it? Why is it so nice?

Seller as Partner

Most sellers are resistant to any kind of creative financing. That's one reason I never use that phrase. The vast majority of Realtors will tell you that you can't buy real estate with nothing down. About 95 percent of the time they're right.

But *you're* searching for the 1 to 5 percent of sellers who desperately need to sell *now*—and are willing to try unconventional solutions. Then the following strategy can be very useful.

Suppose the seller has a property worth $100,000 with an underlying loan of $90,000 and an equity of $10,000. He's really desperate to sell. If he lists the property with a Realtor, he'll have to pay most of his equity in commissions and closing costs—leaving no money for himself. Here's the script for you and the seller:

"Mr. Seller, I'm going to make you two separate offers for your house. The first offer is for $95,000. I'll take over your first mortgage and give you $5,000 cash. The second offer is for $101,000—$1,000 above your asking price. Instead of cash, I'll give you a promissory note❖ for $11,000 with an interest rate of 10 percent. Let's look at both offers as if they were investments.

"Five thousand dollars cash kept in a bank CD bearing 5 percent interest would become $8,144 in ten years. An $11,000 secured note bearing 10 percent would become $28,531 in ten years.

"In fact, it would take seventeen years of compound growing❖ for the first offer to equal what I'm willing to give you with offer number two. I really hope you'll consider offer number two, because we both can win."

Many times, the seller can be informed as to the benefits of a *Nothing Down* deal.

Can you see how enlightened the second offer is? You're offering the seller more money! By the way, when the buyer said, "I'll take over your first mortgage," of course, *you* know by now that she really meant that she would take over the payments in a subject-to arrangement.

Realtor as Partner

Here's one of the sweetest ways to turn your Realtor into your partner, and you can just hand her this book and have her read it herself:

Let's assume the same facts as in the previous strategy, but now the property has already been listed with a Realtor. After closing costs and $6,000 in real-estate commissions, the seller has zero equity. In reality, the Realtor has the most to profit from the sale. Here's your script with the Realtor:

"Ms. Realtor, the seller is going to end up with little or nothing from this transaction, and the longer this house remains on the market, the deeper the seller goes in the hole. Here's what would help: I'll take over the first mortgage. I'll pay closing costs for title transfer and so on, so the seller can walk away from this deal happy. As for commissions, instead of $6,000 in cash, I want to give you a note for $8,000 with an interest rate of 6 percent secured by the property. I'll also give you a guaranteed listing when I sell the house anytime down the road. I'm ready to close immediately."

This technique has a greater probability of success if the Realtor involved is also the listing broker, so she doesn't have to split commissions with other agents or brokers.

Wow, the Realtor is going to make not only an automatic $2,000 more but also all the interest until the note is paid off. All the Realtors I've spoken to said they'd be happy to do the deal. (Do understand that some won't be able to if their brokers won't allow it.)

Buyer as Partner

Whenever you make an offer to buy a property at a certain price in a certain number of days, you sign an offer to purchase❖. It's a short-term option, really. It's a legally binding document that obligates the seller to sell to you within a specific time. Maybe you offered to buy a $200,000 home with a closing date ninety days in the future. You then have a ninety-day option on this property with a locked-in price of $200,000. But what if someone calls you during this ninety-day period (before you have actually taken title to the property) and offers you *$220,000* for your contract? Could you sell your contract to this new buyer and pocket the $20,000 profit? Absolutely! The new buyer will complete the purchase instead of you. To strengthen your legal position, be sure to include these three words after your name in the purchase offer: *and/or assigns.* That phrase gives you the right to purchase a property and/or to assign your contract to another party. (Check with your attorney about the details.)

I know quite a few investors who are multimillionaires, and all they ever do is find great deals, get them under contract, and assign the contracts to other investors. This is the strategy called "assigning❖," or an "assignment of contract." Are you starting to think about the wealth of possibilities?

What would you attempt to do if you knew you could not fail?
—SIGN ON THE WALL AT MY DOCTOR'S OFFICE

Word Wizard

___ Promissory Note   A document that shows an amount one person *promises* to pay to another.

___ Compound Growing   Compound interest; how interest increases; interest paid on accumulated interest as well as on the principal.

___ Offer to Purchase   A document where you make an offer to the seller and he accepts it or declines it.

___ Assigning   Getting a property under contract and then selling it to another investor by selling him the contract ("selling him the paper").

Quiz Wizard

1. What are some reasons that a seller might be willing to be your partner?
    a. He could make more money by giving you better terms.
    b. He could possibly have some tax advantages by doing seller financing.
    c. He could find a way to retire to Florida.
    d. He could have a better plan for his IRA.
    e. He could make new friends.

2. Why would a Realtor be motivated to be your partner?
    a. She would be able to see that you could match her 401(k) plan.
    b. She would like to be a part of your team in order to get more business from other investors in your group.
    c. She might like to pretend to conduct herself in an enlightened way after reading *The One Minute Millionaire*.
    d. She could make more money because you would list the house with her when you sell it in the future.
    e. She could make more money by letting you pay her over time.

3.   What is it called when a buyer becomes your partner using the strategy described in this helping?
      a. Lease-option.
      b. Assignment of contract.
      c. Offer to purchase.
      d. Seller financing.
      e. Simultaneous closing.

4.   Did you notice that you're getting a much bigger real-estate vocabulary, and there are hardly any words for you to look up?
      a. Yes.
      b. No.

Turn to page 437 for the answers.

Whiz Wizard

1.   Take your Realtor to lunch and show her this section. It would be very sweet if you gave her a copy, but I wouldn't want you to think I was trying to get you to buy another book (wink!).
Done _____

2.   Get together with the person you're teaching and let her pretend to be a seller. Talk her into letting you take over payments on her existing mortgage and then letting you pay her interest-only payments for five years with a lump-sum payment at the end. Show her how much more money she'll make on the asking price of her home. Then switch around, and you be the seller and your partner be the buyer, doing the same deal. After that, both of you pretend to do an assignment of contract, talking it through in both directions, with you assigning a contract and then her assigning the contract.
Done _____

3.   Teach the concept of sellers, buyers, and Realtors as partners to someone else so that he or she understands it.
Done _____

HELPING 42

These Ain't Ya Ordinary Loans

Bob Allen has told me personally that never in his wildest dreams could he have envisioned the kinds of loans that are available today when he was writing the original *Nothing Down*. In those days, you had to put down 10 to 30 percent for conventional loans. Period.

These days, there's a *Nothing Down* loan program on every corner. Maybe your *bank* doesn't have a zero-down program, but your friendly mortgage broker does. In fact, he'll likely have multiple ways for you to borrow money with zero down. One hundred percent financing is the fashion of the day. There are even 100 percent loans for investors.

There's a lot more to learn than I can teach you here, and, frankly, what I teach you today might not be accurate tomorrow. The lending business is a fluid, changing, morphing, and molting thing. Lending trends respond to what goes on in the world, from global right down to citywide. You might start off applying for one kind of special loan program only to discover that twenty-eight days later that program has different requirements or even has disappeared all together.

That is why you want a great, honest mortgage broker on your team. You need her to keep you advised of what's going on in the lending world. She should be able to help you find cool and groovy new programs as they surface, and she should help you decide which ones suit your specific needs. And those needs aren't determined just by your credit scores, they're determined by the nature of the deal: Are you going to keep it forever? Are you going to keep it for one year? Are you going to keep it one week? Are you going to live in it?

Loans for People Who Don't Have a JOB

When I lost my job—or rather, when I knew the end was near—I went out and got a line of credit on my home. The reason I did that was that I believed that without a job I'd never be able to get a loan again. Well, I've never held a job in the last six years, and I have had over forty-five loans. How is that even possible? Now are you starting to believe me when I say these ain't ya mama's loans?

For example, there are loans where you just state your income. Nobody calls up your boss, nobody asks for pay stubs. You just say what is necessary to qualify for the loan. Yes, it has to make some logical sense. You can't say you make $50,000 per month if you have no spare change anywhere to back that up. I'm just saying you don't have to have a job to get a loan. You can use "stated income❖" loans.

Not only that, you don't have to show the lender all your tax returns and tell him what color underwear you had on three Thursdays ago if you do "no-doc❖" or "low-doc❖" loans. There are an awful lot of terms in the lending industry that we need to catch up on, and their jargon changes all the time as well.

To help you get the swing of things pretty fast, I've created a special bonus for you, a taped interview with one of my favorite mortgage brokers. Mary Turner was one of my students who had never bought a property, even though she was in a related business. Now she has multiple properties securing her future. She's one of the most experienced lenders around, and I've asked her the questions that I know are on your mind. It's the same questions women in my audiences have been asking over and over again. So enjoy listening to the bonus tape with these questions in front of you, so you can take notes. She really makes things easy to understand. You'll find the download link in the Whiz Wizard.

These are questions you can ask your own lenders, too.

Bonus Interview Questions

1. What are the make-or-break points in a person's FICO score for being able to get real-estate loans?
2. What can you do for someone whose score is under 650?
3. Please explain a stated income loan. It looks like the person is lying if she states a certain income but has no job.
4. Who could do a stated income loan?
5. I've heard of SISA❖ (stated income, stated asset) and SIVA❖ (stated income, verified asset) loan programs. If a person is doing stated income, how would she decide whether to do stated asset or verified asset?
6. What's a no-doc loan? Are you saying there are really *no* documents?
7. OK, then what's a low-doc loan?
8. How fast can a person get a loan?
9. If you do stated income, stated asset, will the loan process go faster?
10. When should a person try to do a 100 percent loan?
11. Do you have any loans that would get a person more than 100 percent? Do you have any where a person could get the money to do the fixing up needed?
12. Would a person have to live in the property, or are these loans you're talking about for investors?
13. What is an adjustable-rate mortgage (ARM❖)?
14. What are the different numbers we hear about, like 5/1, 3/1—what do all those numbers mean?
15. What's an option ARM❖ (also known as a power option ARM)? What other names does that go by?
16. What's a negative-amortization loan❖? When would a person be safe using one?
17. What's LIBOR❖ (London Interbank Offered Rate)? What are the other indexes like LIBOR?
18. What is loan processing?
19. What's loan underwriting?
20. How many mortgages can a person have?
21. What are the differences between an owner-occupied loan and a non-owner-occupied loan? How about a second home? And how many second homes can a person have?
22. Is it really OK to take over payments on a seller's loan even if it isn't assumable?

23. What common mistakes do new investors make? What's your pet peeve with investors applying for loans?
24. What's your best piece of advice for our women readers?
25. How can a person make up her mind among all these programs?

If you can count your money, you don't have a billion dollars.

—J. PAUL GETTY

Word Wizard

___ Stated Income	A loan for which you don't have to prove your income.
___ No Doc	A loan with very little documentation required.
___ Low Doc	A loan that requires a little more documentation than a no doc.
___ SISA	Stated Income, Stated Assets (no verifying).
___ SIVA	Stated Income, Verified Assets (they verify your assets).
___ ARM	Adjustable Rate Mortgage (the rates can change at specific times).
___ Option ARM	An ARM with several different ways you can choose to pay each month.
___ Negative Amortization Loan	A loan that tacks some of your payment due onto the end of the loan.
___ LIBOR	London Interbank Offered Rate. One of several indexes for lenders.
___ Pre-Qual Letter	A letter from your lender that tells your prospective seller or builder what amount you are potentially qualified to obtain on a loan.

Quiz Wizard

1. Do you have to have a job to get a home loan?
   a. Yes.
   b. No.

2. Can an investor get 100 percent for a property she doesn't plan to live in?
   a. Yes.
   b. No.
   c. Maybe, it depends.

3. If a woman works as a waitress, and she's doing a stated income loan, can she state that she makes $5,000 per week?
   a. Yes.
   b. Probably not.

Turn to page 437 for the answers.

Whiz Wizard

1. Go to www.ND4W.com/lenderMP3 and download the bonus MP3 of the interview with the lender. Listen to the interview in your car while you're driving over the next week.
   Done _____

2. Call your lender of choice (I'm assuming you already have a mortgage broker on your team, because it was part of your homework—ahem!) and ask him to find out how much you can prequalify for. Get a pre-qual letter❖ from him. Ask the broker if he can give you the letter based on a credit report that you've pulled yourself, so that he doesn't have to initiate any extra inquiries on your report. Ask what the guidelines are for 100 percent financing while you're at it!
   Done _____

3. Teach the concept of loans today to someone else so that he or she understands it.
   Done _____

How to Be a Great Borrower

There's a lot more to borrowing than having a good credit score. Let me help you be popular with your lending team. You want to make everything easy and efficient for the mortgage broker, and even more importantly, for the processor and the underwriter. Here are the things you should be prepared to deliver quickly and easily at all times.

That's right, keep these things ready in advance, and you'll find your loans go through better and better. You'll develop a reputation for having your financial world organized. You'll demonstrate that you understand the lending process and that you're cooperating as a part of *their* team to get your loan packaged and processed to everyone's best advantage.

And don't ever forget, your lender wants to get the loan done for you because that's his very livelihood. When you don't provide what he needs for the loan to go smoothly, you're digging into his pockets. Lenders make money by lending you money, so they're very motivated to get the job done. If you can show them you understand how to speed up the process, you're going to be very popular!

If you'll remember all the way back to module 4, I showed you how to use PaperPort. Now is the time when either PaperPort or Adobe Acrobat❖ will be very helpful to you, because you'll want to be able to email portable document-format (PDF) files❖ of all your data. It is the very fastest way to get things to your processor and underwriter, and they'll come to respect you for your preparedness. That respect will actually influence how your loans go.

Here are the items the lender may most often request from you:

1. A completed 1003 form❖, or standard loan application.
2. Signed and dated authorization and certification disclosures, their required forms.
3. Bank statements, usually for two months, sometimes more.
4. Copies of checks written to mortgage companies, sometimes going as far back as a year.
5. Copies of mortgage statements, sometimes going as far back as a year.
6. Payment histories, also called verification of deposit❖, or VOD❖.
7. Copy of a recent trimerge credit report❖.
8. Proof of seasoned funds❖.
9. Utility bills to prove your primary residence.
10. Letter from your CPA❖ or tax preparer saying how long you've been self-employed and how long you've been at the same location.
11. If you own a corporation that's involved, copies of its articles of incorporation❖.
12. A copy of your net worth❖ statement.
13. A copy of your Schedule of Real Estate Owned❖.
14. Copies of trusts❖ or LLCs❖ if you have any properties in asset protection entities❖.
15. A letter explaining any unique circumstances. Sometimes a woman might want to show a history of her name changes, especially if there've been a lot of them (wink). I personally send a letter explaining my background as an investor and what my company does.

And if you're going full doc:
1. Last two years' W-2❖ forms for all borrowers.
2. Last two years' tax returns.
3. Recent pay stubs showing year-to-date❖ earnings.
4. Last three months' bank statements, all pages, for all

liquid-asset❖ accounts (bank statements, checking, 401(k), stocks, bonds, and so forth).

I go online to my bank once a month and download all my statements and copies of mortgage checks and file them on PaperPort. I'm not saying that you have to do that too, but it sure does make life easier when people want that stuff. I keep my tax returns in PaperPort too. And every time I pay a mortgage payment, I scan the statement into PaperPort. Tonight, before I wrote this helping, I had to send the most recent copy of every statement for every house. That's *a lot* of paperwork, and it was all there, just waiting to be emailed in about ten minutes. Don't you think the lender knows I'm a professional? They'll know *you* are too if you anticipate his or her needs.

My best suggestion is a simple one: Call the lender several times and ask if she needs anything else from you. It'll help cut down on last-minute emergencies!

And last but definitely not least: When something goes awry, just remember that Karen said to think like a problem solver. Ask your lender to help you think like a problem solver. You're gonna find yourself owning that property and being very, very proud of yourself!

Deal first, funding follows.

—KAREN NELSON BELL

Word Wizard

___ Adobe Acrobat	A software program that lets you create PDF files.
___ PDF Files	An abbreviation for *portable document format,* a file format developed by Adobe Systems. PDF captures files from many desktop publishing applications, such as Word and Excel, making it possible to view them as created. To view a file in PDF format, you need the free Adobe Acrobat Reader. To *create* a file in PDF,

___ Processor

___ Underwriter

___ 1003 Form

___ Verification of Deposit (VOD)

___ Trimerge credit report

___ Seasoned Funds

___ CPA

___ Articles of Incorporation

___ Net Worth

___ Schedule of Real Estate Owned

___ Trust

___ LLC

___ Entities

you'll need a more advanced version (not free).

A person who gathers together all of the information needed before it goes to the underwriter.

A person who examines all of the data gathered by the processor to evaluate if your file indicates that you'd be a person who would pay back the loan.

Standard loan application form.

Some proof (usually by a bank or lender) that you've got the money you say you have, or you've paid the money you say you've paid.

Your credit report from all three bureaus.

Money that has been in your possession for a specified amount of time, usually two to six months.

Certified public accountant, a person who does accounting and has passed some tests that got him certified.

Documents showing the setup of a corporation.

How much you have versus how much you owe; whatever is left over after you pay all your debts.

A list of all the properties you have with the mortgages listed; also shows how much is owed, what the values are, and so on.

A legal device used to set property aside from one's own self.

Limited liability company, a hybrid between a partnership and a corporation.

Legal structures that could be thought of as an artificial person examples include corporations, LLCs, partnerships.

___ W-2

An IRS form that an employee receives from the employer at the end of the year to show earnings and all deductions.

___ Year to Date

If something is written in the middle of a year, the data are only from the beginning of the year to the current date.

___ Liquid Asset

Assets you can get your hands on in a fairly short period of time, such as checking accounts, savings accounts, IRAs, 401(k)s, stocks.

Quiz Wizard

1. Why do lenders need to have so much data?
    a. They need to know if you're likely to pay back the loan.
    b. They have to follow certain laws that make them ask for certain stuff.
    c. They need to minimize their risk.
    d. They can help to minimize *your* risk.
    e. They're paper pushers who are overanalytical.

2. Why do lenders want you to get your data to them as soon as possible?
    a. Their bosses are breathing down their necks.
    b. Their own paycheck depends on the loans they write.
    c. Your loan puts money in their pocket.
    d. They want to close as many loans as they can every month.
    e. They're salesmen, selling you money, and they want their commission.

3. As an investor, should you keep all your financial files in order and up to date all the time?

      a. Yes.
      b. Yes.

Turn to page 437 for the answers.

Whiz Wizard

1. Go to www.ND4W.com/loanapplist and get the special report ti-
   tled "Application Checklist." Read the text describing what the
   lender wants you to know, under "Keys to Fast Loan Approval."
   Done _____

2. Go to www.ND4W.com/loanappMP3 and download the MP3 of
   the interview with Mary Turner. Listen to it in your car while
   you're driving over the next week. It's about twenty minutes long.
   Done _____

3. Find the following items and put them someplace where you can
   get your hands on them quickly: two years' of tax returns, proof of
   payment of your mortgage or rent for one year, and two months'
   of bank statements. It's a start!
   Done _____

4. Teach the concept of how to be a great borrower to someone else
   so that he or she understands it.
   Done _____

Nothing Down without OPM (Really!)

The best way to remember something is to learn it through a story. We remember the principles we learned from the tales we read as children, yes? Let me tell you three stories to help you begin to think in new ways about how to buy real estate when you haven't got two nickels to rub together.

The Horse Property

My old friend, let's call him "Roger," had lived in a nice four-bedroom home on a half acre for several years with his wife and children. When they divorced, it was painful, and he moved across the country, partly for work and partly to revitalize his life. He had done well enough to move and start a new business without having to sell their lovely home, so he rented it out, using a property management company. The company didn't do a very good job: The rent didn't even cover the mortgage—especially since the property managers took 10 percent off the top—plus the renter paid late more often than not. When Roger found out that the renter was leaving without notice, he had had enough. Even though he had a fair bit of equity, he couldn't take the aggravation any longer. I think the house also reminded him of another time that he wanted to forget.

He said, "Karen, just take it over and get it off my shoulders. If you ever sell it or refinance it, send me $10,000. If you don't, then we're still square."

The property was worth $345,000, and he owed $275,000, so he was walking away from $70,000 of equity. He knew it; he didn't care. He informed the management company and the renter that he was selling the property, my husband and I made arrangements to pick up the keys, and the renter gave us a tour of the place. It was in nice shape, and there wasn't much to do except clean up. We put up a handmade sign, and in seventy-two hours we had new renters all tucked away in their new home. That's a truly *Nothing Down* deal with no money changing hands. Oh, yes, we had to rent a trash bin to remove the renter's stuff he had strewn around the huge yard; that was $200 we put on a credit card and paid back with the renter's deposit. Still a *Nothing Down* deal! And we got a $300 positive cash flow right from the start! Still do!

When Roger heard about the escalating prices in Las Vegas, he expressed a little regret. The house is now worth over $450,000, but he knew he did the right thing for that moment in his life. I told him I'd teach him what we're doing, and he said he'd come out for a class one day. We did refinance the property after a couple of years, and when we did, we took about $30,000 for ourselves and gave Roger his $10,000 as promised.

The Truck Driver

This next story is kind of sad, because the sellers really were in such a jam; they were running from their problems. Whereas the deal with Roger came from word of mouth alone, this property came into our lives because someone gave "Doug and Cindy" our card. They don't know who gave it to them, and neither do we, but we're glad they did. I always think of a business card as an extension of word of mouth!

Doug was a truck driver, and one night during the summer he got arrested for riding his motorcycle while intoxicated. Beer and bikes can be dangerous in many ways, and this time it lost him his job, because a truck driver can't have a DUI (driving under the influence) on his record. He and Cindy both drove trucks, but with Doug's DUI, they couldn't make ends meet to pay the mortgage payments, and they were six months behind.

On the day Doug called, he said, "I'm leaving for Mississippi tonight; gonna find a company that doesn't know about my DUI and get back to work. I was stupid, I'm never gonna do that again, but I gotta go find some work for me and my family. I don't care what you do with the property, just let me sign something, and I'll leave the keys in your mailbox."

Their house was a large townhome in the best part of the city, and they were just walking away. How sad. I wish they could have taken this course and rebuilt their lives. That was certainly a true *Nothing Down* deal, wasn't it?

It's still hard to believe that people can have so much stress that they would prefer to walk away, but I've seen it over and over again, not only in my own life but for other investors as well. And the people always end up writing back that they were so grateful and relieved.

Duncan's Birthday Surprise

My favorite story is about Roy and Ellen. It was in the spring, and I was trying to find some real estate to give Duncan for his birthday. (We pledged to give each other real estate for every birthday, anniversary, and Christmas, so we'd know that we would buy at least four properties every year! You should take the same pledge!)

I found an ad in the Las Vegas *Review-Journal* for 9.3 acres of land in a bedroom community outside of Las Vegas called Pahrump. It's a wild and wooly place where they still have legal prostitution, but civilization is creeping in, and almost all the big builders in Nevada are developing huge communities there. I called Roy on the phone, and he told me how to get there so that I could take a look at it.

It was nice compared to the other parcels for sale nearby. It had two wells, power, and phone lines already on it. It seemed like it was underpriced by about $20K compared to the others.

We got there too late that day to connect with Roy, so we made plans to drive the forty-five minutes over the mountain again the following weekend, which was the weekend of Duncan's actual birthday. I was pretty excited! Roy was a gentleman in his seventies, and he seemed so nice, I thought we could make a pretty good deal even if we paid him full price.

When we got there, Roy said, "Well, some fellers from L.A. came over this mornin', and they said they'd pay me all cash and beat anyone else's bid."

I figured we'd wasted a tank of gas, but Duncan said, "Well, Roy, I'm here, so why don't we walk the land?"

He and Roy got out of their trucks, and Ellen and I sat and chatted while they walked the perimeter of the desert landscape surrounded by California mountains. When they got back to the truck after about forty minutes, Roy said, "Duncan, let's go over to the casino and get us a $4.99 buffet and work this deal out. I'd like to sell it to ya." Duncan had won out over an all-cash, top-dollar offer from the other investors. They didn't *listen*. And honestly, Roy simply liked and trusted Duncan.

I tried to hide my surprise, and we rolled off to the little local casino to finish our negotiations. It turns out that Roy didn't want all cash. If he took all cash, he'd have a tax problem, so he let us pay *him* through a title company instead. He also said that he wouldn't mind letting us pay the down payment over six months' time, so there was no need to come up with a down payment.

I was stunned! Roy not only sold it to us, he sold it at his original asking price (which was quite a bit below market value) *and* gave us 100 percent seller financing. He let us pay him for the first mortgage, and he let us pay him over time for the down payment. We never had to go to a bank, and, amazingly, I need to show more ID when I buy a loaf of bread at the store.

By the way, the value of the parcel went from $130K to $500K in a year! We had planned to live on it but decided to build homes on it instead. (That's a whole different game from investing.)

The thing I love most about this *Nothing Down* story is that I watched my own negative viewpoints evaporate in the presence of my partner's more creative and positive mind-set. Like Bob Allen says, all the techniques in the world won't turn you into a successful investor until you shift your thinking. That day really shifted mine, and now, when I catch myself with a gloomy perspective on a deal, I just ask myself, "What does the seller need from me that could move this deal? And whatever it is that he needs, *where can I get it?*"

Sound familiar? I hope so!

The meek shall inherit the Earth but not its mineral rights.

—J. PAUL GETTY

Quiz Wizard

1. In the first story about the horse property, what motivations created Roger's willingness to give me such a good deal?
   a. Divorce
   b. Transfer
   c. Management problems
   d. Cash flow problems
   e. Vacancy

2. In the second story about the truck driver, how did we find the deal?
   a. Word of mouth
   b. Business card
   c. Foreclosure list
   d. Newspaper
   e. Realtor

3. In the third story about Duncan's birthday surprise, what factors caused us to get the deal over previous investors willing to pay all cash and beat any offer?
   a. Listening
   b. Communication
   c. Affinity
   d. Trust
   e. Understanding

Turn to page 437 for the answers.

Whiz Wizard

1. I got the deal in the first story by word of mouth. Today's homework is designed to get you the same thing. I want you to call twenty-one people and tell them you're a real estate investor! That's three people a day over the next week. OK, you can sign

off on this lesson after the first six, but you promise, promise, promise to keep going until you get to twenty-one, right?! Right! Done _____

2. I got the deal in the second story by handing out business cards. Hand out one hundred cards this week, and promise, promise, promise to hand out one hundred *every* week until you have all the deals you desire. It's time to start getting into real action now, because you're almost finished with the seventh module, and you actually know everything you need to get started! There's more to learn, but you can really, really get started right now!
Done _____

3. I got the deal in the third story by looking in the paper. Today's homework is truly designed to get you the same thing. I want you to call twenty-one ads and have a quick conversation! That's three ads a day over the next week. OK, you can sign off on this lesson after the first six, but you promise, promise, promise to keep going until you get to twenty-one, right?! Right! See? We're gonna kick some butt, you and I!!! There, I finally said it. We—I mean *you*—have to finally kick some butt in the physical universe!
Done _____

4. Teach the concept of *Nothing Down* without OPM to someone else so that he or she understands it.
Done _____

5MM Time Capsule 7

5MM Module 7, Helpings 38–44

Here's your familiar checklist of what your seven lessons included in module 7. Check off each item that you know you can easily explain to someone else! If you can't, then check back through the text. Use this list as an opportunity to review!

Helping 38:
___ How to get great money to flow to your deals.
___ How to get investors to invest with you without your having to beg.
___ Why your partner in a pocket is better than a fifty-fifty partner.
___ The two rules that will keep you out of credit trouble from now forward.

Helping 39:
___ How to get OPM in an hour.
___ Sixteen more *Nothing Down* strategies.
___ Who your private lenders are, and why they want to invest in your deals.

Helping 40:
___ The greatest secret weapon in the world of *Nothing Down* financing.
___ What a lease-option sandwich is.

___ The big differences between *buying* with a lease-option and *selling* with a lease-option.

___ Why you don't want people to buy your house!

Helping 41:

___ Why your buyer would want to become your OPM partner.

___ Why your seller would want to become your OPM partner.

___ Why your Realtor would want to become your OPM partner.

Helping 42:

___ Why you don't need a job to get a loan.

___ How to tell your lender what you earn without having to prove it.

___ How to get a loan with no income, no assets.

___ What these strange acronyms mean to your profit: SISA, SIVA, LIBOR, ARM.

Helping 43:

___ How to get your lender to put your deal at the top of his to-do pile.

___ What to have on hand for loans in half the time of your neighbor.

___ How to increase your lendability by increasing your credibility.

Helping 44:

___ How you could do a *Nothing Down* deal even without any OPM.

When you've checked off every item, you can get started on module 8 on fixing stinky houses (without ever lifting a finger)!

Bobservations

The subject of how to find and use other people's money still fascinates me today. I'm always amazed at the bright ideas students and fellow investors come up with that provide a creative twist to my own inventory of strategies. The toolbox just keeps getting bigger and bigger.

It would be interesting to follow the history of *Nothing Down* investing from the time I wrote the original book to the present day. I didn't invent *Nothing Down,* I invented the *phrase.* Then I brought the concepts to the general public and made it easier for ordinary people to grasp.

The concept of using someone else's resources to leverage your own probably started when the first farmer borrowed his neighbor's rooster to "finance" some action in the henhouse. Then he paid the neighbor back interest in the form of eggs.

And as you might guess from this module, there are as many *Nothing Down* techniques as there are people living in properties.

If you continue to refine your talent for *listening* and *understanding* at the heart level, you'll come up with a list of more *Nothing Down* ideas than could ever fit in one book. Just think of this module as your starter kit. Be sure to write and let us know some of your own solutions!

MODULE 8

FIXING AND STUFF

HELPING 45

Turn a Stinky House into a Stunning Home

Yesterday, I was inspecting a property I'm thinking of buying from another investor on an assignment of contract, and I was startled by how differently we viewed the property. He felt it was almost a walk-in-and-do-nearly-nothing house, and I felt it had upward of $10,000 worth of repairs to make it tolerable or attractive to any woman.

Then my potential OPM partner went to look at it, and he too thought it had very little work to do. I guess women really see things differently. I saw ugly four-by-four-inch white porcelain tiles on the kitchen counter with moldy grout lines and funky dents all over the master bath vanity. Any woman I know would despise it. And who buys houses? We do!

Your advantage in the "Stinky House❖" business is that you can see clearly what other women will see. You understand automatically and instinctively what home buyers (read "women") want.

I call them Stinky Houses because most houses that have been left in disrepair usually smell bad, either from smoking tenants, pets, water damage, or even just from "hard living."

At one of our weekend boot camps, I asked one student if she was considering the Stinky House we had just seen as a possible investment for herself. I was excited for her to make a lot of money with it.

She said, "No, it's just not my style."

I thought that was odd, because the house was an incredible opportunity and a very, very good investment from a Bargain Finder point of view, so I asked her what it was about it that didn't seem to be "her style." I thought she understood the Stinky House strategy.

She said, "Well, it's very cluttered, and it really stinks."

Of course, after that comment, we had a long chat about not investing on emotion and according to what *you'd* like to live in. An expert investor sees the clutter and thinks, "Oh, goodie, no one else will see beyond the mess, and I'll be able to scoop up this deal." Clutter gets handled by hiring two college students to haul it off. When I smell a stinky house, I think, "Hooray, I can fix that easily, but no one else will see what I see, and I can get a great discount!"

Stinky Houses are potential gold mines to me!

In the early days of my investing career, my husband and I did all the work ourselves. We painted, scraped, hauled, polished, repaired, spackled, installed nice fixtures, and when all was said and done, we felt quite pleased with ourselves to have contributed to someone's lovely home.

Now I hire people at good prices to do the work for me, but it was nice to know that I could get in there and fix up a fixer-upper. For you, I think you should have someone else do everything! Why do I say that? *Because you already have too little time.* You and I are doing this program together because the idea of a 5-Minute Mentor seemed right for you. You probably don't need to spend your time fixing a broken door handle when you could be opening the door to another deal. Get it?

You'll get used to looking with a very discriminating eye when you view a property. I'm going to give you a checklist, and you should print it out and take it with you on a clipboard when you're viewing a home. By the way, your checklist will let the seller know you aren't going to be fooled by emotions, you're an analytical buyer looking at the facts.

Once you've made your initial observations, if you guesstimate that even with repairs the deal is good, now bring in your handyman to give you the real data on what it will cost. Tell him that you'll use him to do the work, and he'll do the bid for you for free. Let him know you'd like a real bid on both materials and labor for what you're going to pay him, and you'd also like a retail bid so that you can demonstrate the retail (therefore *higher*) cost of repairs to the seller in case you need a persuasion tool.

Tip: Ask the handyman if you could get a better deal by buying the materials yourself. Sometimes he can get it cheaper and sometimes you can! I *live* at Home Depot and Lowe's. I know when the sales are going, and so should you!

How will you find a handyman or other vital trade person? Can't you just hear my answer before I say it? Word of mouth! You know how I love word of mouth. Ask your Realtor, ask your investor friends, ask your neighbor. Look in the services directory of your newspaper and then compare that to the services directory of your *Nifty Nickel, Thrifty Nickel, PennySaver*—whatever giveaway weekly you have in your hometown.

Have courage if you have to wade through several referrals, and smile even if they don't work out—it's just part of the investor's life. Keep using the same resources to develop more and more contacts.

If you enjoy the work, by all means, get right in there. I *love* to paint! That's my thing! I also love shopping for nice knobs and door handles, pretty light fixtures, and bathroom appointments. Do the parts that you enjoy and delegate the parts you don't, and make sure you're spending your own time on the things that will make you the most money.

A word on paint: neutral❖, neutral, neutral. Well, that was three words, but neutral is the only way to go. You may personally be very tired of neutral, but here's the deal: When it's neutral, the buyer can envision her color on top of it. When it's not neutral, and it's distinctive, if the buyer doesn't like it, she has trouble envisioning something else. You may not like cream-colored walls, but do it anyway! No blue carpet, no pink tile, no yellow window coverings. Yes to beige carpet, yes to tan tile, yes to cream blinds!

Did I mention that you should use neutral colors when you're dressing a house for sale or rent? Neutral!

Here's one thing you can do that you might not have thought of: Look up! Look to see if there are any stains on the ceiling. If there are, it may be a sign of water damage and a potential leaky roof. Flush the toilets, turn on the showers, run the dishwasher and the disposal. You basically want to try everything that moves. Turn on all the lights as you walk through each room.

If there is a great deal of clutter, imagine the room as though it were empty. If it stinks, imagine sparkling clean surfaces with fresh flowers on the countertop. Look beyond the cosmetic deficiencies and let your creativity envision a space where the new residents will be ecstatic. If you have vision with a Stinky House, you can turn it into a Stunning Home without ever having to do a lick of work. All you need is the viewpoint that it can be done! You'll manage your crew and tell them what to do, but you'll be busy making more deals.

Stinky House = Stunning Home = *ka-ching!* ❖ I LOVE Stinky Houses! I hope you will too!

Every house started out as a lovely home where people imagined they'd live happily ever after. Restoring charm to a broken property is the equivalent of restoring a dream to a broken heart. I love the transformation.

—KAREN NELSON BELL

Word Wizard

___ Stinky House   A house that has cosmetic defects as well as possible structural defects; it usually smells bad too, but it doesn't have to smell bad to earn the title.

___ Neutral   Colors that are not vibrant; anything in the range of "blah," from white to tan; earth tones; not red, blue, yellow, purple, pink.

___ *ka-ching!*   The sound of the profit you can make on a Stinky House.

Quiz Wizard

1. Why should you be happy when you find a Stinky House at a good price? (Choose one answer only; the best answer!)
   a. Because you've been trying to quit smoking, and it really helps you stay true to your commitment.
   b. Because you love to paint and decorate.
   c. Because you know you can turn it into a profitable deal.
   d. Because it means you've got something to do to fill your spare time.
   e. Because the stinkier the house, the more other investors will miss the deal.

2. What colors are best for dressing a house for sale or rent?
   a. Lavender.
   b. Lemon.
   c. Lime.
   d. Crimson.
   e. Neutral.

3. Should you do the fixing up on a Stinky House yourself?
   a. Yes, if you just can't bear the thought of not doing it because you love all the elements of creating a lovely space.
   b. No, if you don't have the time but would like to have the incredible profits.

Turn to page 437 for the answers.

Whiz Wizard

1. Go to www.ND4W.com/stinkyhouse and get the file called "Stinky House Checklist" to read and to use. I put it there as a MS Excel document, so you can tweak it to suit your personal needs, and you can fill it out on the computer and save it with your reference files on the house. Because it's Excel, you can put your pricing right in it. It's not fancy, but it sure is efficient.
   Done _____

2. Look in all your resources you learned in module 2 to find a fixer-upper. Visit at least one Stinky House before you move on to the next section. If it's a good deal according to your Bargain Finder, you may feel like making an offer. Screw up your courage and ask, "Would-ja take?"
   Done _____

3. Teach the concept of fixing Stinky Houses to someone else so that he or she understands it.
   Done _____

If You're Scared to Be a Landlord

There are some changes in the world of landlording that make the process so much easier than you probably think. Let me help you through your concerns or fears. I'll state the concern, and then I'll state the solution. Remember, we all have to accumulate some income-producing assets in order to pay for our future days.

"What If the Tenants Don't Pay Some Month, and I Have to Cover the Mortgage Payment Myself?"

When you get a renter or a lease-option tenant, you'll be getting the first and last months' rent, a security deposit❖, and, if it's a lease-option, the option payment. Use the money for the first month's rent to pay your current mortgage, and put the last month's rent and deposit in an account where you can save some "buffer❖" money. Robert Allen recommends having three months' of buffer for each property, but you won't have that in the beginning. Just keep that last month's rent and the deposit so that you won't panic when the tenant doesn't pay on time.

If you get an option payment, sometimes it can be enough to pay a whole year of payments in advance, but if you need the money for other things in your life, just put a portion of it away in the buffer account❖.

No one I've ever met started out with a big buffer account, but it will grow. I've got a one-month buffer for forty properties, and I've never, ever, ever been late on a mortgage payment.

"What If the Tenant Turns Out to Be a Rotten Egg❖?"

Before you put the tenant in the house, there's one thing you can do to radically diminish your likelihood of rotten eggs and bad apples: do a background check❖. Have him sign a page that says you can do a background check and a credit check. Look for criminal activity, look for lawsuits with landlords, call his references. Don't just call his last landlord, because he might have stiffed the last one, and she's just glad to get rid of him. Or the reference might be his uncle. Call *all* the references.

How do you do the check? You let someone do it for you, and that person becomes a part of your team. I use a private investigator who works for attorneys. It costs me $60 for each tenant, and it's really, really worth it. The only times we've had problems with tenants have mainly been the times we forewent the background check.

One time, the tenant owned two jet airplanes, and he put down a $10,000 option payment. We didn't think we'd have to do the check. He turned out to be one of our naughtiest renters, and if we had checked, we'd have seen the trail of troubles he had in his report.

You can find companies that do these checks by looking in your telephone book under credit services, or you can go to www.Landlord.com for some excellent resources. I really love Landlord.com (they don't know me from Adam), because it has such a content-rich site. You can learn just about everything you'd ever need to know about being a professional landlord, right down to the state by state laws.

"I Don't Want to Fix a Toilet in the Middle of the Night"

Here's the solution: Get a home warranty❖. Home warranties are the only way to go. You can get a home warranty for $30 to $50 per month (tack it on to the price of the rent). Whenever something goes wrong, you call the company, and it sends someone out for a small deductible (usually $45), which the tenant pays if *they* caused the problem.

When I bought the big mansion that turned me into a millionaire, there was a home warranty on the property. Thank goodness, because two months after buying it, the double air conditioners went on the blink. The home warranty folks sent out a repairman, and the next day, it still wasn't working, so they sent him out again. He came out for three visits and finally ended up replacing the units. That $45 we paid as the deductible saved us from having to spend $7,000 for new units. Wow!

"I Don't Want the Tenants to Know Where I Live, and I Also Don't Want to Go Pick Up Rents"

I used to have all my tenants either hand carry or mail the rent to my post office box. They don't know where I live. You can get a personal mailbox someplace close to your home or office, and the tenants will mail their rents there. You won't be inviting renters to your home. If their rents aren't in the mailbox by 5:00 p.m. on the first of the month, they get a late charge.

I'm in the process of converting to a system where tenants can elect to deposit their rent directly into my bank account. I've set up a business checking account just for one purpose: to receive rents and then transfer them into my regular account. The tenants can go to the branch nearest them, make their deposit, and get a receipt to show the time and date they paid their rent!

"What If Something Happens to the Property?"

You're going to get a special insurance policy called a rental dwelling policy❖, and it will cover your house with the renter in it. In fact, if you use a home-owner's policy for a rental dwelling, you may never be able to get paid on your claim. The right policy will also cover you for intentional vandalism (but not "hard living").

The other thing you're going to do is ask your renter to acquire a renter's policy❖. It costs only about $120 per year, so if he balks at it, you can use that as a sign that you don't want him in your property. If he won't pay $10 a month to safeguard his *own* belongings, what responsibility level will he have with *your* property? Their policy also covers anything that happens that is the tenant's fault, such as a fire in the kitchen.

The next piece of insurance you need is an umbrella policy❖, which will cover you in case a renter thinks you've harmed him and wants to sue you. Your umbrella policy will cover all your homes. The coverage should be in the amount equivalent to your net worth, but it should start at $1 million. It's very inexpensive, and you don't want to be without it.

In fact, you mustn't go without any of these three forms of insurance, and the three will layer your protection.

"I Wouldn't Have a Clue What to Do If I Had to Evict❖ Someone"

Well, you'll have to take a more professional outlook, because you need to research the steps, but then you can have someone else do the actions. You just do some paperwork and contact the authorities. The authorities are the ones who will do the actual eviction, not you. It's different in every county, but it could be the sheriff who actually goes to the house and locks the doors, after removing any animals left behind. After you put the proper paperwork in place, you'll be at a distance from the process.

I do suggest Landlord.com for all kinds of advice on the procedures in your own home state.

"How in the World Do I Attract Tenants?"

First of all, you'll be reading the chapter on marketing very soon, so you'll know how to attract great tenants. Whether you like marketing or not, you will want to learn some basics to give yourself the advantage over all the other landlords looking for tenants! In the meantime, take a look at www.rentclicks.com or www.rent.com (an eBay site). It'll give you some confidence!

You can also hire someone else to do it for you. You can use a rental management company, or you can see if there is a service like the Renter Mentors, such as we have in Las Vegas (www.ND4W.com/rentermentor). A property manager❖ is a Realtor who has taken a special class and gotten a separate license, and she must also work for a broker as opposed to being independent. They typically charge 8 to 10 percent of the gross rents every month, so I prefer to train my own assistant to do the job. I give my assistant a modest wage but a big bonus when a house rents or sells. She gets to do all the work and gets a nice reward.

She meets the prospect at the house, takes the applications and the deposits, and meets tenants when they move in to do a walk-through and take photos. She calls the home warranty company when necessary and coordinates all the repairs. She stays in communication with the renters and keeps them happy. She just doesn't collect the rent. If she did that, she'd be working as a real property manager, and she'd have to have a license as described above. She *assists* me, so she's an assistant, not a property manager.

I believe you should begin by managing your properties yourself so that you can discover what good managing is. That way, when you hire someone else, you'll know if he or she is doing a good job. Many investors think there is no such thing as good property management companies, but if they're "home-grown," they can be wonderful! Once you get ten or more properties in your portfolio, you may want to start grooming someone to help you. I also believe that you should look at your duties as a landlord as professionally as you can. Network with other investors to find out what their successful actions are. Stay in touch with internet resources such as www.Landlord.com or www.MrLandlord.com.

Here are some tips on being a landlord that have worked for me:

- Offer to give tenants free air filters every month or every two months. That way, you or your assistant can go inspect the home without calling it an inspection.
- Give them a nice welcome mat as a gift when they move in. It's a little touch, but it sets the tone that you are different from other landlords.
- I'm keepin' a list and checkin' it twice, so I can always send a holiday gift and thank-you note to tenants who have been good.
- I keep a white board in the office with all the houses on it.

When the rents come in, they go on the board. Around the fifth, I can look and see who hasn't paid, so I write them a "five-day pay or quit❖." That's the way the system works in my county. They have five days to pay or leave the property. My tenants know they can call me and work things out, but legally I now have the right to move them out.

If you only have one rental property, when something bad happens, you think it's the end of the world. If somebody does a lot of damage, you probably would decide that renting isn't for you. But if you have ten properties, and something goes wrong, you just figure it's the cost of doing business. You still have a property that's appreciating more than you had to spend on repairs, even if the repairs ate up your profit margin for the year. By the way, let's review that you will be getting insurance specifically designed for rental properties. You're going to get a Rental Dwelling policy that you'll pay for (make sure you cover the house as a rental and not a residence, or you may not get your claims paid). You'll also have the renters pay for a Renter's Insurance Policy, which will cover their own belongings and any damage that they might accidentally do. Last but not least, ask for a Liability Umbrella over all your properties to cover you from assorted problems, accidents, or lawsuits.

My career as a landlord started quite naturally when my dad became terminally ill and moved in with my husband and me. We put a renter into his home to help defray his medical costs. A few years later, when the mortgage was finally paid off, we earned $1,100 every month free and clear. Some people in this country are living on that much. It's a tough life with that little dough. What if, when you're in your senior years, you already have four homes bringing in rent free and clear?

That's another retirement strategy that I really love. One extra home will probably cover the cost of the basics, the second home might give you enough to afford gas for the car, the third home will bring you enough to take care of your family, and the fourth one will be your secret little stash! Ahhh, I can see it now! Can you? Actually, my vision is a lot bigger than that for me and for you; I see a future of great abundance for you and all your family.

Income-producing assets can make that vision come true!

An empty house is better than a bad renter.
—LYNN KOON-CONRAD, MULTIMILLIONAIRE REAL-ESTATE INVESTOR

Word Wizard

___ Security Deposit	Money that a person can get back if he keeps the house clean; cleaning deposit, pet deposit, smokers' deposit are examples.
___ Buffer	Something to put a protective barrier between two other things.
___ Buffer Account	A safety savings account in case the renter fails to pay.
___ Rotten Egg	Naughty renter.
___ Background Check	Investigation into a prospective tenant's criminal history, housing history, credit history.
___ Home Warranty	A policy on the property that handles things when they need repair.
___ Rental Dwelling Policy	The insurance policy you have to have on a rental dwelling. Don't use a homeowner's policy on a rental dwelling, or you most likely may not be able to collect when it comes time to file a claim.
___ Renter's Policy	A policy that the renter takes out to protect his own belongings and his own actions that cause damage.
___ Umbrella Policy	A policy that goes over all your properties to protect you from legal liabilities.
___ Evict	Force a tenant to move out because he didn't comply with the contract.
___ Property Manager	A Realtor who has studied to be a licensed property manager and has received her license and works for a broker.
___ Five-day Pay or Quit	A specific legal process in some counties where the landlord gives the tenant five days to do one of two things: either pay up or move out.

Quiz Wizard

1. Which of the following things will help you if a tenant doesn't pay on time?
    a. A buffer account.
    b. A savings account.
    c. The tenant's deposit.
    d. The tenant's last month's rent.
    e. The tenant's option payment.

2. What are some things you can do to improve your likelihood of selecting good tenants? (This is a trick question.)
    a. Do a background check.
    b. Hire a private detective to follow them.
    c. Do a credit check.
    d. Only rent to people who have credit scores over 700.
    e. Don't rent to people whom you instinctively don't trust. However, we're sure not to discriminate.

3. What are the three types of insurance that will help you the most as a landlord?
    a. Rental dwelling policy.
    b. Life insurance policy.
    c. Renter's insurance policy.
    d. Liability umbrella policy.
    e. Long-term care insurance policy.

Turn to page 437 for the answers.

Whiz Wizard

-   Go to www.ND4W.com/landlords and get the file called "References for Landlords" to read and to use. Then read it and use it!
    Done _____

-   Go to www.Landlord.com and/or www.MrLandlord.com and look all around. Find the laws for your own state, just so you know what they are. Sign up for anything they offer for free

(you know how websites change all the time, so I don't know for sure what they'll have).
Done _____

- Teach the concept of fearless landlording to someone else so that he or she understands it.
Done _____

New Construction and Out-of-State Buying

Buying houses that aren't even built yet—buying "dirt"—is possibly the best-kept secret in creative real-estate investing, but you have to do it the right way. Let me help!

When builders runs out of dough for their new home development (and they always do), they become motivated sellers. They can also get very motivated when their inventory of homes is too high, and they need to move on to the next phase to abide by the contracts they have with *their* lenders.

If you find such motivated builders, then you might consider doing business with them. (Oh, yes, we still want to stick to our rules of dealing only with Don't-Wanters, and if the builders are treating investors disrespectfully, move on.)

You can consider buying new construction under these circumstances:

1. *If* the homes are in an aggressively appreciating market❖, *and*
2. Generally, *if* you can buy in the earliest phases❖ of construction, *and*
3. *If* you can do it using OPM,

311

THEN a new home is one of the easiest ways to jump-start your investing career.

Here are the advantages to buying new construction, followed by the disadvantages:

Pros

- There isn't any negotiating. You decide if you want it, and you buy it!
- You can use your Realtor. It doesn't cost extra, and she represents your interests, plus it gives your Realtor a nice chunk of change as thanks for all those comps.
- Prices can appreciate in days, weeks, or months instead of years, even before it's built! The builders are artificially pushing up the price for you (and for them).
- New homes appreciate faster than older homes.
- You don't make payments until the home is built, giving you time to find a buyer or a renter. (Be cautious with builders who ask you for money during the building period. I won't say don't do the deal, but do very scrupulous research on the builders and the project.)

Cons

- The actual cash profit to you is deferred until the home is built.
- The investment is speculative❖.
- Someone has to qualify for the home loan right away.

So how would you decide if you wanted to buy it? You'll be turning to your old friend, the Bargain Finder. However, you'll tweak it a little bit to use with new construction.

Using the Bargain Finder with New Construction

Location. Make sure it's a 3 or going to become a 3. You'll avoid buying homes on a busy highway, near a sewage treatment plant, or twenty miles out of town.

Condition. Make sure it will be a 3 by asking your Realtor to identify which builders are good and which builders are naughty.

Price. Make sure it'll be a 3 by the time it's built by looking at the track history of the developer and the area. Are the prices going up by $10,000 every phase? Is land in the area going up? Price is driven by the price of land more than the cost of lumber and goods, so if you know that land prices are skyrocketing, that's a good sign.

Financing. Find a way to do it with OPM, so it rates a 3. I'm buying six homes in one state that will close in about ten months. They're going up by $10,000 per phase. By the time they close, there's every chance they'll be worth $50,000 more than I paid for each one. That'll be a nice $300,000 in the spring, if I sell them all. I bought them with 100 percent financing.

Flexibility. Find a builder who really is a Don't-Wanter because he needs more money to build more houses. When the builder says that you have to be the owner, or you can't sell for a year, or you have to pay triple what the owner-occupied buyer pays for earnest money, then just use my favorite four letter word: next!

Here Are Some Points for You to Remember with New Construction

- Remember that the model home has upgrades that will cost you extra, like tile floors, better carpet, window coverings, backyard landscaping, and fancy fixtures. I typically upgrade the carpet pad, the entry tile, and the garage door opener. Sometimes I'll also upgrade the kitchen tile, depending if the home is slightly above the median price range.

- Stay in the price range that is the easiest to rent or resell: $200 per month cash flow or better, 10 percent or better below market if flipping.
- Choose floor plans with good traffic flow, garage to side or back when possible.
- Avoid paying lot premiums❖ unless it's for an incredibly good positioning such as a spectacular view, abundant landscaping, true privacy, and so on.

Buying new homes isn't a strategy out of the original *Nothing Down* book. This technique is actually speculation❖, which is opposed to Robert Allen's view of investing. He believes you should make your profit on the day you buy the property, either because you know you've got so much equity you can flip it, or you've got a positive cash flow on the rental.

You see, with new construction, things could go wrong. The market could cool off. A bubble could burst. You could be caught with a home you can't sell and payments you can't make. Here's the simplest way to guard against that: Buy in a price range low enough that you can rent it out if you can't sell it. Prices will eventually go up again, and you'll have had someone else paying the mortgage all that time.

But even though you understand the hazards, the lure of this kind of investing is powerful. I know, because I've made millions using the new-home technique. I bought ten new properties one Memorial Day weekend (it was Duncan's birthday, so you know what I had to do!)

The problems of buying new construction compound if you're buying in a city other than your own. If you live in a place where prices are so high that you can't begin to dream of covering the mortgage with rents, you may be looking to other locations. Me? I'd be moving to a better investing city, but that's me.

So if you're buying out of state, please, please, please make sure you have a team in place. That's the real solution. You need a Realtor you truly trust, not a stranger, and she needs a team who will do your design choices, do your walk-throughs❖, help you sell or rent, and so forth. You also want someone who can accurately inform you about the demographics of the area, so you can speculate intelligently. You don't want to get there after all the investors have swooped up the good stuff; you want to get there *ahead* of the curve❖.

I've had students buying new construction in various cities tell me, "This is too easy. I want to do it the hard way." They had a different song to sing eight months later when they became asset millionaires!

I've put together a checklist for buying new construction. I hope you'll enjoy it and use it. It's an awful lot of fun to close on a house and sell it on the same day for a lot more than you paid for it!

If you are distressed by anything external, the pain is not due to the thing itself but to your own estimate of it; and this you have the power to revoke at any moment.

—MARCUS AURELIUS, ROMAN EMPEROR

Word Wizard

___ Aggressively Appreciating Market	Any market that is going up by 10 percent or more could be considered aggressive. California, Florida, and Nevada have seen appreciation as high as 30 percent to 50 percent in one year!
___ Phases	Builders only build a certain number of houses at a time; if they have eighty houses to build in the development, they might build them in eight phases of ten each.
___ Speculative	Not a sure thing.
___ Lot Premiums	Extra money added to the base price of a new home for its especially nice location.
___ Speculation	The act of buying based on some future predictions as opposed to current hard numbers.
___ Walk-throughs	Going through a new house just prior to closing so you can look for defects. There is typically a second walk-through after you've created a to-fix list for the builder.
___ Curve	The shape of a graph that's going up; "ahead of the curve" means ahead of the big appreciation and way before the decline of the graph.

315

Quiz Wizard

1. What are some things you should have if you're going to buy new construction?
    a. An aggressively appreciating market.
    b. A motivated seller.
    c. Access to properties in the earlier phases.
    d. A list of colors from the prospective renter.
    e. Access to other people's money.

2. What are some disadvantages of buying new construction?
    a. The investment is speculative.
    b. The houses don't close quickly.
    c. Someone has to qualify for the home loan right away.
    d. There's no landscaping.
    e. The actual cash profit to you is deferred until the home is built.

3. What parts of the Bargain Finder could you skip using to analyze new homes?
    a. Location.
    b. Condition.
    c. Price.
    d. Financing.
    e. Flexibility.
    f. None of the above.

Turn to page 437 for the answers.

Whiz Wizard

1. Go to www.ND4W.com/downloads and get the file called "New Construction Checklist" to read and to use. Then read it and use it!
    Done _____

2. Call your team Realtor and tell her you're interested in looking at some new construction. Even if you're in an area where you know you won't be buying, get out and look at some model homes. It's a

ton of fun! Ask the Realtor if there are any neighborhoods appreciating rapidly. Then ask if there are any neighborhoods in a price range low enough to make good rentals. Go see at least one neighborhood! Notice how they decorate the models!
Done _____

3. Teach the concept of new construction and out-of-state buying to someone else so that he or she understands it.
Done _____

5MM Time Capsule 8

5MM Module 8, Helpings 45–47

Here's your familiar checklist of what your three lessons included in module 8. Check off each item that you know you can easily explain to someone else! If you can't, then check back through the text. Use this list as an opportunity to review!

Helping 45:
___ Why Stinky Houses are potential gold mines.
___ How to figure out what the repairs on a property will cost.
___ How to use color to improve your property's salability or rentability.
___ Why you need to look up!
___ Techniques for looking past the stinky first impression to the stellar profits.

Helping 46:
___ How to keep from having to worry if your tenants don't pay on time.
___ How to find and keep wonderful tenants.
___ How to be a fearless landlord.
___ Why you won't ever have to go fix a toilet in the middle of the night.
___ How to get the rents coming in without your going to get them.

___ The three kinds of insurance every landlord needs to insist on for safety.

___ How to get over the worries of having to evict a tenant.

___ KNB's tips for smooth renting.

Helping 47:

___ Three things you absolutely must see before you buy new-construction homes.

___ Five advantages to buying new construction.

___ Three important disadvantages to buying new construction.

___ How to analyze whether the new construction you're looking at is a good deal or not.

___ Four reminders for better deals in new construction.

___ How to safeguard yourself from the dangers of speculation.

___ How to protect against a bursting bubble.

___ How to make your out-of-state investment work for you.

___ A checklist in outline form of the steps involved in buying new construction.

___ Why the people who worry about the bubble will be crying while you'll be buying.

We're nearing the finish line! Yippeeee! Hooray! Hoorah!

When you've checked off every item, you can get started on module 9 on getting those houses sold or rented faster than anyone else on the block!

Bobservations

My motto has always been: Make your money on the day you close. In other words, have your profit already built in. If you buy at a deep discount, your profit is there winking at you. If you buy with a low loan payment and high rents, your profit comes in from day one. Some people have argued that you don't really get your profit on the day you close. I understand that argument, and in truth, you get the money when you sell or rent the property. Some people even say you can't call your appreciation profit, because it's projected profit, not real money. I understand and don't disagree.

I simply want you to think in terms of getting a good deal. If you buy at a deep discount, then if you turned around the next day and sold, you'd have your profit.

With new construction, you have to wait and see. That's what speculating really is: waiting to see if your predictions come true. It's a much riskier style of investing than what I have always taught. We've seen a lot of beginning investors get themselves into trouble by not knowing the guidelines Karen has set out for you in this module.

I'm delighted for you to become wealthy by acquiring new construction, but please stay conservative by using your Bargain Finder as described here, so that you don't become one of the fatalities in a false run-up in prices due to dilettante investors' greed for instant gratification.

MODULE 9

FARMING

HELPING 48

Classy Classifieds

(Bright Ideas for Using Your Local Newspaper)

It doesn't matter how clever you are at finding a great deal and funding a great deal if you can't farm the great deal after you've acquired it. If you can't sell it to someone or rent it to someone, you'll become a Don't-Wanter as fast as you can say "mortgage payment."

I was never interested in marketing before, but I studied it with Robert Allen through the Protégé Program. I found out that it might be the most important element of good real-estate investing.

Once, I begged one of the other instructors (Denise Michaels) to just do it all for me, and she wisely refused, saying that I needed to understand what good marketing was, so that when I did hire someone, I'd know if he was doing a good job. Bob also taught me that when the marketing is a true reflection of your personal core values, it's much, much more effective. You know what? He's 100 percent right. In the process of learning how to do it, I came to enjoy it! Bob and Denise made it seem like so much fun!

There's one fundamental of farming or marketing so important, that if you were taking notes, I'd have you create one page with this one concept on it:

Test/Tweak

Test. Tweak. Test. Tweak. Test. Tweak. Test. Tweak. Test. Tweak.
Test. Tweak. Test. Tweak. Test. Tweak. Test. Tweak. Test. Tweak.
Test. Tweak. Test. Tweak. Test. Tweak. Test. Tweak. Test. Tweak.
Test. Tweak. Test. Tweak. Test. Tweak. Test. Tweak. Test. Tweak.
Test. Tweak. Test. Tweak. Test. Tweak. Test. Tweak. Test. Tweak.
Test. Tweak. Test. Tweak. Test. Tweak. Test. Tweak. Test. Tweak.
Test. Tweak. Test. Tweak. Test. Tweak. Test. Tweak. Test. Tweak.
Test. Tweak. Test. Tweak. Test. Tweak. Test. Tweak. Test. Tweak.

Fill up one whole page with test❖ and tweak❖, if that will help
you remember the concept. In marketing, you're never really finished. The world changes, and therefore so does marketing. All marketing really means is communicating to the *world,* but you'd better
think about reaching *one* person. It's the individual person who will
respond to your communication.

So test your marketing, see how it does, gather statistics, and if it's
not working to your liking, then tweak it here and there to see what
you can do to improve your results.

When you saw the chapter title, maybe you thought to yourself,
"Hmmmmm, I already know how to use a newspaper. What can I
possibly learn?"

I'm going to give you several bullet points, and you can use them
as you see fit. It might surprise you to see some fresh viewpoints on
the daily classifieds!

**Find Out How the Alphabetization Works, Then Use It to
Place Your Ad in the Top Ten.** You may think that alphabetization goes a, b, c, d, e, f, g, but it doesn't. It goes *0, 1,
2, 3, 4, 5, 6, 7, 8, 9,* a, b, c, d, e, f, g. In fact, in *my* newspaper,
it goes **! $ #* before the numbers! Find out what works in
your paper, and use that knowledge to place yourself at the
top of the list of ads in the section you're advertising in. If
it's a house in the northwest, let it read: "NW: ** Awesome
Bargain, . . ."

Place Your Ad in "Homes for Sale" and "Homes for Rent."
I double the number of people who see my ad over my
competitors by placing the home in both categories. If I

want to sell the house, naturally I put it under "Homes for Sale." But I also put it under "Homes for Rent" and say, "Rent to Own." If I want to rent it or lease it, I also advertise under "Homes for Sale," and once again I use the magic phrase "Rent to Own." That means double the traffic to my ad!

Use Short Ads. First of all, short ads are nicer on your pocketbook. Second, they force you to think concisely, and third, it's easier on the eye of the reader. Use short ads!

Have a Call to Action: "CALL NOW." I'm going to be talking about *them* and *they* a lot during this module. *They* are the people who do statistical analysis of marketing. *They* say that you should have a "call to action." In other words, tell your buyers what to do. It increases the effectiveness of your ad! And use ALL CAPS to tell them!

Use a Personal Name: "CALL KAREN NOW!" *They* say that using a personal name increases the rate of response. I also have heard *them* say that using a woman's name *doubles* the rate of response. Lucky for us!

Best Four-letter Word: FREE. If you're thinking, "Karen, I don't have anything to give away free," how about this: You could give away a free DVD player, and when the buyer or renter gives you her deposit, you can hustle on over to Costco and get the DVD player for $49.95. You can also offer free rent, meaning that the free month is the thirteenth month, if the tenant has paid on time. You can also give tenants free coupons good for $100 each to use any month they need help with the rent—but they can use them only if they've been paying on time! Another free item: Free prequalification for a loan. (Your team lender will be glad to help you, because he'll get the business.)

Run Your Ad for the Whole Week, Not Just Wednesday and Sunday. If you can afford it, it's good to run it the whole week. What if someone needs to buy or rent on Tuesday, and your ad isn't in there?

Use an Answering Service That Gives Callers All the Details and Then Directs Them to Your Website and Your Phone Number. I go back and forth on this idea, because I know that so many people are tired of navigating the instructions on complicated answering services only to end up getting disconnected or never finding a human. If you're friendly and like talking to people, you'll get a better response dealing personally. That's why the opposite recommendation is next:

Don't Use an Answering Service for marketing the property! Suzan Hudson says to *always* answer your phone, just because no one else does. She always makes the deal.

Use a Short Time Frame ("Must Sell This Weekend"). When you put urgency in the ad, it makes buyers think you're going to give them a good deal. And you are!

Use the Auction Technique. There's a book called *How to Sell Your Home in 5 Days,* by Bill Effros. It's an interesting book, and I've seen it work. Test. Tweak.

Advertise an Open House. Offer free refreshments, like lemonade and cookies. Everyone knows you can buy lemonade and cookies at the convenience store for ninety-nine cents, but doesn't it sound like a fun party?

Use Your Foreign-language Skills. If you have a second language, let everyone know! You can market to people who are dreaming of finding someone where they don't have to struggle with their English!

If You Use an Ad That Says You Buy Houses, Put "Extensive References." When you're advertising to capture pre-default and preforeclosure properties, use references. If you don't have any, use your CPA, your attorney, or join the Chamber of Commerce or the Better Business Bureau! Remember this sample ad:

"0 Stress, 0 Cost to You. Sell in 72 hours. Foreclosure OK. Can even help you move. Husband/Wife team in LV since '67. Extensive references avail. Call Karen now, 999-999-9999.

Use One of these Classic Ads:

- "I'll Give It Away Before She Gets It!"
- "Illness Forces Sale—I'm Sick and Tired of It!"
- "Butt Ugly"
- "Kick Me While I'm Down!"
- FREE HOUSE with Purchase of Lawn
- GARAGE SALE—House Included!

Give the Buyers a Great Deal. My favorite strategy is to buy low and sell low. If I can advertise that I'm selling at $15,000 below true market value, I'm going to sell very fast! Tell them about your great deal!

Avoid Using Jargon Like "OWC" or "FSBO," or even "Lease-Opt." This is another one of the most important lessons you can learn from this section. I remember teaching in Denver, and a student asked what *OWC* meant. One fellow said it meant "old world charm." The rest of the class told him it meant "owner will carry." He said, "Wow, you mean the owner will actually help me carry in all my boxes?" Now, if a student of real estate doesn't know what OWC means, what chance do your buyers have? A confused mind says no, so no fancy terms. Say: "Owner willing to finance privately"—or something else that says exactly what you mean.

TEST. TWEAK. TEST. TWEAK. TEST. TWEAK.

I have often found that there is nothing more flawed and unreliable than conventional wisdom.

—J. PAUL GETTY

Word Wizard

___ Test Try out your marketing and keep statistics on how well it does.

___ Tweak Change your marketing a little bit to see if you can improve it.

Quiz Wizard

1. What's the most important concept to remember in your marketing?
   a. Test.
   b. Tweak.
   c. Test and tweak.
   d. Test & tweak.
   e. Test/tweak.

2. What's the most important concept to remember in your print marketing?
   a. Use language the reader can understand.
   b. Don't use language the reader can't understand.
   c. Avoid jargon.
   d. Include pretty pictures.
   e. Who, what, where, when, why, and how.

3. What's the best four-letter word in marketing?
   a. Fear.
   b. Nice.
   c. Hope.
   d. New.
   e. Free.

Turn to page 437 for the answers.

Whiz Wizard

1. Go to your local classifieds and read the ads to see if you can figure out how the alphabetization works.
   Done _____

2. Call your local classifieds to ask if you can get a rate sheet. Ask if
   they charge by the word or by the line. Ask if you can get a business account to pay with. Ask if you can have one rep handle all
   your ads. When they ask if you're a Realtor, say no (unless you
   are); prices can be higher for professionals.
   Done _____

3. Teach the concept of farming and marketing with classifieds to
   someone else so that he or she understands it.
   Done _____

Fancy Schmancy
On-site Marketing

What the heck is on-site marketing anyway? It's the stuff you put on the front lawn and down the street! I thought *on-site* sounded fancy!

Once again, this lesson contains some fundamentals I hope will remain ringing in your ears for the rest of your investing career.

Use Huge *Bold* Legible Letters. There's nothing worse for buyers than having to get out of their cars in the rain, snow, sleet, hail, or heat in order to read the phone number on a sign, written in a pathetic little scrawl. Legible! Bold! Big! Readable! If you don't have nice sign-making skills, buy vinyl letters from Home Depot or Wal-Mart. Big black ones!

Use Multiple Signs. If you're old enough to remember the Burma Shave signs, you'll recall that the effectiveness was in the repetition. They placed several small signs along a stretch of road instead of one big sign. Each sign bore a line of a humorous rhyme, before ending in the product name.

One day I was driving south on Jones Boulevard, and I saw a cinder-block wall of a neighborhood with four brightly colored signs stuck in the backyard. I made a screeching U-turn and went down a cul-de-sac that I'd never seen in my thirty years in Vegas. The signs on the wall said, "For Sale by Owner," "4 Bedrooms," "3 Baths," and something else that I don't recall because I was in a hurry to get to the property.

The signs had been edged in Day-Glo paint, as if a party were just about to happen. The signs on the front lawn said the same thing, but there was one more: "Please. Take a flyer. Seller financing available."

Because of that one sign, several things happened. First, I became aware there was a flyer. I hadn't seen the container or realized there was something I could read. Second, I was invited to step on the land (I don't like trespassing). Third, I had been informed that maybe I could afford this house no matter how bad my credit was.

Use multiple signs!

Use Bright Colors. One time, I saw a FSBO sign that had been made to look like a professional real-estate sign. It was black and white, and it very discreetly informed me that the house was for sale by owner. I think I'm the only one who knew that it wasn't a regular deal. Buyers want to look for bargains, and FSBO signs need to scream, *"By Owner!"* Use colors that sell well (think Campbell's soup cans), like red, yellow, white, black. Don't use pink, lavender, or lime! Day-Glo works great (kids' finger-paint colors)!

Use a Container with Brochures in It. You can buy the signs at Home Depot or a sign store. They also sell several styles of containers for your brochures.

Also Place the Brochures Inside the Windows, Front and Back. For some reason, the brochures disappear fast. Maybe it's some buyer not wanting anyone else to find out about the property, so he takes them all. Maybe it's the neighborhood kids using them for scratch paper. Maybe it's a chronically competitive Realtor who doesn't want buyers to know about your property. Therefore, make them in black and white, but put a color copy of the front and the back in the front window. It means people will be able to see the price and the amenities, and when they call you, they already know they can afford it.

Use One Sign to Say "Please Take a Flyer." I really like the idea of one sign saying something about the flyer. It makes the buyer comfortable to come walking on your land. It helps you screen out people who aren't genuinely interested.

Handwritten Is Better. One time, Duncan made a huge four-by-eight-foot plywood sign to sell a house we had on a gravel road off a busy street. I told him, "Honey, that's the ugliest sign I ever saw!" The property sold in seventy-two hours! Handwritten (and legible) is better!

Learn the Signage Laws. Remember my multimillionaire investor friend, Tammy Billington from Phoenix? She doesn't even use the newspaper. She's a professional Realtor/investor/property manager, and she just puts signs out everywhere. But make sure you find out the signage laws in your district and follow them. Let's be the "other" investors, who do things according to the laws of the land! Tammy does, and it sure works for her. When we tried her method, we saw incredible results! Signs everywhere will do the trick for you too!

If you want to get rich, find something no one wants anymore and make it valuable by what you do to it.

—WALT DISNEY

Quiz Wizard

1. What's the most important concept to remember in your on-site marketing?
    - a. Artistic.
    - b. Attractive.
    - c. Legible.

       d. Unusual.

       e. Feminine.

2.   What are some effective on-site marketing tools? (Trick question, answers not all in the text. Put your thinking cap on!)

       a. Multiple signs.

       b. Wheelbarrows.

       c. Flyers in containers.

       d. Flower pots.

       e. Bright colors.

3.   Which is better?

       a. Handwritten and legible.

       b. Professional.

Turn to page 437 for the answers.

Whiz Wizard

1.   Go to Home Depot or Lowe's and buy a For Sale sign, a For Rent sign, and some black vinyl letters. You're going to need them pretty soon! OK, you don't have to actually pay for them and bring them home if you don't want to, but find out where they are and how much they cost!
Done _____

2.   Call a local sign shop to find out what it would cost to make up some signs with colored edges, sized like a regular Realtor's sign, saying "Take a Flyer" and "Seller Financing Available." You don't have to buy them, but find out if they're inexpensive in your area (like they are in mine).
Done _____

3.   Teach the concept of on-site marketing to someone else so that he or she understands it.
Done _____

Fabulous Flyers

For this lesson, I'd like for you to follow along with the sample flyer. You'll be collecting other people's flyers, and I'm sure you can tweak the sample out to be very attractive indeed, especially if you have any skills in computer graphics (which I don't). The sample will allow us to discuss some fundamental principles.

You'll notice that the flyer is two sided. You want to take advantage of all the space on the flyer that you couldn't take in your classified ad. You'll also notice that I've included several photos; in fact, the more the merrier. Remember, black and white for the flyer tube and color for inside the front window, so when prospective buyers (or competitive-minded Realtors, or kids with crayons) take the whole stack, you're still able to give the data!

Give Your Flyer a Headline and Put the Address at the Top. The buyer may be collecting flyers all weekend, and if she can't remember your address, she may forget you entirely.

UNIQUE HOME
FOR SALE OR RENT!

100 Lovely Home Road

Give the Buyer a Call to Action Right Away:

**MOVE IN TODAY TO THIS STUNNING HOME
WITH UNIQUE FEATURES**

Use Different Fonts, but not more than three or four. Use different sizes and thicknesses to break up the look.

CALL ME AT 555-555-5555 NOW TO ASK ABOUT HOW YOU CAN MOVE INTO THIS IMMACULATE HOME TODAY WITHOUT QUALIFYING AT A BANK. THE SELLER WILL FINANCE YOU EVEN IF YOUR CREDIT ISN'T PERFECT. (OR RENT: $1,485/MO, RENT TO OWN ALSO AVAILABLE.)

Give the Buyer the Price and Its Relationship to Comps. That way, you won't have to deal with people who can't afford it. They'll disqualify themselves. (See next page.)

ROBERT G. ALLEN AND KAREN NELSON BELL

OFFERED AT $219,900

($7,000 UNDER CURRENT MARKET VALUE)

Put Some Items into Boxes or Frames:

> - **The backyard is home to tons of mature, blooming, and graceful landscaping.**

> - **This beautiful waterfall and double lagoon create a private oasis in the middle of the desert.**

> - **The attention to detail extends around the sides of the house as well.**

Put the Features of the Home into Bullet Points, using descriptive language when possible or reasonable. They say you should use an odd number of bullet points for maximum response. I say they must have more time on their hands than I do. (See next page.)

Features:
- Three attractive bedrooms
- Two bathrooms with tiled floors and many upgrades
- Spectacular custom-designed waterfall and two lagoons
- Family room with great fireplace
- Ceiling fans
- Beautiful custom tiles (14x14 inches) in kitchen and family room
- Granite countertops in kitchen
- Luscious and no-sweat carefree desert landscaping, lots of mature plants in perfect condition
- 1,704 square feet of luxury living space
- Two-car garage finished with cabinets and built-in shelving
- Laundry room with almost-new washer and dryer
- Huge refrigerator and brand-new dishwasher
- Built in 1999—just THREE YEARS NEW!

- Close to a lovely park with walking trails
- Close to shopping, movies, golf course, schools, and library
- Remarkable appreciation in this popular, upscale neighborhood
- Meticulous miniature gardens in back

Finally, put a Call to Action that lets folks know you can help them move in even if they don't have perfect credit.

CALL ME RIGHT NOW AT 555-5555
TO SEE HOW YOU CAN MOVE IN TODAY!

Have some fun making your flyers eye-catching and appealing. Once you create one effective flyer, you can use it as a template for additional properties. Save each one as a separate computer file.

Enjoy letting your creativity run free! You can even use your scrapbooking skills if you happen to be talented in that area. I personally enjoy this particular handicraft, since it's the only one I seem to have any talent for. I know one woman who used her scrapbooking abilities to create charming envelopes to hang on the doorknobs of homes where she was marketing flyers. It gave the communication a look that was inviting and nonthreatening, and made the flyer much more likely to be read instead of tossed. You could use stamping techniques to provide interest and color without the expense of regular color printing.

Boys will be boys, but girls will be women.

—ANONYMOUS

Quiz Wizard

1.   How many bullets should you have on your flyer?
     a. An even number of bullets.
     b. An odd number of bullets.

2.   What are some effective flyer marketing tools?
     a. Multiple fonts.
     b. Different fonts for every paragraph.
     c. Photos.
     d. Bullet points.
     e. Flowery language.

3.   What data will you want to include on your flyer?
     a. Address.
     b. Price.

c. How to contact you.
d. Appealing features of the property.
e. Reason for selling.

Turn to page 437 for the answers.

Whiz Wizard

1. Using the sample flyer as a template, create a flyer for a house that you may have for sale or rent right now. If you don't have one on the market yet, write a flyer for the home you live in, even if you don't own it. If you live in an apartment, write a flyer for your dream home! You'll use it as a template for future flyers.
   Done _____

2. Get a copy of *The Ultimate Sales Letter* by Dan Kennedy from your public library or Amazon.com and check your own sales flyer against each chapter's primary points.
   Done _____

3. Teach the concept of flyers to someone else so that he or she understands it.
   Done _____

HELPING 51

Marketing Online

Almost a year ago, a student in one of my audiences, who also happened to be a Realtor, told me that they thought that in ten years there wouldn't be any more Realtors. He said that everything will be done on the internet. That's why he was taking the class on investing, because he felt he was headed toward involuntary retirement.

I don't agree that there won't be any Realtors, but I can certainly say that since the 1990s, the web has become vitally important for anyone doing any kind of real-estate business. Especially with the advent of virtual house tours—where a video camera takes you from room to room via the internet—people are more and more willing to purchase a property without ever seeing it.

Here are some points to help you on your path to internet marketing:

Get a Website Where You Can Display Your Properties. It has come to this: If you don't have a website, you won't be taken seriously as a professional. Even if you're not up on computers or savvy on the internet, you'll want to develop a loving relationship with these tools, because they allow communication, just like the phone. Remember the days before faxes and cell phones? How did we manage? There are many free ways to get a website, and I put my first one up in two hours. I did it without knowing much of anything. Let someone who loves doing all the website stuff help you! You can find free website templates by searching the internet or visit www.clicksitebuilder.com, or www.go-daddy.com.

Get a Digital Camera with a Wide Angle Lens So the Pictures Look the Most Spacious. If you look at beautiful pictures in the *Ladies' Home Journal,* you'll see practically the whole room. However, your own camera probably won't let you take in the entire space. That's because most cameras don't have extreme wide angle. At the very least, get yourself a digital camera, but if you want to take photos that really showcase your real estate, ask for interchangeable lenses with an extreme wide-angle lens.

Use the Services of a Company That Does Virtual Tours for FSBO Sellers. I found a company in my town that goes out and takes a ton of excellent photos for you and then mounts them on its own website. It was called www.vtpix. com. See if there's one in your area too.

Vmail. There's a new way of sending emails, and by the time this book is in your hands, I expect it will become the norm of how people communicate. It's called vmail, a new and easy way to send videos in an email that requires no downloading on the part of the receiver. I foresee vmail becoming a huge boon to real estate professionals in multiple ways. Imagine: (1) You can video the interior of your property and talk about all its best features and benefits, so that when an interested buyer or renter calls, you ask them, "May I send you an email?" Now they can visit the property without having to use up a tank of gas, and you can find out if they are seriously interested. (2) You can turn the video camera on yourself and explain seller financing or lease options in a way that allows the potential buyer to get a feel for your sincerity and credibility. I like vmail even better than the robotic "virtual tours," because it's so much more personal. For a business that depends on relationships and trust, vmail can't be beat. To learn more, you can visit www.ND4W.com/vmail. I've been using it awhile, and I even do my instant messaging with video!

Use Free Websites Like CraigsList.com or Others in Your Area. CraigsList.com started in San Francisco, and now it's all over the country, at least in the major cities. If it's in your town, great! You can list real estate there for free for ten days, and I also find people who can't afford ads in regular classifieds tend to post there. Are bargains lurking? The address is www.CraigsList.com.

Use eBay for Real Estate. In the past, I wouldn't have bothered to include this tip. Now eBay is one of the biggest sellers of real estate in the world! Treat yourself to a visit to eBay (http://pages.ebay.com/realestate) to check it out—you'll be very surprised! I have friends who market their properties only on eBay and do quite well! You can also use www.rentclicks.com and www.rent.com (an eBay site) to market rentals.

Use FSBO Websites. There are a gazillion FSBO websites, and many of them will do a deal with you to list your property on the Multiple Listing Service for a flat fee as well. We sold two properties from one ad on www.ForSaleBy Owner.com last year.

VistaPrint Does Email Replication of Your Biz Card. You can get an email replica of your business card to put at the bottom of all your emails so that everyone will know what you're up to. (You know how I love word of mouth.) Go to www.vistaprint.com.

Put a Signature File at the Bottom of All Your Emails Telling What You Do. This is the simplest free way to do a little internet marketing. Every email system has a way to put a signature file at the bottom of every email you send. Prowl around until you figure out how to do that, and let everyone know what you do with every email you send. As those emails get passed around, it will help you create a little bit of free marketing!

One of the nicest things about problems is that a good many of them do not exist except in our imagination.

—STEVE ALLEN, COMEDIAN

Quiz Wizard

1. Should you get a website to market properties now even if you don't have any properties to market yet?
   a. Yes.
   b. No.

2. Should you have a digital camera as soon as financially feasible?
   a. Yes.
   b. No.

3. What are some websites you'll be visiting this week?
   a. www.craigslist.com
   b. pages.ebay.com/realestate
   c. www.ForSaleByOwner.com
   d. www.vtpix.com
   e. www.clicksitebuilder.com or use www.google.com to search for other free site builders

Turn to page 437 for the answers.

Whiz Wizard

1. Sign up for a free website somewhere on the internet and put an hour into building your first page. By the way, I recommend that you sign up for your own name at www.godaddy.com or another vendor that sells domain names.
Done _____

2. Go to http://pages.ebay.com/realestate and look at ten properties. Print out a few ads that are well written, so that you can use them as inspiration when you're ready to sell on eBay!
Done _____

3. Teach the concept of online marketing to someone else so that he or she understands it.
Done _____

Will There Be Realtors a Decade from Now?

Some real-estate gurus teach that an investor should avoid working with Realtors. I guess they feel that their commission❖ erodes too much of the profit. Here's *my* take on using Realtors: They're professionals, and they get the job done. If I've got a property that doesn't seem to be moving fast with all my cool and groovy strategies, I send it over to my team member, whose job it is to know how to get that house sold.

You know what happens when I do that? It puts money in the pocket of one of my valued team members. You know we like putting money into our team members' pockets, right?!

Use a Realtor You've Developed a Relationship with, Who Is Part of Your Team. If you've been doing your action steps along the way, this is no problem for you. You already have a real team member who wants to help you. Give that person your business.

Use the Realtor Who Has Helped You to Buy the Property—Let Her Know You'll Let Her List It When You're

Ready to Sell. Your Realtor can help you decide whether to sell at full retail, and how long that might take, or to sell at a discount to get the job done in thirty days.

Remember, Realtors Are Professionals to Whom You're Delegating Part of the Workload So That You're Free to Do Deals! Some savvy investors I know don't do any marketing themselves. If you've bought well and have a deal that has plenty of equity in it, let someone else do the selling while you're busy buying!

Ask for Discounts after You've Done Some Business. This is trickier. You can't ask a brand-new Realtor with whom you have no track record for discounts. Realtors work very hard, and they deserve their pay for doing all the dirty work.

When can you ask for a discount? When you've demonstrated that you're going to be doing multiple deals with them. When you've brought them some of your other investor friends as contacts. When you know them well enough to know that the answer will probably be yes. A reasonable discount might be 1 percent. Remember, the Realtor can't say yes to your request if her broker won't let her.

But also remember, if you're really giving her a ton of business, she could surprise you. One Realtor gave me a listing for free as a thank-you for all the biz I brought her during the prior month. I only had to pay 3.5 percent to the listing Realtor❖. That's networking!

Ask If They'll Do the Realtor-as-Partner Technique where she makes more money if she carries her commission over time on an interest-only note. Show her this book and the section where it discusses Realtor as partner.

Here are some tips from one of my favorite Realtors, Brid'Jette Whaley. One of the reasons I'm such a fan is that she gave me my best month ever, when we sold several properties at one time, and I made $300,000 in one month. It was obviously a good month for her too! That was an incredible experience that I'll never forget! Brid'Jette suggests the following for dealing with real-estate professionals:

1. **Use Your Realtor to Help You Set Realistic Expectations.** In other words, let her help you decide what pricing is true and fair. When buying, let her help you understand what offers are likely to be accepted and why.

2. **Make Your Requests Considerate and Realistic.** When you ask a Realtor to make ten offers at 30 percent below market value, you're demonstrating a lack of consideration for her time and a lack of understanding of the way you get the deep discounts. There has to be a truly motivated seller on the other side to get a discounted property, so asking someone you've never had communication with to lower his price drastically is an insult to the seller. It also wastes the agent's time.

3. **Ask if You Can Get in Communication with the Seller.** This will work sometimes, and sometimes it just won't happen. I know that if I can talk to the seller, I can use all the strategies you've been learning to find out his or her real motivations, and I can construct an offer based on the communication. Make it clear that you don't want to go around the agents, you just want to talk to the seller with both of them present.

Remember the time I asked my Realtor, Brid'Jette, if I could speak to the seller we were working with? We had offered the seller her asking price of $500,000 for five acres of land, and she had turned down the offer because we wanted a ninety-day escrow, and she wanted thirty days.

When the escrow went sour with the buyer to whom she did say yes, she called Brid'Jette and said she'd sell me the property for $365,000 if I'd close in thirty days, all cash. I told Brid'Jette I still needed at least sixty days to do my research, and I instructed her to offer $400,000 and sixty days. The seller still said "no."

I finally asked Brid'Jette to see if I could talk to the lady. Brid'Jette tried to warn me that it was no use, but I was determined. We called the seller's Realtor together, and wow! I never spoke to such a rude person in my life! She told me unpleasantly and in no uncertain terms that I wasn't going to talk to the seller because the seller didn't want to be talked to, and that the terms were absolutely nonnegotiable. If you'll recall, I ended up with a $135,000 discount by *not* talking to the seller.

What's the moral of this story? Maybe there's more than one.

a. Trust what your good and faithful Realtor tells you.
b. Sometimes you can talk to the seller, and sometimes you can't.
c. You can get deep discounts when you work off what the seller needs, so let your Realtor do her job.

4. **Always Keep Your Relationship Honorable.** If you try to go around a real-estate agent, you can guarantee a bad reputation. It's a real no-no. We don't go around our agents. Period. I wanted to have this commandment read as "Never go around your Realtor," but that sounded negative—"never do this, never do that." So: Always keep your relationship honorable. Operating the enlightened way really will turn out to be the best business strategy there is!

In the beginner's mind there are many possibilities, but in the expert's mind there are few.

—SHUNRYU SUZUKI, ZEN TEACHER

(That's why I *love* teaching beginners, says KNB!)

Word Wizard

___ Commission
The money a Realtor takes as his fee for helping a client buy or sell a house; sometimes he does both, when he represents the buyer and the seller simultaneously.

___ Listing Realtor
The Realtor who represents the seller; some Realtors specialize in getting people to list their houses with them.

Quiz Wizard

1. Should a savvy real-estate investor bother with using Realtors?
   a. Yes.
   b. No.

2.   Should you always ask a Realtor for a discount?
     a. Yes, it means more profit to the bottom line.
     b. Yes, but only when you've developed a good relation-
         ship with the Realtor.

3.   What are some ways to work well with Realtors?
     a. Respect their time.
     b. Respect their advice.
     c. Bring them chocolate.
     d. Honor the relationship by not going around them.
     e. Introduce them to your friends, investors and otherwise.

Turn to page 437 for the answers.

Whiz Wizard

1.   Call up the Realtor on your team and ask her if you can take her
     to lunch, your treat. When you're at lunch, show her this helping
     and ask her to comment on it. Ask her if her broker would allow
     her to give you any discounts at some point in the future. If you
     haven't already done so, you can also show her the section on
     "Realtor as Partner" from module 7.
     Done _____

2.   Tell your Realtor that you have only eight helpings left in your in-
     vesting lessons, and you want to do a deal before you're finished.
     Ask her to help you find something in the following areas: new
     construction that's appreciating well, vacant homes with out-of-
     state owners, sellers willing to finance, lease-options, homes that
     have been on the market too long, listings that have recently ex-
     pired from the MLS. Tell the agent you'll also ask her to market
     the property when you're ready to sell it.
     Done _____

3.   Teach the concept of using Realtors to someone else so that he or
     she understands it.
     Done _____

Dress Your House for Success

Some of the things you find in this helping will seem so simple to you, you'll wonder why they needed to be in a lesson. Many women—not all, but many—are so good at creating and caring for a beautiful home that these lessons will only reinforce what you already do every day. For others, like myself (I'm orderly in my mind, but somewhat disorderly in my home), these ideas will seem fresh, logical, and easy to implement.

If you live in a market where it's hard to sell a property because the area is sluggish, or if you live in a market where it's hard to sell because the area is so *hot,* these strategies will give you that extra advantage over the seller down the block.

1. Make sure the house is 100 percent clean. Check under the sinks and behind the toilets.
2. Make sure it smells good; even put apple-pie potpourri on the stove. (*They* have discovered that apple pie is the single best smell for selling!)
3. Quick pickup: new wider baseboards, new switch plates, new handles and knobs, new light fixtures. Don't buy the

cream-colored switch plates, use pure white, as it looks cleaner.

4. Put the pets in contained areas. Even if the buyer says she loves dogs, put yours in a separate location during the visit.

5. Create the look that says, "We're happy, and we have leisure time." (A book open on a chair, a craft project in the laundry room). One expert investor went so far as to put a copy of *Paradise Found* on the chair along with a comfy throw blanket.

6. Remove all clutter. Make it as spare as possible. Think "model home."

7. Place a box of chocolates and a pitcher of lemonade in the kitchen.

8. Hide toys, toilet brushes, plungers, toothbrushes, medications, litter boxes, pet dishes.

9. Remove personal photos. People need to imagine their *own* belongings, so you want to depersonalize it from *your* stuff while simultaneously personalizing it as a wonderful environment.

10. Use feng shui to create a good aura: fruit bowl in kitchen and so forth. Check www.ND4W.com/fengshui to get some wonderful ideas from my personal feng shui adviser on applying this ancient Chinese tool to real estate.

11. Remove a piece of furniture—overly tight spaces are a turnoff.

12. Take down worn drapes; bare windows are better than worn-out furnishings.

13. Empty the closets by two-thirds to create a plenty-of-storage feel. Color coordinate the hanging clothes.

14. Line up the towels by their decorative bands. Some of you already do this. For those of us who don't, it will create the illusion that our lives could be orderly if we just bought this nice house with the towels all lined up.

15. Take small appliances off the kitchen counter. Reducing items triples the illusion of work space.

16. Reduce the inventory in the cabinets to make it seem roomier. Line up items with their labels out and grouped, like in the grocery store.

17. Take out the dining room table leaves and remove all but four chairs. Set an attractive dinner table for guests.

18. Paint where needed.
19. Add fresh flowers.
20. Play soft music.
21. Make sure the front door is sparkling clean with nice hardware.
22. Mow and fertilize the front yard. Special tip: Edge it for an extra-tidy look.
23. You can create a nice window treatment without spending big bucks by creating a valance and leaving the windows free of drapes or blinds.
24. Take doors off hinges. Did you ever notice that model homes have no doors on anything except the front, back, and garage? I've never had to do this, but if I were in a very, very difficult market, I'd sure try it!

Do you notice that the tips are slanted toward a home that you own and are trying to sell? When you're an investor, you'll often have a property that's empty. I believe you should create miniature "stages" upon which you subtly persuade the potential buyer that this home is happy, warm, tidy, and gracious. You're selling a lifestyle, not a house. You're creating emotions, unlike when *you* buy. You're selling the ideas of the benefits of living in this beautiful home.

Therefore, if the house is vacant, get yourself some items to make it look welcoming. The prospective buyer will know that no one really lives there, but it will have a homey look. Here are the things I keep and move from house to house when I'm selling. By the way, if the buyer wants the items left behind, no problem: I spent only $200 to $500 to market that property!

1. Wicker chair
2. Wicker table
3. Lamp
4. Book
5. Throw blanket
6. Silk plants
7. Silk flowers
8. Area rug
9. Cookbook on cookbook stand
10. Fancy oil bottles with designer flavorings inside
11. Candles (not lit—thinking of safety)
12. Bowl of candies or plate of cookies

13. Glass pitcher of lemonade (like Mama made)
14. Apple-pie potpourri
15. Fancy kitchen towels
16. Bathroom hand towels
17. Bathroom soaps in soap dish and matching tissue box
18. Throw pillows
19. Table and chairs for the buyers to sit and sign contracts
20. Plants in pots outside

For many women who enjoy interior design and homemaking, this step is a real pleasure. I confess this may be one of my favorite steps in the process. I love to paint, and I love to put on the loving touches. But I also love the part where they sign the contract!!!

Finally, remember that public relations❖ means *your relationship with the public!* Marketing❖, advertising❖, PR—it all comes down to your communications with other human beings. Applying the Golden Rule really works great; sellers do business with people they like, and buyers do business with people they like. Treat your buyers graciously, as if they were guests in the home and potential new friends. Every now and then, it will turn out that you indeed create a relationship that will last beyond the sale. Enjoy the fact that we're in the *people* business!

No one can possibly achieve any real and lasting success or "get rich" by being a conformist.

—J. PAUL GETTY

Word Wizard

___ Public Relations (PR)	Persuasive communication with other human beings; relations with the public.
___ Marketing	Persuasive communication with other human beings.
___ Advertising	Persuasive communication with other human beings.

Quiz Wizard

1. What are some ways to dress your house for success?
   a. Remove all clutter.
   b. Make sure the house is 100 percent clean.
   c. Put nice furniture in each room.
   d. Put photos of your family to create trust.
   e. Replace aging light fixtures and switch plates.

2. What are some items you could use to dress a vacant home?
   a. Wicker chair.
   b. Wrought-iron headboard for bed.
   c. Dining room table.
   d. Throw rug.
   e. Hand towels.

3. Overall, what's the most important part of marketing? (Kind of a trick question.)
   a. "Setting the stage."
   b. Expensive floral arrangements.
   c. Your communication and intention to help.
   d. Writing clever ads.
   e. Paying to have a great website created to show your properties.

Turn to page 437 for the answers.

Whiz Wizard

1. Call your Realtor and ask her to take you to a new construction site that has nice model homes. Stroll through every model and notice how the designers created the feeling of emotions for each one. Ask your Realtor if any of the homes would be a good buy for an investor looking for excellent appreciation during the building period. Enjoy!
   Done _____

2. Look in your local paper to see if there are any open houses. Go to a few and see if they used any of the strategies from this lesson.

If any are FSBOs, go through your scripts to see if there is a potential deal there for you.

Done _____

3. Teach the concept of dressing your house for success to someone else so that he or she understands it.

Done _____

5MM Time Capsule 9

5MM Module 9, Helpings 48–53

Here's your checklist of what your six lessons included in module 9. Check off each item that you know you can easily explain to someone else! If you can't, then check back through the text. Use this list as an opportunity to review to see how smart you've become!

Helping 48:
___ The single most important thing you can do to make your marketing the best it can be
___ Why the ABCs you learned in school aren't the same ABCs in marketing
___ How one strategy can double the amount of people who see your marketing
___ What a "call to action" is and why you need it
___ The best four-letter word in marketing
___ How to create instant "references"
___ How to avoid confusing your buyers

Helping 49:
___ How Burma Shave–type ads can work for you
___ How to make buyers feel safe at the front door
___ Why homemade is better than pro for on-site marketing

Helping 50:
___ How to create a flyer that creates sales
___ Where you can put your flyer to create a never-ending supply of data for the buyer

Helping 51:
___ How to get a free website for marketing your properties
___ How to market for free on the internet
___ Why eBay is the newest internet trend for big profits in real estate

Helping 52:
___ How you can use your Realtor to free up your time for more deals
___ How to get discounts worth thousands of dollars from your Realtor
___ Four secrets your Realtor wishes you knew
___ The golden rule of working with Realtors

Helping 53:
___ Twenty-four tips for quick sales
___ Twenty inexpensive things you can buy to help sell your home fast
___ What the true core of good marketing is

You've come quite an admirable distance in the fifty-three helpings. I hope you're suitably proud of yourself and your studies. I'm excited that you've made it this far, and you will, without any doubt whatsoever, make it the whole way through the materials!

When you've checked off every item, you can get started on module 10, in which you'll learn how to make $40,000 in less than ninety days using none of your own cash or credit!

Bobservations

We live in a world where marketing rules our existence to a larger degree than we would imagine or than we would necessarily like to believe. And since we're marketed to so pervasively, we seem to have become immune to much of the communications we're bombarded with daily. It takes more cleverness on the part of the marketers to pierce the barriers we've all put up to prevent marketing overload.

Whether you succeed in your real-estate investing career will depend not on the things you think it will. You believe you must master every technique in the catalogue to acquire properties. Yes, that will help you. Here are the two things that will really determine your success:

1. Your willingness and ability to market (both to acquire properties, and to sell or rent them)
2. Your mind-set

If you're good at getting deals but not good at selling or renting them, you'll eventually go under.

You're coming to the end of the how-to helpings in this book, so you're nearly ready to acquire some real estate! Make a pledge now to do whatever it takes. That's what Karen did. Whatever it took, she was willing to learn and willing to apply.

I can hardly wait to hear your story about how you bought your first house before you ever even finished *Nothing Down for Women*!
"I'll Do Whatever It Takes."

MODULE 10

FUN FINALE

$40,000 in Ninety Days, Step One

(Let's Do a Deal Together)

If you are reading this section out of sequence, please go back.
The information has been layered on the data from past helpings.
Please read this section after you've completed the others.

Ready to have some more fun?! Not only will you learn how to make $40,000 in ninety days or less without using your own cash or your own credit, in the next seven helpings you're going to learn a fundamental principle so powerful you'll never forget it. It's a principle that will make you the queen of *Nothing Down*!

I'm going to share a strategy with you that I learned from my mentor John Childers. He was one of the early *Nothing Down* experts who became one of Robert Allen's friends and business associates in the eighties. He's now a multi-multimillionaire who currently teaches seminars to people who want to become professional speakers. He was my real-estate teacher in the early days of my experiences with Robert Allen's Protege Program, and about a year after studying with John, I was honored to take over teaching his classes, along with my husband, Duncan. He and Bob's longtime friend Tom Painter were my first real-estate "professors."

Not only did John teach me this technique, he also taught me how to teach it to you, and he told me I could share it with you in this book. It has never been put into print before now. You are about to learn:

The Inosculation❖ of Funds

Now, you know that I like to clear up words so they don't confuse us. That's a whopper, isn't it? Inosculation. To inosculate❖. What in the world does that mean?! Here's what the dictionary says:

> in·os·cu·late, v. in·os·cu·lat·ed, in·os·cu·lat·ing,
> in·os·cu·lates. 1. To unite parts such as blood vessels,
> nerve fibers, or ducts by small openings; 2. To unite so as
> to be continuous; blend.

And what does that have to do with real estate? Well, I'm going to ask you to suspend your need for the answer to that question until helping 60. Now that you've heard the definition, just forget about it! It'll make sense to you when we're all done!

OK, here we go!

How would you like to do a real-estate deal with yours truly? Seriously.

If I Put Up All the Money, and You Do All the Work, Can We Split the Profits Fifty-fifty?

If there's any doubt in your mind that the answer should be yes, you need to go back and reread module 7.

By the way, do you care *where* I get the money? Frankly, I don't have enough cash sitting around to take care of millions of readers, so I'm going to have to use my normal strategies of using other people's money. Is that OK with you? I promise it will be legal, so you shouldn't care where I get it, right? I'm going to use everything I know about other people's money so that I can keep my part of the agreement to put up all the money.

Would You Come Out of Pocket $200 for Incidentals?

I don't want to be messing around with sending a lot of little checks all over the country. If you come up with $200, and you can get it paid back when we close, then it'll still be a *Nothing Down* deal. If you can't find $200, refer back to module 7 again and locate a friend who'll let you put it on her credit card, and then give her $400 in return. After all, you're going to ultimately make $40,000, so that should be totally fine, right? Right!

I need for you to sign a contract between us:

I, _____, DO HEREBY SWEAR THAT
I WILL DO EVERYTHING THAT KAREN TELLS ME TO
DO, EXACTLY THE WAY KAREN TELLS ME TO DO IT.
OTHERWISE, THE DEAL IS OFF.

SIGNED,

_____

(I tried to get Duncan to sign this contract, but he wouldn't do it! LOL!)

The reason for the contract is, John Childers and I have both have experience and know this deal inside and out. You don't. I need for you to just do it the way I'm going to lay it out and not add or subtract anything to it, OK? Later, when you've done a few deals using the Inosculation of Funds, then you can tweak it and do variations on it. For now, it's my way or the highway! OK? OK!

Here's the actual first step of the strategy. By the way, you'll notice I couldn't have taught it to you until now, because there are elements in this instruction that you wouldn't have been able to understand fifty-three lessons ago. In fact, if you've skipped ahead and are reading this out of order, I think you'll be frustrated.

Here's Step One: Find a Vacant FSBO Property Worth $200,000 That Rates a 12 or Higher. Not a Full Rehab Fixer-upper, not a Preforeclosure.

Fifty helpings ago, you may not have known what a FSBO is; you wouldn't have known why we want a vacant property; you wouldn't have known what a "12" is or why we want it; you wouldn't have thought about buying at $200,000 in the bell curve. You also may not have known what a rehab or a preforeclosure was.

By the way, if your city doesn't have any houses in the $200,000 range, go through this exercise as if it did, so you can understand the principle. Then apply it to the median-range price for your area. I picked that price because it makes the math easy to see. (Remember, I'm not very good with numbers.)

> *When I examine myself and my methods of thought, I come to the conclusion that the gift of fantasy has meant more to me than my talent for absorbing positive knowledge.*
>
> —ALBERT EINSTEIN

Word Wizard

___ Insoculation   The act of being inosculated, blended together to seem continuous.

___ Inosculate   To unite so as to be continuous; blend.

Quiz Wizard

1. What is the definition of "to inosculate"?
   a. To discombobulate.
   b. To procrastinate.
   c. To blend two things together so they seem to become continuous.
   d. To hyperventilate.
   e. To use a fifty-fifty partner.

2. Why would you want a vacant house for this deal?
   a. Chances are good the house is owned by a motivated seller.
   b. You could get into the property to do any minor fixing up necessary.
   c. You wouldn't want the owner to know what you were doing.

      d. Then you wouldn't have to move anybody's stuff out.

      e. Because Karen said so, and you have to do the deal her way.

3.   Why would you care if the property in this deal rated a 12 or higher on the Bargain Finder?

      a. Because Karen said so, and you have to do the deal her way.

      b. Because a 12 means the deal could possibly be a profitable one.

      c. Because there need to be twelve points in every inosculation.

      d. Because 12 is a lucky number.

      e. Because a 12-pointer would mean that women can do this deal better than men.

Turn to page 437 for the answers.

Whiz Wizard

1.   Look up *inosculate* in the dictionary for yourself. You can also go to www.dictionary.com.

    Done _____

2.   Look in your paper to see if there are any vacant FSBO properties in the $200,000 price range. If there aren't, look in some other cities' papers on line, just to see if you can find one. If you do, call up the owner and do a Bargain Finder to see if it might be a 12 or higher!

    Done _____

3.   Teach the concept of step one of the Inosculation of Funds to someone else so that he or she understands it.

    Done _____

$40,000 in Ninety Days, Step Two

(You Make the Offer)

Are you starting to get excited because you can sense that you're closer to $40,000? Excellent!

Before I give you step two, let's have a chat.

In your own hometown, if you offered one hundred FSBOs 100 percent of their asking price, how many of them would say yes?

Realistically, the answer should be "all of them." Maybe in a very hot area, some people might respond by saying 95 percent, because some sellers might want to wait for a bidding war, but generally the answer would be all of them. (This is a chat, not scientific research, by the way!)

Well, then, let's lower our offer. If you offered one hundred FSBOs 95 percent of their asking price, how many of them would say yes?

To tell you the truth, I don't have the right answer set in stone. I've heard everything from 75 percent to 95 percent. Realtors tell me that it's more likely to be 100 percent, because sellers generally start out at a price that allows them some wiggle room.

OK, what will happen if we go even lower? If you offered one hundred FSBOs 80 percent of their price, how many would say yes? Eighty percent? Fifty percent? Thirty percent? I don't know, but we can be pretty sure that it's a lot less the lower we go.

Now let's make an offer for a deep discount. If you offered one hundred FSBOs 70 percent of their asking price, what results will you get? Twenty percent? Ten percent? Five percent? One percent? How many do you need to say yes to get a deal? *One person!*

Do you get the impression that I'm saying we're purposefully reducing the amount of people in our funnel of possible sellers who we're going to do business with? Nod your head up and down! Yes! We want to do business with that person who is so motivated that we can get a really, really good deal! We need only one person to say yes!

I'm not going to ask you to make an offer at 70 percent, but I do want you to make an offer at 75 percent of market value.

Here's Step Two: Make an Offer at 25 Percent under Market Value.

So let's do just a little math: If you're buying a house valued at $200,000, how much will you offer? The answer is $150,000.

Let's have another chat. In your own hometown, if you were selling a house worth $200,000, and you advertised it at $10,000 under market value, could you sell it pretty quickly? In most places across America, the answer is yes! So that's what we're going to do. We're going to buy the house for $150,000 and sell it for $190,000.

How much profit is that for you?

Did you say $40,000?

Well, what about my fifty-fifty split? Can I trust you? LOL!

Your profit is $20,000. I know you were expecting $40,000, because that's what the chapter title said, but stick with me here. At the moment, your share is $20,000.

I guess we'd better move on to step three quickly.

An idea's worth is directly proportional to the opposition created.
—ROBERT TOWNSEND, FILMMAKER

Quiz Wizard

1. If you buy a house at $150,000 and sell it for $190,000, what is your profit?

    a. $40,000 if you don't have to split with your partner.

          b. $20,000 if you have to split with your partner.

          c. $20,000 on this deal, because Karen is your partner.

2.   Was I serious that I didn't trust you for the fifty-fifty split?

          a. Yes.

          b. No.

3.   What is step two of the Inosculation of Funds?

          a. Make an offer at $157,999.

          b. Make an offer at $149,997.

          c. Make an offer at 25 percent under market value.

          d. Make an offer at $150,000 (if the house is worth $200,000).

          e. Make an offer at 75 percent of market value.

Turn to page 437 for the answers.

Whiz Wizard

1.   Take out a calculator and run through this deal to show yourself the percentages. See what you would have to offer if the house were worth $300,000.

Done _____

2.   Look in your paper to see if there are any vacant FSBO properties in the $200,000 price range. If there aren't, look in some other cities' papers on line, just to see if you can find one. If you do, call up the owners and do a Bargain Finder to see if it might be a 12 or higher! (Isn't that the same Whiz Wizard step that was in the last lesson? Yes it is!)

Done _____

3.   Teach the concept of step two of the Inosculation of Funds to someone else so that he or she understands it.

Done _____

$40,000 in Ninety Days, Step Three

(Get the Contract)

This lesson is going to focus on the contract you're going to be entering into with your seller. I need you to put certain elements in the contract, and you'll recognize them from module 6.

1. I will authorize a ninety-day closing. You need as much time as you can get to do the deal. I could personally do the deal in fourteen days, but I want you to have every advantage, so get yourself a ninety-day escrow. There's one circumstance under which I'll allow you to do a sixty-day escrow: if you can't get one for ninety days! In fact, I'll authorize you to do a thirty-day escrow if you can't get a sixty-day escrow, but try to get all the time you possibly can!

2. Put your new last name on the line where your name goes. Where it says *Buyer*, put *"Your Name, and/or assigns."* If you have any questions on this step, check back to module 6.

3. Let's have another chat. In your hometown, what kind of earnest money would you typically have to put up in order to do this deal—$500? $1,000? $2,000? $5,000? All those answers are "correct." Instead of earnest money, I want

you to get the seller to agree that you will make improvements to the property as your earnest money. Realtors might balk at this, but a *motivated* seller likely won't. I did a deal one time where I had this clause, and I fixed up the place and moved in my renter before we ever even closed the escrow!

4.   Get the following lifeboat clauses:

    a. The Buyer will be allowed to inspect, repair, and show the property.
    b. This offer contingent upon the approval of my partner.
    c. This offer contingent upon suitable financing.

Who is your partner on this deal? KNB! Who does the financing need to be suitable to? Us!

If any of these clauses seem strange to you, please check back to module 6!

If the seller wants to know why you need to show the property, tell him you often have interested parties stop by even before you're finished with all the repairs, and you hope to sell the house quickly. Let him know that you intend to sell the house to make a profit. The owner is happy because he's motivated and is getting what he wants.

Step Three: Get the Contract! (As Outlined Above.)

Change is the law of life. And those who look only to the past and the present are certain to miss the future.

—JOHN F. KENNEDY

Quiz Wizard

1.   Why should you try to get a ninety-day closing?
    a. To give yourself enough time to do this deal.
    b. Because ninety days makes it more legal.
    c. Because Karen said so.

2.   What will you put in the space where your name goes on the contract?
  a. Your name, and/or some signs.
  b. Your name, and/or assigns.
  c. My name, and/or assigns.
  d. Karen Nelson Bell, Aries.

3.   What lifeboat clauses are pertinent to this deal?
  a. The buyer will be allowed to inspect, repair, and show the property.
  b. Subject to termite inspection.
  c. This offer contingent upon the approval of my partner.
  d. Subject to appraisal.
  e. This offer contingent upon suitable financing.

Turn to page 437 for the answers.

Whiz Wizard

1.   Take out one of your sample contracts and write up the deal with "Sally Seller" according to the guidelines above. Practice will make it much simpler when you get with your real seller.
  Done _____

2.   Call at least one FSBO every day and do a Bargain Finder. We're looking for deals for real now, aren't we?! If you get a live one and feel you need help, you can always go to www.ND4W.com and enroll in our mentoring program! Your phone mentors will help you through any steps you can't figure out on your own.
  Done _____

3.   Teach the concept of step three of the Inosculation of Funds to someone else so that he or she understands it.
  Done _____

$40,000 in Ninety Days, Step Four

(Fix It Up)

This lesson is about the fixing up you're going to have done to the house. This is where your $200 might come in.

Do the following fixing up:

1. **Fix the Front Door So That It's Very Nice.** The front door is to the house as eyes are to the soul. If the front door is shabby, buyers will perceive immediately and inevitably that the house is also shabby. If you have to paint it, paint it. If you have to change the hardware, change the hardware. If you have to replace the door, replace it.

I once had a student ask me if he could use the same door on the next deal too! Hmmmm, we did say we were going to uphold our personal integrity. I'll leave that one up to you!

2. **Paint the Front of the House.** With "oops" paint. Why are we going to paint only the front? Ladies, why do we put makeup only on the front? Curb appeal, of course! We're not going to lie to the buyer

about the paint, we just want the first impression to be perfect.

And what is oops paint? It's the paint you'll find at Home Depot or Lowe's or most paint stores over in a corner where they put paint that turned out the wrong color. Maybe Mrs. Adams got home and decided that she wanted navajo white instead of moonlit white, so she brought it back. The store marks it as mistake paint, and sometimes they write "oops" on the can.

What you're going to do is get every can of oops paint you can in every shade of "blah." That means everything from white to tan. Don't worry if it's indoor or outdoor, flat or shiny. Just buy all the ones you can find at great prices and get yourself a big trash can and a broom handle. Pour all the paint in and stir it up. That's your oops paint. Then you can save a one-gallon can for touch-ups, because the color will be changing every time you add more paint!

I painted an entire 5,000-square-foot seven-bedroom home for $40 worth of oops paint. The paint was worth $80 for a five-gallon tub, and I got it for $5 per container. I told you I was the frugal millionaire!

3. **Mow, Water, Fertilize, and Edge the Front Yard.** You'll notice I didn't say "mow the grass." What color are weeds? Green! Don't forget to edge. Remember module 9!

Step Four: Fix It Up.

Change is not merely necessary to life—It is life!
—ALVIN TOFFLER, AUTHOR

Quiz Wizard

1. Why should you be sure the front door looks great? (Trick question.)

    a. Because it tells the buyer what's on the inside.

    b. Because of ancient Chinese feng shui principles.
    c. Because Karen said so.

2.   What do you need for oops paint?
    a. A big trash bin.
    b. A broom handle.
    c. Mistake paint in off-white and beige.
    d. Mistake paint in black and red.
    e. Mistake paint in shades of blah.

3.   What should you do to make the front lawn look presentable?
    a. Put down sod.
    b. Water the foliage.
    c. Plant bushes.
    d. Mow the vegetation.
    e. Edge the lawn.

Turn to page 437 for the answers.

Whiz Wizard

1.   Go to your neighborhood sources for paint and find out if they have oops paint or paint by any other name that is essentially returned cans of mistake paint. Check out the prices.
Done _____

2.   Call at least one FSBO every day and do a Bargain Finder. We're looking for deals for real now, aren't we?! If you haven't found a yes yet, ask your Realtor to help you find something that's a good deal and then analyze it together with the Bargain Finder.
Done _____

3.   Teach the concept of step four of the Inosculation of Funds to someone else so that he or she understands it.
Done _____

$40,000 in Ninety Days, Step Five

(Best Way to Reduce Risk)

Because of my personality, people think I'm a risk taker. But I'm very conservative with my money. I hate losing money! I try to minimize risk at every opportunity.

This lesson is so important that I wish I could have taught it to you sooner. It's fundamental not only to the Inosculation of Funds but to your entire *Nothing Down* real-estate investing system. It's so important that I want to put it on one page, all by itself, in huge, bold letters.

Are you ready to find out this principle that is so important? I'm ready to tell you:

GET YOUR BUYERS FIRST!

That's right. If you have your buyers ready, there is almost no risk to real-estate investing. There's especially little risk if you have *more* than one buyer waiting in the wings. So your job from now on is to get your buyers list!

You didn't think I'd leave you with that advice and not tell you how to get a buyers list, did you? Let me tell you a story:

As you know, Duncan and I liked to give each other real estate for our birthdays, and one year we were in Garden Grove, California, for a special "Wealth Retreat" put on by the Protégé Program. It was my birthday weekend, so Duncan let me choose what we would do for our free time. I chose to go to some model homes so I could see what the styles were in Southern California.

We went to a lovely development, and as we walked into the sales office, we had to sign in. I said to Duncan, "Isn't it sad that ever since 9/11 the security is so tight that we have to be screened just to see a model home?"

Duncan said, "Karen, it isn't security, it's sales. They just want to keep your name and address so they can market to you."

So I pulled out my trusty electronic device and started copying down all the names on the list!

Duncan said, "Karen, stop! You can't do that!"

"Why not?"

"Uh, I don't know, but you just can't!"

Well, I'm not telling you to go take someone else's list, but let me ask you this: Do you live in a house? Could you put a sign in the yard that says "Open House"? If you don't have a house, do you have any friends with a house?

Here's another idea: Put a test ad in the newspaper, and when people call, get them into a conversation to find out what they're looking for. Take names and numbers.

Here's another idea: word of mouth! Didn't you just know I was going to say that?

Step Five: Get Your Buyer First!

When you get your buyers list going, then you call up the buyers who have indicated they would like this house at $190,000, and you say, "Hey Bonnie, I've got a house that seems to be what you're looking for. I'm going to show it on Wednesday at two—can you make it?"

Then you call up Sarah, and you say, "Hey Sarah, I've got a house that seems to be what you're looking for. I'm going to show it on Wednesday at two—can you make it?"

Are you getting the idea? They're all going to show up at the same time, and you're going to use auction mentality to put pressure on them.

"Bonnie, you were the first person on my list, so you have the first right to take this property. I've put all the comps on the table there, and I'm selling for $10,000 under market value, so you're definitely getting a great bargain. Take a look around, and if you want it, great. If not, Sarah gets the next right to say yes."

And so you show the beautiful home to as many buyers as you can get there at two o'clock on Wednesday!

"By the way, Sarah, since Bonnie wants the house, do you want me to put you down as a backup buyer in case anything goes wrong or she changes her mind?"

See how having a whole list is better than having one buyer?

Step Five: Get Your Buyer First!

If you have an apple, and I have an apple, and we exchange, then you and I each still have an apple. But if you have an idea, and I have an idea, and we exchange these ideas, then each one of us will have two ideas.

—GEORGE BERNARD SHAW, PLAYWRIGHT

Quiz Wizard

1. What's the best way to minimize your risk in real-estate investing?
   - a. Get your buyers first.
   - b. Get a buyers list first.
   - c. Get your buyer before you commit to the property.

2. How could you get a buyers list of your own?
   - a. Borrow it from someone else's list if you can.
   - b. Ask your Realtor for her buyers list. (Not!)
   - c. Hold an open house and take names and numbers.
   - d. Place a test ad.
   - e. Word of mouth.

3. What does KNB think is the most important safety feature in investing?
    a. Get your buyers first.
    b. Get a buyers list first.
    c. Get your buyer before you commit to the property.

Turn to page 437 for the answers.

Whiz Wizard

1. Call your team Realtor and ask her for ideas on how you could develop a buyers list.
    Done _____

2. Call at least one FSBO every day and do a Bargain Finder. We're looking for deals for real now, aren't we?! If you haven't found a yes yet, ask your Realtor to help you find something that's a good deal and then analyze it together with the Bargain Finder. Did you notice that this step is the exact same as it was in the last helping? Why? Because you want me to push you!
    Done _____

3. Teach the concept of step five of the Inosculation of Funds to someone else so that he or she understands it.
    Done _____

$40,000 in Ninety Days, Step Six

(Finish the Deal)

We're down to the last two steps, and I'm asking you to hang in with me and stay focused, OK? Great! This lesson goes over your instructions on how we're going to finish this deal.

You're buying a house from Sandy Seller and you're selling the house to Bonnie Buyer. They don't know each other, but they know each other exists. You're buying from Sandy for $150,000 and selling to Bonnie for $190,000. Sandy understands that you're selling the house for a profit, and Bonnie understands that you bought the house for less than you're selling it for. Everyone is happy, though, because Sandy got what she needed, and Bonnie got a $10,000 discount! You and I are happy because we're going to split $40,000!

Here are the individual steps you'll take on step six:

1. **Find a Title Company (Escrow Company or Attorney) Who Can Close Two Deals on One House in the Same Day—One to Buy, One to Sell.** Actually, I've never used a title company that couldn't close two deals like that, but just in case you find one that can't do it, use our favorite four-letter word: next.

By the way, don't call the transaction anything special, like "double close"❖ or "simultaneous close,"❖ or certainly not "Inosculation of Funds." John Childers made up that phrase, so I'm darn sure no one at the title company will know what you're talking about!

2. **Close on the Property. Close with Seller in Morning. Close with Buyer in Afternoon.** Call up Sandy and say, "Sandy, I'm ready to close on the deal now, so can you come over to the title company tomorrow morning around ten? We'll sign all the papers, and then you can pick up your check in a few days when the title officer has it ready."

Call up Bonnie and say, "Bonnie, I'm ready to close on the deal now, so can you come over to the title company tomorrow afternoon around one? We'll sign all the papers, and as soon as it funds, you'll be the proud owner of a great new home! By the way, your lender sent over the instructions for funding, so all you have to do is bring in the cashier's check for the down payment. See you tomorrow!"

Your escrow officer or your attorney (if you live on the East Coast) will know how to do the jigsaw puzzle of all the paperwork.

3. **Put in a "Letter of Demand." Request $20,000 for You and $20,000 for Karen. Instruct the Title Company to Send Me My Check for $20,000.** This is my favorite part! The part where you put in the letter of demand! That's what you do in order for us to get our money. Ask the escrow officer if he has any special forms for the letter of demand. If he does, he'll fax it to you. If not, just write up a letter and say that $20,000 goes to you and $20,000 goes to me! Yea!

What's that?

You say something doesn't make sense? Something's wrong here?

You say you can't figure out what Karen Nelson Bell actually did in order to earn her $20,000? You say I didn't use my money the way we talked about?

Sure I did! You said you didn't care where the money came from, remember?

Where *did* the money come from?

Oh, yeah, Bonnie brought in her cashier's check for the down payment.

Yes, I know I didn't use my credit. I didn't need to, because Bonnie came in with her loan, and that provided the rest of the money needed, right? You said you didn't care where the money came from.

I told you I was going to use other people's money, didn't I? I used Bonnie's money and her lender's money.

OK, let me tell you the secret of what just happened here. Actually, I'm going to make you wait until the next helping!

How's that for a cliff-hanger? See you on helping 60!

Step Six: Close the Deals with Your Buyer and with Your Seller, and Put in a Letter of Demand So That We Can Enjoy Our Profits!

My imagination creates my reality.
—WALT DISNEY

Word Wizard

___ Double Close	Two escrow closings that take place very close together in time.
___ Simultaneous Close	Two escrow closings that take place at the same time.

Quiz Wizard

1. What should you tell the escrow officer you'd like to do?
   a. A double close.
   b. A simultaneous close.
   c. An Inosculation of Funds.
   d. Buy the property from your seller and sell the property to your buyer on the same day.
   e. Go to lunch to celebrate.

2. What is a letter of demand?
    a. A letter of instructions to the escrow officer.
    b. A letter to your ex-husband.
    c. A letter to me for my $20,000.

3. Where did the OPM for this deal come from?
    a. Your pocket.
    b. My pocket.
    c. Bonnie's pocket.
    d. Bonnie's lender.
    e. It's a mystery.

Turn to page 437 for the answers.

Whiz Wizard

1. Call your team escrow-closing person and ask if he could close on your deal with your buyer and your deal with your seller on the same day.
    Done _____

2. Call at least one FSBO every day and do a Bargain Finder. We're looking for deals for real now, aren't we?! If you haven't found a yes yet, ask your Realtor to help you find something that's a good deal and then analyze it together with the Bargain Finder. Do you recognize this Whiz Wizard from the last two helpings?
    Done _____

3. Teach the concept of step six of the Inosculation of Funds to someone else so that he or she understands it.
    Done _____

$40,000 in Ninety Days, Step Seven

(What Did You Really Need?)

You're aware that something odd happened in the last lesson, right? You're wondering why you should send me a check for $20,000 when I "didn't do anything."

Guess what? You're right about one thing: You didn't need my money and you didn't need my credit.

If you didn't need my money, what *did* you need?

You needed my knowledge!

I confess that I played one small loving trick on your subconscious. When I told you that I would come up with all the money, didn't that free you up? Didn't you feel a certain kind of relief that you were going to do this deal without having to find your own money? I needed for you to be immersed in the comfort of only having to find a great deal, so that you could see the mechanics of what it means to have no need for your own cash or your own credit. Now you know the secret that I'm not really going to be your business partner, but that I was using this mental exercise to help you immerse yourself in the delicious feeling of not worrying about having your own cash or credit!

And, oh yes, since I did not in fact bring the money personally, I am going to wipe out your obligation to pay me $20,000, so you just made all $40,000 for yourself, just like I described in the beginning of this module.

Do you see how we inosculated two deals to merge into one continuous deal? Now does the definition make some sense to you?

Please notice that you now actually, really, and truly do know how to make $40,000 without any of your own cash or credit, and it isn't a play on words, it's a real, true technique you're never going to forget. And what is the key element? It's the element I want you to remember for the rest of your investing career:

Fundamental Truth: Your *Buyer* Can Supply All the Elements That *You* Don't Have!

Step Seven: Enjoy the Aha That You *Really* Do Know How to Make Money with No Cash and No Credit of Your Own!

Here's a list of the seven steps you've learned:

1. Find a vacant FSBO property worth $200,000 that rates a 12 or higher.
2. Make an offer at 25 percent under market value.
3. Get the contract.
4. Fix it up.
5. Get your buyers first!
6. Close the deals with your buyer and with your seller, and put in a letter of demand so that "we" can enjoy "our" profits!
7. Enjoy the fact that you now know how to make money with no cash or credit of your own!

I Love You.
  —KAREN NELSON BELL

Quiz Wizard

1. What did you need from me?
   - a. Cash.
   - b. Immersive training.
   - c. Credit.
   - d. Time.
   - e. Knowledge.

2. What is the fundamental truth you learned from the Inosculation of Funds?
   - a. Karen is pretty clever and a little tricky.
   - b. Your buyer can supply the elements you need.
   - c. John Childers must be some kind of genius.

3. Do you really, *really* know how to do a deal with no cash or credit of your own now?
   - a. Yes.
   - b. Yes.

Turn to page 437 for the answers.

Whiz Wizard

1. The most important action step for you right this minute is to *go into action!* You know all the strategies you need to get started, and by now you should have a pretty high level of confidence. If you haven't already got a yes on a deal, write up your pledge to do one specific action every day until you get your yes.
   Done _____

2. To really cement the Inosculation of Funds and its lovely conceptual advantages in your mind, teach it to someone you love. Share your aha with them. Please don't gloss over this step, as it will help you keep this strategy and its fundamental concepts vibrant in your awareness for all your future investing.
   Done _____

3. Continue to use the various strategies in these sixty helpings every day. Reexamine your goals from helping 10 and see if they're the same now.
    Done _____

5MM Time Capsule 10

5MM Module 10, Helpings 54–60

Here's your checklist of what your seven helpings included in module 10. Check off each item that you know you can easily explain to someone else! If you can't, then check back through the text. Use this list as an opportunity to review to see how smart you've become!

OK, now here's the list of what you've learned. With the completion of this list, you graduate!

Helping 54:
___ What the Inosculation of Funds means.
___ How you can earn the right to do a fifty-fifty deal with me.
___ The first step toward making $40,000 in ninety days or less without your own cash or credit.

Helping 55:
___ What percentage of the population will eagerly work with you.
___ The second step toward making $40,000 in ninety days or less without your own cash or credit.

Helping 56:

___ How to reduce the amount of earnest money you have to pay down to $200 or less.

___ What safety clauses you need to do the Inosculation of Funds.

___ The third step toward making $40,000 in ninety days or less without your own cash or credit.

Helping 57:

___ How to get your house painted at a 90 percent discount.

___ Exactly what to fix up if you haven't got much money for repairs.

___ The fourth step toward making $40,000 in ninety days or less without your own cash or credit.

Helping 58:

___ The single most important way to reduce risk in all real-estate investing.

___ How to use that single most important strategy to your best advantage.

___ The fifth step toward making $40,000 in ninety days or less without your own cash or credit.

Helping 59:

___ How to get your money by using a letter of demand.

___ How come you didn't need your own cash or credit to make your $40,000.

___ The sixth step toward making $40,000 in ninety days or less without your own cash or credit.

Helping 60:

___ The single biggest fundamental secret of how to invest with no cash or credit that will work with many strategies.

___ The seventh step toward making $40,000 in ninety days or less without your own cash or credit.

___ What you need even more than money.

You've come quite an admirable distance in these ten modules. I hope you're suitably proud of yourself and your studies. I'm excited that you've made it this far, and you can, without any doubt whatsoever, make it the whole distance to real-estate investor!

I can hardly believe we're at the end of the how-to section, can you? You actually have the steps you need to get started, and the confidence to take the steps over and over again!

If you're working with me in our mentoring program, you'll have a graduation step with a very valuable rewards package. Congratulations!!!!!

Love,
KNB

Bobservations

With the completion of this module, you've learned enough powerful fundamentals to begin investing. It's possible that you've already had someone accept your offer to purchase that first property. Is this everything you'll ever need to know about real estate? No. But it's everything you need to know to get started.

We've delivered the data in a way that you can remember basic concepts. When you need help, you can always return to the helpings, but now they'll be snacks you can nibble on when you feel the need.

Take a "win" on making it this far. You now know more about real-estate investing than the vast majority of America. You're in an elite group of women who have the skills needed to build a financial future beyond the dreams of most, whether male or female.

You may or may not believe me, but I love you. If that seems an odd thing for me to say to someone I haven't met, let me explain why: I respect and honor you for the commitment you made to finish this book. I believe that the time has come for women to ascend to their rightful altitude in this world. I've been around women all my life, and I've been deeply influenced by their strength and love. You have power and innate wisdom, and even when you momentarily forget that you do, you still persist to survive. You deserve to be empowered. Look at all you've done to empower your mates, your children, your friends. Yes, I love you.

HOW TO TURN THIS BOOK INTO YOUR SKYROCKET TO WEALTH

What the Late-Night Gurus
Won't Tell You

First and foremost, they won't tell you that it will take energy on your part.

Typically, they'd like you to believe that your pot of gold lies one hundred yards away, and it's yours if you will only shift the way you think and send them a check. The gurus seldom emphasize the amount of elbow grease that will be required to lift the pot of gold into your own private safe.

Additionally, most get-rich-quick teachers will speak in a negative tone about get-rich-quick schemes, declaring that theirs is no such thing. But they won't tell you that the process of becoming truly wealthy could take you months or years of forming new habits. Yes, Duncan and I became millionaires in 129 days, *but*, and it's a huge *but*, we still didn't have enough cash on hand every month to get by. We struggled to pay every bill, even though we had a $1 million net worth on paper.

As you know, we felt so embarrassingly incongruent when people would congratulate us on our speedy success, and we knew secretly that each month was an exhilarating challenge to meet the demands of the bill collector. Was the experience worth it? Yes, a million times over. We were building our future passive streams of income. It was on paper, and we couldn't spend it, but what better place for your future money to be?!

The Game Is "How Good Can It Get?"

Most people end up spending their nest egg when they need it desperately, and then it isn't there for their future. Why not save it where you *can't* get it very easily?! It took us a full seventeen months to get to a point where our passive cash flow exceeded our bills, and even then, it was modest. We "retired" for a week to prove to ourselves we could, but retiring on $1,000 a month meant that we would be living a poverty lifestyle. When we "un-retired," we knew that the game was then to find out just how good a retirement you could create for yourself.

Learn to Love Hearing "No"

Another thing that TV salesmen won't emphasize is that you may stumble and fall before you soar off into the horizon. You might actually experience disappointments and failures along the way. Bob says you have to make at least one hundred offers before you can be discouraged at not getting a yes. Frankly, I got yesses to a whole handful of offers. Your experience may fall somewhere in between those two extremes. The main thing to remember is that every no puts you that much closer to your first yes. Surround yourself with the great team you will have built while reading this book, and the team will help pick you up when you get discouraged or when something doesn't go exactly the way you planned.

You May Have to Push Past Some Barriers

Sellers can lie, lenders can disappoint you, and houses can turn out to have problems nobody ever anticipated. You need to hear that. Then you need to hear that through all the frustrations I've experienced, the benefits have overridden the barriers. Remember that the times when I goofed were the times when I didn't take Bob's advice (like "buy within a fifty-mile radius of your home," and "buy within the price range that normal people can afford").

The Perpetual Professional Student

Another very, very interesting thing that seminar speakers generally gloss over is the fact that you'll very likely have to continue spending more money on your continuing education if you want to be fully, completely trained in any subject. My parents probably spent more than $100,000 for my college education, which didn't prepare me at all to make a living. I don't regret the education, as it served me in many other ways, but it sure as heck didn't train me to make money. Then, thank goodness, I signed up for a $4,000 program that turned me into a millionaire. I just need to let you know that I spent another $100,000 over the next few years, studying anything and everything that resonated for me, seeking to expand my abilities to create abundance. Actually, I expect to continue my education for the rest of my life, and now, instead of being labeled a "professional student" with the pejorative connotation of sloth in tackling the real world, I'm labeled a success.

The seminar industry has more to offer me than my college education did in terms of how to make my life work out the way I want it to. I can study real estate, I can study how to keep myself motivated, I can study internet marketing, I can study—well, the list goes on and on. And my teachers aren't sitting in an ivory tower talking theory, they're people who succeeded in their field and now show others how to walk in their footsteps.

I love it! Am I a seminar junky? No, because that term refers to a person who attends seminar after seminar, waiting for something to click. I consider myself a "professional seminar student," because I won't sit around waiting for something to happen, I'd rather go out and apply what I've learned to see if it really works. Take what you're learning from any mentor and *apply* it. Let's get into *action!*

I've saved the most important point for last: What late-night TV gurus won't tell you is that $1 million won't be enough.

It's such an important point that I'm going to give you a whole segment on this topic alone!

A Million Isn't Enough

You might be thinking to yourself, "Hmmmm, by the time I reach retirement age, $1 million won't take me very far. Even if I'm getting 4 percent interest in a safe investment, who'll be able to live on less than $3,400 a month twenty years from now? That will be poverty level by then."

The people who are considered fabulously wealthy today are the billionaires. Being a millionaire is almost common. Did you know that there are 161 new millionaires every day in the United States?

We need a new term. Multimillionaire won't be quite good enough either. Having a few million lying around will be nice, but if you want to have a comfortable retirement for you and your family, let's start talking in terms of megamillionaire.

A megamillionaire will have a net worth of at least $100 million. That's my new definition, and that's the new standard for goal setting. Let's set our sites to become megamillionaires, and in another twenty years, that won't even seem outrageous to you.

When Napoleon Hill wrote *Think and Grow Rich* in 1937, $1 million was a real $1 million. In today's dollars, it would compare to one hundred times that, $100,000,000.

Megamillionaires

Why am I telling you this? Is it just to depress you? You don't have $1 million net worth yet; maybe you even have a negative net worth. Why should you worry about becoming a megamillionaire when you can hardly bring the picture of $100,000 into focus?

I'm telling you this because most late-night TV gurus won't. You deserve to hear the truth. When I first became a millionaire, it was in equity. It was on paper. It felt great, but it hadn't changed my lifestyle yet. And I was happy to leave it on paper, because I was building for the day when it *would* make a change in my lifestyle.

Here's what I think you should do as you begin to form your goals: For every house you buy to turn around and sell, buy one to keep. Build your future passive income at the same time as you make those cash dollars from buying and selling. Then in your second year, every time you buy one to sell, buy *two* to keep. Year three, buy *three* to keep for every one you sell.

What I'm recommending here is a case of "Do as I say, not as I did." I concentrated solely on *keeping* properties, and in the first five years I only sold five properties total! Are you surprised?

As you move determinedly forward to become a "state of the art" investor, always remember what you learned in these pages: that it's even better to be a "state of the heart" investor!

We Believe in You

Don't worry if you don't believe in yourself. I believe in you enough for both of us. Bob and I want you to start now to build for that beautiful time in your future when you are a *megamillionaire,* and your passive income gives you the strength to care for yourself and your family with such ease and grace that you'll be seeking ways to pay it forward out into your community, out into the world. I see you on our team. We're ready when you are!

State of the heart wins over state of the art every time.

—KAREN NELSON BELL

Turning Naysayers into Yeasayers

You may have naysayers in your life who will tell you all the reasons why you can't invest in real estate and make it work. They'll tell you all the reasons why you can't do any number of positive things, because if you do go out and accomplish something good, it will constantly remind them that *they* did *not*.

You might think that the worst person to have as your naysayer is your spouse or partner, but it's even worse when the naysayer is *you*!

Here are some negative things your naysayers may tell you about the *Nothing Down* style of investing. I've culled them from articles in money magazines and websites that purport to protect you. It's very difficult to sort out the truth, and ultimately you'll have to observe your own results and decide for yourself. In the meantime, I'm going to share my own responses with you to use if you feel the need to defend your new adventure. (The best response will be to survive, thrive, and prosper!)

Nothing Down investing doesn't work. It won't work for you.

First, I believe there is simply confusion about the term. In my world, the term means acquiring property by using other people's resources. For some people, it means acquiring property with 100 percent financing. Borrowing money to acquire assets. That's what we're talking about here.

Even the loudest critics, if they are knowledgeable, will have to admit that there's nothing intrinsically wrong with buying real estate by borrowing the resources to do so. In fact, investors have been buying property for nothing down for a very long time. It wasn't until Robert Allen came on the scene and gave it the name *Nothing Down* that it became controversial. But there's really nothing controversial about leveraging resources to get what you want!

Critics typically say that testimonies from *Nothing Down* investors are lies, but there are thousands of students who can tell you their stories. Once you've seen some testimonials, you *still* have to go into action and apply the strategies *yourself.* Does everyone succeed? Of course not. But those who do succeed are willing. Not everyone is willing to take action and commit to persist. Here's an idea: wait until you have your *own* testimonial to tell your *own* naysayers.

Nothing Down investing takes advantage of people, especially people in trouble.

I personally think this criticism is fair. I've seen investors use these powerful strategies to become rich at the expense of others. As I lay out the fundamental rules for my style of *Nothing Down* investing, I urge you to please follow the commandment that says "Never harm another in a real-estate deal." The techniques you're learning will give you knowledge that will put you in a high stratosphere compared to uninitiated home owners. With the power of your knowledge will come the responsibility to use it sagely, with compassion and integrity. You can use it for powerful good as well. You'll never go wrong helping someone out. You'll always go right by making sure everyone wins.

Nothing Down investing only puts money in the pockets of the seminar gurus and not yours.

I've been a student, and now I'm a teacher. I do make a living by writing and training. I believe in multiple streams of income, especially since Bob's book with that title changed my life. I work in three areas: real-estate investing, public speaking and writing, and entertainment. I can't imagine having to defend the fact that I work hard for my living and that I have multiple interests.

The real problem revolves around the issue of whether the *student* will make any profit. Whether *you* will make any profit. I'm going to do my best to show you clearly how to maximize the probability of profit. Together we can prove whether or not this concern is real.

If the teacher is so rich, why are they working at selling you information?

This is a good question, in my view. My own personal answer is that I'm not one of the big boys—you didn't know me until you picked up this book. I don't know any woman who would chastise me for continuing to build a strong, safe retirement. I'm trying to build as good a future for myself as I can so that I can do as much good all around as I can. Yes, good for myself, but good for my family and friends, good for my community, good for my fellow humans.

Imagine telling Oprah she should stop now because she's got enough. The game for me is to see just how good it can get and how much good I can do. I hope one day you'll come to know me by my actions.

Nothing Down teachers won't tell you their mistakes.

Oops, I already told you about the Idaho debacle and you heard about my "big house" booboo too. There's no hiding. If you want to read about my mistakes (and learn from them like I did), go to www.ND4W.com/nonos.

Karen Nelson Bell is just a glorified piano player with no background in real estate.

Guilty. I had zero training for this job. The world of arts and enter-tainment is three planets away from the world of finance. I still find strategies that are new to me, and if I tried to tell you I know every-thing there is to know, I'd make a fool out of myself. Maybe that's why some people like learning from me, because they get the feel-ing that if KNB can do it, surely they can do it too. I don't have a degree in real estate, I'm not a licensed real-estate agent, and I'm not setting myself up as the expert of all experts.

The one thing I'm an expert in is how *I* did it. And every day, I'm expanding what I know, so that I can keep on my toes as an investor and as your teacher. Obviously, I invest part-time. You can't invest full-time if you're also making TV shows and speaking at seminars. Here's the problem that's followed me all my life: I'm too interested in too many things. Maybe you are too. Maybe you'll decide to invest part-time, and maybe you'll fall in love with it and go all the way. Isn't it nice to know that someone you know (me) became a multimillionaire by doing this part-time?

Maybe I'll end up going to *your* seminar someday. That wouldn't be any wilder than the fact that this piano player is writing this book! And even though I might be your first teacher, I doubt that I'll be your last!

You're going to change into a greedy fat cat, obsessed with material possessions.

Well, you may indeed change, but as Bob says, "Money just makes you more of who you are to begin with." If you're already greedy and obsessed with keeping up with the Joneses, that characteristic could increase. If you already think about taking care of everyone around you, that characteristic could be amplified as well. This one is up to you. May I suggest that you use your spiritual or religious foundation to help you keep the perspective you want for yourself. If you don't want to become something undesirable, you don't have to. Pray on it, meditate on it, dream on it, and keep your abundance in line with the integrity of your convictions.

Those who say it cannot be done shouldn't interrupt the people doing it.
—BUMPER STICKER

The Simple Secret
of Speed Shopping

When people ask me how it all happened so fast for me, how the real-estate business turned me and my husband into millionaires in such a short time, my immediate answer is one word: *action.*

Well, really, *intention* comes first. You intend to accomplish something. Then must come action. Without action, your intention will be relegated to daydreams.

What can I do to nudge you, guide you, or push you into action? Do you want me to be your kicker-of-the-derriere? Then reread *Nothing Down for Women,* but this time, really *do* the Whiz Wizard steps. You're going to be amazed at your own results. I personally don't see how you could do those actions and not end up with a profitable deal!

By the way, I personally used the method that Bob likes to call "Ready, Fire, Aim." I wasn't really prepared, with all my tools in place, when I did my first deal, and, yes, I was scared.

Let's go shopping! *Let's go shopping!* Let's *really* go shopping! I'd rather shop for houses than for shoes, how about you?! I need the houses to put the shoes in! Think of me as your personal shopper!

Isn't it ironic that going shopping can help you achieve a bright financial future? Because we're shopping for things that go *up in value*! So speed on into action toward your ultimate goal of owning income-producing assets! Let's go speed shopping! Let's buy a great deal every month for the next twelve months! Then see how your net worth looks!

When I joined the Protégé Program, there were only two trainers available on the subject of real estate. (Now there are more than a dozen or so to choose from.) I listened religiously to John Childers on Tuesday evenings and Tom Painter on Saturday mornings. Then I spent the week in between doing every scrap of homework they gave me. Now I can look back and tell you exactly which deals were the results of exactly which homework.

When John told us to make one thousand business cards and hand them all out, the homework resulted in our first deal, with $75,000 in equity and $18,000 in cash. Wow! That's an incredible return on a $19.95 investment for a stack of ordinary business cards.

If you'd like to have some extended assistance with your action plan, I'd love to welcome you to the current evolution of the Protégé Program, where there are now over 30 classes in real estate, stock-market investing, business building, information marketing, multilevel marketing, and internet marketing. I teach a portion of the curriculum, and I'd love to have you join me. To find out more about the Protégé Program, visit www.EnlightenedWealthInstitute. com/ND4W.

Love,
KNB and Bob

P.S.: Remember, with *Nothing Down for Women,* you hold in your hands everything you need to get started. If you've enjoyed the 5-Minute Mentor method of learning, and if you want to stay on the fast track to more advanced materials, we're ready when you are!

> *Nobody succeeds beyond his or her wildest expectations unless he or she begins with some wild expectations.*
>
> —RALPH CHARELL, AUTHOR

Contact Us for Bonus Resources

There's so much I have to tell you, it wouldn't all fit in this book! Visit us at www.ND4W.com to see more information on the subjects addressed in the book and additional related subjects, including "Handling the Devastation of Death and Divorce," and "Real Estate Doesn't Discriminate (How to Turn Your Problems into Your Rocket Fuel)," as well as some essays by my stellar friends and associates: "Feng Shui: Hocus Pocus or Science?," "Testosterone Free Marketing," and "A Realtor's Take on Nothing Down." You can also read some amazing stories from women just like yourself who've made extraordinary changes in their lives with real estate. Visit us at www.ND4W.com/giftbag to download everything you want!

We'd also love to hear from you! In fact, if you have a story that you'd like to share, we want to hear it!

Here's how you can reach us:

Email: BobandKaren@ND4W.com

Websites: www.ND4W.com

www.TheEnlightenedWealthInstitute.com/ND4W
www.FiveMinuteMentor.com

Mail:

ATT: Karen Nelson Bell
The Enlightened Wealth Institute
5072 N. 300 West, Suite 110
Provo, UT 84604

Phone: 1-800-371-9876, extension 444

In Person: The Enlightened Wealth Institute holds Wealth Retreats several times each year. Look on any of our websites for the dates and locations, and come join us. There's always a special time when we meet and greet our friends, so walk up and say hello. We'd love to meet you.

Acknowledgments

I want to acknowledge the body of work created by Robert Allen, which inspires and enables common people to make uncommon wealth in the field of real estate. I also thank Mark Victor Hansen for showing me how to *give* and love doing it. Both Bob and Mark are men of honor who put their philosophies into action.

Thanks go as well to Tom Painter and John Childers for enduring my relentless curiosity during all my early real-estate classes. The inspiration of these men fills every page of this book.

I'll be thanking my late husband, Duncan Guertin, forever for demonstrating that life is a game to be played with zest and joy!

And lastly, I thank the Enlightened Wealth Institute for creating the incredible Protégé Program, where I learned how to design an abundant future. I thought I had signed on to study how to make a fortune in real estate. I ended up learning how to live a life that matters. What I must do now is follow the models set forth by my mentors.

These wonderful friends and associates assisted in myriad wondrous ways in bringing me to this book and this book to you:

How grateful I am to the best literary agent in the world, Jillian Manus, who worked valiantly to give *Nothing Down for Women* a chance; the wisest senior editor in all publishingdom, Fred Hills; the kindest adviser and editor that I could wish for, Emily Loose; and my incredibly knowledgeable copyeditors, Philip Bashe and Celia Knight.

Thanks to my business partners and voices of reason, Suzan Hudson and Frank Woodbeck, for their loving guidance of the MPC Action Weekends; to Denise Michaels, the author of *Testosterone-Free Marketing: The Yin and Yang of Marketing for Women,* for kicking my determination up a notch; to Devra Robitaille, the author of *Quantum Feng Shui, Hocus Pocus or Science?* for spiritual sisterhood.

I'm extremely thankful for the team who helps me operate my businesses: Nick and Samantha Nierop (the Renter Mentors), and Teresa Serrano.

To the original Inner Circle, I'm deeply grateful to everyone for their tender care when Duncan passed away. And for the ongoing fervent support of my endeavors, I particularly thank Pat Burns, Michelle Burns, Tad Lignell, Robby LeBlanc, Paulie Sabol, Heshie Segal, Eric Lingenfelter, and Larry Chao.

These Realtors kept me actively buying, and I applaud them for taking the time to become students and investors themselves, so they "get it": Brid'Jette Whaley, Melissa Helmkamp, Lisa Middleton, Liz Crowder, Stacey Tyler, Aaron Hixon, and Lynn and Elaina Saperstein.

And thanks, Genie Corcoran, for allowing me to put our TV show *Tales from the Story Genie* on the back burner while I finished this book.

Glossary

Abundance	The concept that there is so much good in the world, all intended for us to enjoy and to share, that there is more than enough to go around for everyone forever.
Accounting	Keeping financial affairs accounted for in an orderly fashion.
Acknowledgment	A written authentication that the signer understands what they're signing.
Acronym	Letters that stand for something besides the word itself.
Addendums	Additional stuff, pages added on after the body of the contract.
Adobe Acrobat 6.0	A version of Adobe Acrobat that lets you create PDF files.
Advertising	Persuasive communication with other human beings.
Affluence mentality	The mindset that it is your responsibility to develop, so that you can create a wonderful affluence that will allow you to do

	great and noble things for yourself, your family, your community, and your fellow man (one woman's opinion).
Aggressively appreciating market	Any market that is going up by 10 percent or more could be considered aggressive. California, Florida, and Nevada have seen appreciation as high as 30 to 50 percent in one year!
All cash	Some wealthy investors have big bank accounts, and when they say "all cash" they mean they're going down to the bank and withdraw the amount of their offer and fork it over to the seller. *We* mean that you're going to give them "all cash" from somebody *else's* bank account! See module 7 for funding strategies.
Alzheimer's	Mental confusion, usually in older people.
And/or assigns	A phrase that you put after your name on a contract to indicate that you have the right to assign the contract to someone else, whether it be a person, a company, or any other entity.
Appraisal	A opinion report created by an appraiser describing the value of a property.
Appraiser	A professional observer and analyst of the values of homes.
ARM	Adjustable Rate Mortgage (the rates can change at specific times).
Articles of Incorporation	Documents showing the setup of a corporation.
As is	The seller won't be doing any fixing up; all the responsibility for anything you find wrong will be yours.
Asset	In this context, something you own that produces income.
Asset-backed debt	A loan that is secured by something tangible owned by the borrower.
Assigning	Getting a property under contract and then selling it to another investor by selling him the contract ("selling him the paper").

Assumable loan	A loan that a new buyer can take over, if they put their name on it, usually by going through the loan application process. In other words, a loan which the lender will allow you to take over and make payments on; can be qualifying or non-qualifying, meaning you might have to prove your credit-worthiness if it's "qualifying."
Auto title loans	Loans made on a free-and-clear car; very expensive and dangerous, but quick and confidential.
Background check	Investigation into a prospective tenant's criminal history, housing history, credit history.
Back-up offer	An offer made if the first offer is rejected, which the seller can hold on to and come back and say yes to, if they don't get any other offers that are better.
Bank REO	A property that didn't sell at the foreclosure auction; it goes back to being owned by the bank; Real Estate Owned.
Bankruptcy	A legal procedure that allows a person in debt the chance to wipe out all their bills; other kinds of bankruptcies allow a person to re-organize their bills so they can have a chance to pay them back.
Bargain Finder	Robert Allen's amazing rating system for analyzing whether a deal is a good one or not; giving scores to Location, Condition, Price, Financing, and Flexibility, and then analyzing how the deal will make a profit.
Barter	Trading; exchanging services or goods for another person's services or goods.
Bird dogs	People who keep a look out for good deals for you in exchange for some compensation.
Bird dogs, 2	Anyone who will be on the lookout for properties for you in exchange for some

	kind of thank-you payment (postman, neighbor kids, other investors, college students, relatives).
Bond	A piece of paper that represents ownership in the worth of a city, county, state, or nation.
Bubba	Name for a caricature of a man who's big, burly, and kinda dumb.
Bubble	Markets in which speculative investment drives prices higher than usual demand can sustain; the prices go up and when the bubble bursts, they go down.
Buffer	Something to put a pad between two other things.
Buffer account	Money to put a pad between the renter not paying and you having to pay the mortgage; a safety savings account.
Cash at closing	Money you get back if you finance or refinance a property for more than the original loan amount it had on it.
Cash out	Money you can get back when you get a loan on a house that has sufficient equity.
Cash-out refi	A kind of refi where you can get money, actual cash, if you have enough equity in the property.
Catawumpus	All lopsided and out of whack. In a diagonal position or arrangement.
Clark County	The county in Nevada where Las Vegas sits; prostitution is not legal in Clark County.
Close	Get the deal all finished, all wrapped up, completely done.
Closing	The time when all the paperwork is finished, all the signatures in place, all the details worked out, and the money that has to change hands has done so.
Closing costs	The expense of creating and completing a home loan, paid when the loan is done; has different meaning in a different context.
Closing costs, 2	The costs incurred to get a deal closed;

loan fees, document fees, transfer taxes, arbitrary fees snuck in by the title company and/or the lender, anything extra added on to the price of the property itself.

Collateral | Something a person pledges when they borrow money, something valuable that the lender can keep if the borrower doesn't pay them back.

Collateralize | To put something tangible of value up to be held by a lender, so that if the borrower defaults, the lender gets to keep the thing.

Commission | The money a Realtor takes as their fee for helping a client buy or sell a house; sometimes they do, when they represent both the buyer and the seller simultaneously.

Common-law spouse | A husband or wife who doesn't have a marriage certificate but lives as if there were a legal marriage.

Competent | Able to make sound decisions.

Compound growing | Compound interest; how interest increases; interest paid on accumulated interest as well as on the principal.

Condo | Short for Condominium; housing similar to apartments, but owned by the tenants instead of rented; sometimes, apartment complexes are converted into condominiums.

Congruent | When things seem to be in alignment, when they correspond, when they match; when what you say matches what you do.

Consideration | The exchange paid for the thing . . . whether in money or something else, some other form.

Consumer credit | The credit that most Americans have in the form of credit cards, gasoline cards, department store cards, etc., which they use to buy consumable goods or services.

Contract for sale	An agreement between the parties saying that the seller wishes to sell and the buyer wishes to buy, and here's what they've agreed upon.
Contractor liens	When a person makes a contract to build a pool or a room addition, for example, if they don't pay for it, the builder (contractor) goes down to the county and records a lien against the property so that the owner can't sell it until the contractor gets paid.
Conveyed	Transferred.
Corporation	A business structure.
Correspondent lender	A mortgage brokerage company that already has developed lines of credit with big money lenders, so they don't have to go outside their own company to find the loans for you.
Cost of living	What it costs to live in America; there's actually a Cost of Living Index that takes into account the price of everything we buy and figures out if we're paying more or less than we did last year or last month.
Counteroffer	What the sellers might say if they want to sell but don't quite like your offer yet.
County records	Public records held at the building of the county's court house; viewable by the general public; records such as property ownership, divorce decrees, bankruptcy proceedings, etc.
CPA	Certified Public Accountant; a person who has been certified by the state and is able to do accounting and tax preparation.
CPA, 2	Certified Public Accountant; a person who does accounting and has passed some tests required for certification.
Creative deal	A real-estate deal that doesn't follow the typical retail real-estate world's pattern; a deal where Other People's Money is

	used in inventive ways that are not common knowledge except to smart real-estate investors.
Creative financing	A phrase that has come to refer to all of the wonderful strategies that Robert Allen first presented to the world in his bestseller *Nothing Down*.
Credit	In this book, credit means how you rate in the eyes of lenders, as represented by an artificial number known as your "score."
Creditors	Companies or individuals you owe money to.
Custom home	A home built specifically to the preferences of one owner, not as part of a housing tract.
Declaration page	*See* Distress letter.
Deduction	Amounts of money that you can legitimately remove from your total income for the year, so that you end up paying less taxes.
Default	In this book, the meaning refers to a situation where a person hasn't paid his home loan in a timely fashion; he's usually ninety days late, and the default would start on the 91st day. The time a home goes into default differs according to locale.
Deferred maintenance	A fancy name for fix-up work that hasn't been done; procrastination of the proper upkeep of a house.
Dementia	Mental confusion, usually in older people.
Depreciation	A unique type of deduction that the IRS lets you take regarding your real-estate investments, subject to rules.
Distress letter	A letter from the seller to "whom it may concern" that says they weren't pressured, forced, or coerced into selling their property.
Don't-wanter	A seller who has some kind of problem that makes him more anxious to sell

	than a typical homeowner; he doesn't want to own that house any more.
Double close	Two escrow closings that happen very close together in time.
Down	*See* Down payment.
Down payment	The cash money that lenders often require before they will give a home loan.
Dry wall	Building material used to create walls in houses.
Due on sale clause	A clause in almost all loans that says if the property is transferred to another owner, the lender can request that the loan be paid in full.
Elevator speech	What you would say about your business if you met someone in an elevator and only had thirty seconds to get them interested in your product or service.
Entities	Legal structures that could be thought of as an artificial person; for example, corporations, LLCs, partnerships.
Equity	The difference between the value of a house and the amount of the loans on it; if a house worth $100,000 has a loan on it for $60,000, then there's $40,000 of equity.
Evict	Force a tenant to move out for not complying with the contract.
Excel spreadsheet	A nifty way of keeping track of stuff, especially when there are lots of numbers involved ("Excel" is a particular brand of spreadsheet made by Microsoft); if you haven't learned how to work with spreadsheets, you may want to have your eight-year-old teach you how . . . It's easy once you learn it, and it'll help you a lot in your future real-estate investing career; a great way to track Notice of Default lists and FSBO lists.
Exercise your option	To say yes, you want to buy the property.
Exit strategy	A phrase that means what your plan is for getting out of something, in this case, out of the debt you created.

Farm	To communicate to potential sellers, buyers, renters; to do the necessary marketing in order to find, fund, flip, rent, etc.
Finance	To obtain a loan for a property.
Find	To locate motivated sellers. In our way of investing, it's not finding houses, it's finding people with problems.
Five C's of Credit	Character (Credibility), Capacity, Collateral, Capital, and Conditions.
Five-day pay or quit	A specific legal process in some counties where the landlord gives the tenant five days to do one of two things: either pay up or move out.
5 percent	A number that tells how much percentage is being charged to borrow money; like the rate on a credit card or the percentage rate on a bank savings account.
Fixer-upper	A property that needs more than just a little cosmetic work; potential for deep discounts on a fixer-upper.
Flip	To buy a property under its real value and sell it for more than you bought it.
Fluffy card	The kind of informal sales-y brochure card you would give to a potential motivated seller, or someone who might know a motivated seller; a card that tells the recipient what's in it for them.
Foreclosure	What happens when a home owner doesn't pay their mortgage over a period of time, and the lender takes the house away from them and sells it by auctioning it off to the highest bidder.
Foreclosure, 2	1. A legal procedure that happens when a person doesn't pay their home loan over some months' time, and the lender either threatens to take the house away or actually does end up taking the house away; there are four stages of foreclosure. 2. The ultimate penalty when home owners don't pay their mortgage payments; they get evicted and they lose their home.

Foreclosure auction	The day the property gets auctioned off to the public.
401(k)	A form of retirement plan in the workplace where the employer could match your contributions if they choose.
FSBO	For sale by owner, a designation that means the seller is not using a licensed real-estate professional to help them sell their property.
Fund	To gather together all the financial resources necessary to transact a deal, and in the 5MM Method, using other people's money.
Grant, bargain, sale deed	A deed resulting from a bargain between a buyer and a seller of real property, resulting in a sale.
Green-built	Designed and built to be energy-efficient as well as creating as little damaging impact on the environment as possible; environmentally conscientious.
Home warranty	A policy on the property that handles things when they need repair.
Hope & Help	The real true product of the enlightened real-estate investor.
House of ill repute	A place of prostitution.
HUD	Short for U.S. Department of Housing and Urban Development; HUD's mission is to increase homeownership, support community development, and increase access to affordable housing free from discrimination.
HUD foreclosure	A home that was covered by HUD, one that got foreclosed on and went back to ownership of the lender; available for purchase by bid through HUD authorized Realtor.
I don't have enough money	Something you don't ever say, something you don't ever think, something you don't even understand anymore; something you've replaced with "Where can I get it?"

Immediate occupancy	Vacant property!
Immersive	To immerse: To cover completely in a liquid; submerge. To baptize by submerging in water. To engage wholly or deeply; absorb: scholars who immerse themselves in their subjects. So an immersive style of training would engage you completely, almost surrounding you in the experience.
Incredulity	The condition or quality of not being able to believe something.
Infinite rate of return	The incredible kind of ROI you can get when you use Nothing Down strategies, where no money at all comes out of your pocket.
Inflation	A time in the nation's economy when prices are going up, up, up.
Inosculate	To unite so as to be continuous; blend.
Inosculation	The act of being inosculated, blended together to seem continuous.
Interest only	Home loans that let you pay a payment of interest only with no amount going toward actually paying off the loan; this kind of loan makes the payments very low in the early years; they generally are interest only loans for a limited number of years.
Interest rates	How much money you have to pay to borrow the money you need; the rates change every day slightly and they vary up and down through the years; the higher the interest rates are, the more clever you have to be in your strategies.
IRA	Investment Retirement Account, a form of retirement plan that allows for some tax advantages. There are several different kinds, each with different tax strategies.
IRS codes	Regulations having to do with real estate; tax liabilities or tax benefits having to do with real-estate investments.

J. Paul Getty	(1892–1976) Fabulously wealthy U.S. oil industrialist.
Jumbo CD	A Certificate of Deposit in a bank that is quite large, usually $500,000.
K	A slang term for "a thousand" as in "$10K" or "ten thousand dollars."
Ka-ching!	The sound of the profit you can make on a Stinky House.
Lease-option	In this usage, lease is another word for rent, and option means "privilege." In a lease-option, a person can rent for a while, and after some time, they have the privilege to buy the house if they choose to (or not).
Lease-option sandwich	To buy a property on a lease-option and then sell it on a lease-option.
Legal description	The way the property is described in the actual book at the county recorder's office; sample: *APN: 139-20-716-363, District: LV Subdivision: CORTE MADERA AMD Map Ref: PB B0087 P0047 Sec/Twnship/Range: PART OF N2 SE9 S20 T20S R61D Abbreviated Description: PLAT BOOK 92 PAGE 32 UNIT 155 BLDG 7 City/Muni/Twp: LAS VEGAS.*
Legalese	Fancy legal language that lawyers use.
Lending guidelines	The points of interest that matter to lenders when they look at you and your ability to pay back a loan; the guidelines change whenever the lenders feel like it, so you'll need to know what the prevailing guidelines are. Years ago, investors had to put down 20 to 30 percent in order to get a loan . . . now, an investor can even find 100 percent financing on residential properties. More commonly, investors can get loans with only 5 or 10 percent down. That's a big change from fifteen years ago.
Letter of duress	A letter signed by the seller that confirms that you didn't force him into sell-

ing his property. It usually states that the seller understands clearly that you expect to make a profit on the house.

Leverage
A way to get more power to move things; a way to get more power to buy things; the money lent on something, the loans on something.

LIBOR
London Inter-Bank Offering Rate; one of several indexes for lenders.

Lien
A debt owed that has to be paid before the property can be sold; it could be a mortgage or loan, it could be an obligation to pay back taxes, it could be a legal judgment, or it could be an old bill due to a pool builder. When I went to www.Dictionary.com for this word, there were *so many* definitions. The clearest one said: "the right to take another's property if an obligation is not discharged."

Lifeboat clause
A clause in a contract that allows the buyer to row away if the ship starts to sink; a clause that allows the buyer to change her mind and not do the deal.

Line of credit
A form of credit that lets the borrower use any portion of the whole amount and then pay it back, then use it again and pay it back again, in whole or in part, over and over.

Liquid asset
Assets you can get your hands on in a fairly short period of time.

Listing Realtor
The Realtor who represents the seller; some Realtors specialize in getting people to list their house with them.

LLC
Limited Liability Company.

LOL
Internet abbreviation for "Laughing Out Loud."

Lot premiums
Extra money added to the base price of a new home for its especially nice location.

Low-ball
A really low offer, such as 20 to 30 percent off the market value.

Low doc	A loan with a little more documentation required than a no doc.
Market value	The amount people are actually willing to pay for similar houses.
Marketing	Persuasive communication with other human beings.
Megamillionaires	People with a net worth of $100 million or more—a term coined by KNB.
Mentor	A teacher who will *tell* you how, *show* you how, and *monitor* how you do it; a person who cares about your results.
MLS	Multiple Listing Service; the place where the normal retail real-estate world lists all the houses that are for sale; Realtors can search this database using special search criteria; you can find all the properties listed on the MLS by going to www.Realtor.com, and you can search, but not in as detailed ways as a Realtor; and these will not be FSBOs; you may still find motivated people who have listed with a Realtor.
Mortgage	A home loan; it's called different things in different states; for now, just know that it's a loan on a house.
Motivated	Having an urgent reason to do something; a seller could be motivated to sell either at a better price or better terms because they have a big problem of some kind; a real-estate student could be motivated to study because they have a problem (like not enough money) or because they are passionate about something (like keeping their family's financial future safe).
MS Excel	A spreadsheet that can contain financial data or any other data; used by most lenders, easy to learn, and great for tracking all aspects of your properties and your net worth.
MS Money	A financial software program developed

	by Microsoft; the version called "MS Money for Home Office" compares to QuickBooks; I use it because it syncs nicely with my little handheld computer; I can't live without it.
MS Outlook	A personal productivity software developed by Microsoft; calendars, contact files, notes, email, I use it to keep records of all my houses, along with their directions and maps, names of lenders, names of renters, etc. I can't live without it.
Negative amortization loan	A loan that tacks some of your payment due onto the end of the loan.
Negotiations	The communication back and forth between the sellers and you as you try to figure out how to solve their problem at the same time as making it a worthwhile investment for you; win-win is your goal.
Net worth	How much you have versus how much you owe; whatever is left over after you pay all your debts.
Neutral	Colors that are not vibrant; anything in the range of "blah" from white to tan; earth tones; not red, blue, yellow, purple, pink.
New construction	Homes being constructed by builders *right now*; never been lived in; may be in the beginning stages and the house isn't a house, it's dirt; new communities or developments where you can buy a home before it's built, pick out the carpet colors and design upgrades; some builders won't let investors buy and some will.
No doc	A loan with very little documentation required.
NOD	Short for Notice of Default.
Nonqualifying assumable loan	An assumable loan where the buyer puts his or her name on it, but does not have to qualify for it through the loan application process.

Nothing	In this context, *nothing* means *not yours*.
Nothing Down	No down payment paid by you, but paid by some other resource.
Notice of default	A public statement by letter and/or newspaper to home owners, letting them know they've gone too long without paying their home loan, and now they'll have a certain amount of time to catch up their payments or else they'll lose their home in a foreclosure auction; also known as NOD.
Nye County	The county in Nevada where prostitution is legal.
OBO	Or best offer; indicates the seller's willingness to negotiate.
Offer	What you say when you tell the seller you would like to purchase the property, and for how much and under what circumstances.
Offer to purchase	A document where you make an offer to the seller and they accept it or decline it.
OPM	Other people's money. Not your money. Bank's money, friends' money, relatives' money, mortgage company's money, and so on.
Outside the bun	A play on "outside the box," from a commercial for Taco Bell, meaning creative and innovative thinking.
OWC	Short for owner will carry.
Owner will carry	The seller will "carry" or "hold" the home loan or the down payment or both, so that the buyer doesn't have to go to conventional financing resources.
PaperPort	An organizing software developed by ScanSoft; great for keeping all your documents generated by your real estate, plus all the documents you need often for the lending process; many uses, business and personal; I can't live without it.
Partner	A person who supplies something you

don't have: money, credit, time, knowledge.

PDF files — An abbreviation for *portable document format,* a file format developed by Adobe Systems. PDF captures files from many desktop publishing applications, such as Word and Excel, making it possible to view them as created. To view a file in PDF format, you need the free Adobe Acrobat Reader.

Permission letter — A letter signed by the seller that grants you permission to speak on his behalf to the lender. Without the letter, the lender is not allowed by law to speak to you.

Phases — Builders only build a certain number of houses at a time; if they have 80 houses to build in the development, they might build them in 8 phases of 10 each.

Points — A percentage point charged as a fee on a loan; equal to one percent.

Positive cash flow — When rent comes in, the amount of money left over after all the expenses, including mortgages, are paid.

Power option ARM — An ARM with several different ways you can choose to pay each month.

Pre-default — The time during which a home owner falls behind in payments, but before the bank sends them a Notice of Default.

Preforeclosure — The period of time between the arrival of a Notice of Default and the actual auction.

Preforeclosure, 2 — The period of time when the home owner who hasn't been paying their mortgage has the chance to make up all the payments and avoid having their house sold at auction.

Prelim — Short for Preliminary Title Search ("Can you do a quick Prelim for me?").

Preliminary title search — The title search that gets you going during your due diligence period; it helps you decide whether you want to proceed with the deal.

Pre-qual letter	A letter from your lender that tells your prospective seller or builder what amount you are potentially qualified to obtain on a loan.
Price	The amount agreed upon between the seller and the buyer.
Proceeds	The money that comes as a result of a sale.
Processor	A person who gathers together all of the information needed before it goes to the underwriter.
Profit potential	How much money you predict you'll make when you sell or rent.
Property manager	1. A real estate agent who has taken a special course in order to become a licensed property manager, who also works for a broker (not out in the field by themselves). 2. A Realtor who has studied to be a Licensed Property Manager and has received their license and works for a broker.
Property profile	A more formal synonym for the Bargain Finder.
Property split	Dividing up a larger property into smaller separate identifying units, such as making a six-bedroom home into three separate condos, or dividing two acres into ten parcels.
Public relations (PR)	Communication with other human beings; relations with the public.
Purchase agreement	*See* Contract for sale.
QuickBooks	A financial software program developed by Intuit, similar to their consumer product called "Quicken"; the most popular bookkeeping software for small businesses.
Quitclaim deed	A deed releasing whatever interest you may hold in a property but making no warranty whatsoever. It quits whatever claim you have to the property. The least powerful deed, since it doesn't make any guarantees.

Real-estate agent	A person who has gone to school to learn how to help people sell their homes; a salesperson who brings sellers and buyers together.
Real-estate broker	A real-estate agent who has taken more training to learn how to run an office with other agents working for them.
Real Estate Owned	REO, the actual real estate that the bank owns; technically, there's another phrase, OREO, Other Real Estate Owned, which means all the properties that they repossessed. REO actually means the properties the bank owns, in other words, their own assets, like the bank building; most people just use the term REO.
Realtor™	A trademarked word for a real-estate agent who belongs to the National Association of Realtors™.
Realtor fees	Typical fees that go to Realtors are 6 to 7 percent of the deal; if a $100,000 house is sold through Realtors, the fee would be $6–7,000; the buyer's agent and the seller's agent split the fee, usually in half; an agent representing both sides gets the whole fee; the agents must give a sizable percent to the broker who owns the agency they worked for.
Re-fi	Short for refinance.
Refinance	To obtain a new loan on a property that you already have a loan on.
Rental dwelling policy	The insurance policy you have to have on a rental dwelling; don't use a homeowner's policy on a rental dwelling or you most likely may not be able to collect when it comes time to file a claim.
Renter's policy	A policy that the renter takes out to protect their own belongings and their own actions that cause damage.
Rent-to-own	An agreement between the renter/buyer and the seller that allows the renter to buy the property at some time in the future;

	sometimes a portion of the rent goes toward their eventual down payment.
REO	Short for Real Estate Owned.
Repaired value	The amount of money a buyer is likely to pay for a house once the fix-up is done, based on what similar homes in similar condition have sold for.
Repo	Short for repossession.
Repossess	A legal process used by lenders to take back a property; the owner possessed it to live in, then when they didn't pay, the lender *repossessed* it.
Retail	A seller who wants to sell so badly they're willing to work out special terms in financing.
Retail real estate	The normal real-estate market, where people buy and sell homes using traditional methods; the focus is typically more on the house itself and not the unusual circumstances of the sellers and buyers.
ROI	Return on investment; the rate of benefit you get from an investment, expressed as a percentage.
Rotten egg	Naughty renter.
Scarcity mentality	The trick your mind can play on you just beneath your awareness that causes you to operate on old and useless programming, saying that there isn't enough.
Schedule of real estate owned	A list of all the properties you have with the mortgages listed, also showing how much is owed, what the value is, etc.
Seasoned funds	Money that has been in your possession for a specified amount of time, usually two to six months.
SEC	The Securities and Exchange Commission; the federal agency created by the Securities Exchange Act of 1934 to administer that act and the Securities Act of 1933. The statutes administered by the SEC are designed to promote full public

disclosure and protect the investing public against fraudulent and manipulative practices in the securities markets. Generally, most issues of securities offered in interstate commerce or through the mails must be registered with the SEC.

SEC rules
: Regulations set by the SEC that must be followed when using a public communication line when you're trying to raise money.

Security deposit
: Money that a person can get back if they keep the house clean; cleaning deposit, pet deposit, smokers' deposit are examples.

Self-directed IRA
: An IRA that you can use to invest in a lot of financial instruments, and in particular, real estate. You can't use it for your own home.

Seller financing
: An arrangement between the buyer and the seller where the buyer pays the seller for all or part of the amount owed for the home; the buyer doesn't have to go get a bank or mortgage company to lend them the money; often the buyer doesn't even have to have good credit.

Short sale
: When the lender is willing to sell the property for less money than is owed on it.

Simultaneous close
: Two escrow closings that happen at the same time.

SISA
: Stated income, stated assets (no verifying).

SIVA
: Stated Income, Verified Assets. (They verify your assets.)

Social Insecurity
: A play on words, suggesting that Social Security might not be there for the younger generation to enjoy.

Social Security
: A government program designed to give "secure" retirement funds to people who have paid into its program during their lives; mandatory investment taken out of a person's paycheck.

Sole remedy	The only way for a conflict to be resolved.
Speculation	Buying a property that you predict (and hope) will grow more valuable.
Speculation, 2	The act of buying based on some future predictions as opposed to current hard numbers.
Speculative	Not a sure thing.
Spread	The amount of buying based on some future predictions as opposed to current hard numbers.
Stated Income	A loan in which you don't have to prove your income.
Stinky House	A house that has cosmetic defects as well as possible structural defects; it usually smells bad too, but it doesn't have to smell bad to earn the title.
Stipulations	Things that have to occur before something else occurs ("I stipulate that you clean the carpets after you move out or before I move in").
Stock	A piece of paper that represents a piece of ownership in a company's worth.
Stock market	The place where people trade stocks and bonds, etc.
Strategies	Specific plans for buying real estate in specific creative ways.
Stuffy card	The kind of formal card you would give to a professional in a conservative field like banking, lending, title insurance, etc.
Subject to	An escape clause that a buyer can put in a contract, such as "subject to my attorney's approval," or "subject to suitable financing."
Subject to, 2	An investing strategy based on the clause "subject to existing financing" that means the buyer will take over the payments of the existing loan.
Sublease	When a lease tenant leases to someone else.

Sublet	To sublease.
Subliminally	Communication that gets received slightly below the analytical awareness of the person receiving it.
Surveys	When experts look at a piece of land and report what they see; usually done by surveyors or engineers.
Sweat equity	The value a person puts into a property by doing labor themselves.
Take title	A phrase that means how the title will be when it's recorded: will it be in a personal name, several names like husband and wife, or a business name? ("How will you take title?").
Tax-free	Money that comes into your account that you don't have to pay taxes on.
1003 form	Standard loan application form.
1031 Exchange	A real-estate tax strategy that allows a person to defer taxes until later.
Terms	The arrangements concerning where, to whom, and how payments get made.
Test	Try out your marketing and keep statistics on how well it does.
The curve	The shape of a graph that's going up; ahead of the curve means ahead of the big appreciation and way before the decline of the graph.
The $5,000 Rule	The amount of money the general public considers is a great discount on a house.
The Money Pause	The five seconds of silence after you ask a seller what they're hoping to get for the property, followed by *Shzzschhhh* and possibly followed by the seller expressing a willingness to negotiate.
Title	A piece of paper that confirms who the true owner of a piece of property is; it could be a piece of paper that confirms the true owner of other items as well, such as a car.

Title, 2	The piece of paper that tells who the legal owner is to a thing (like the title to your car). It's usually (but not always) recorded on the county records.
Title company	A company that provides title insurance (actual insurance that the title is free and clear, and can be transferred from the seller to the buyer); a title company performs many other services for Realtors and investors, buyers and sellers.
Title defects	Any circumstances that prevent the title company from insuring that the title really is free and clear.
Title search	Looking around to see what data is connected to the title, for example, are there any mortgages, are there any liens? The search can be done by a private party, but it's usually done by professionals at a title company.
Townhouse	A property that is connected to other ones like it; not a separate single family home.
Tri-merge credit report	Your credit report from all three bureaus.
Trust	A legal device used to set property aside from one's own self.
Tweak	Change your marketing a little bit to see if you can improve it.
(A) Twelve	A house that rates well enough on the Bargain Finder to make it eligible for consideration as a potential deal.
24 percent per annum	24 percent per year, or 2 percent per month, interest rate on a credit card.
Umbrella policy	A policy that goes over all your properties to protect you from legal liabilities.
Underwriter	A person who examines all of the data gathered by the processor to evaluate if your file indicates you'd be a person who would pay back the loan.

Urban	Referring to city as opposed to suburbs (sub-urban) or countryside.
VA loan	VA is short for Veterans' Administration. A home loan given to a veteran that doesn't require a down payment except for one dollar. It has various rules and regulations for eligibility.
Verification of deposit	Some proof (usually by a bank or lender) that you've got the money you say you have or you've paid the money you say you've paid.
Vivid Vision	A beautiful technique I learned from Robert Allen and relearned from Mark Victor Hansen that lets you luxuriate in your perfect future five years down the road in order to begin actually creating that very future.
VOD	Verification of Deposit.
W-2	An IRS form that an employee receives from the employer at the end of the year to show their earnings and all the deductions.
Walk-throughs	Going through a new house just prior to closing so you can look for defects; there is typically a second walk-through after you've created a to-fix list for the builder.
Warranty deed	A deed in which the seller warrants or guarantees that a good title is being transferred to the buyer.
Where can I get it?	The sentence that instantly transforms you into "Super-Solver," the super-heroine who goes around finding solutions everywhere.
Wholesale seller	A seller who wants to sell so badly they're willing to reduce the price.
Win-win-win	Triple win; better than win-win; the bank wins, the seller wins, the buyer wins.
"Would-ja take?"	Would you take? A way of making an offer; "Would-ja take $9,000?"

www.LandVoice.com	A company that delivers FSBO leads to your inbox daily.
Year to date	If something is written in the middle of a year, the data is only from the beginning of the year to the current date.
Your new last name	A phrase that you put after your name on a contract. *See* "And/or assigns."
Zilch, nada	Nothing.

Quiz Wizard Answers

Helping 1
1. b, d, e
2. b
3. a, b, c, d, e, f

Helping 2
1. a, b, c
2. c
3. [Write your own answer]

Helping 3
1. b, d, f
2. c
3. d

Helping 4
1. c
2. [Write a paragraph]
3. a, b, c, d, e

Helping 5
1. d
2. c
3. b

Helping 6
1. b, e
2. c
3. c, d

Helping 7
1. I = Income;
   D = Deductions and Depreciation;
   E = Equity;
   A = Appreciation;
   L = Leverage;
   S = Safety
2. b
3. b

Helping 8
1. d, e
2. c
3. b

Helping 9
1. c
2. a
3. [Write a paragraph of text]

Helping 10
1. a
2. a, c, e, g
3. b

Helping 11
1. a, b, c
2. b, d, e
3. a

Helping 12
1. a, c, e
2. a, c, e
3. b

Helping 13
1. b, c, d
2. d
3. c

Helping 14
1. a, b, c, d, e
2. b, d, e, f
3. a, b, c, d, e

Helping 15
1. d
2. b
3. c

Helping 16
1. b
2. a, b, c, d, e
3. e

Helping 17
1. f
2. g
3. b

Helping 18
1. f
2. b, c, d, e
3. a, b, c, d, e, f

Helping 19
1. f
2. b, c, e, f, g
3. a

Helping 20
1. a
2. c
3. d

Helping 21
1. b
2. c
3. d

Helping 22
1. b
2. c
3. d

Helping 23
1. b
2. c
3. d

Lesson 24
1. b
2. c
3. d

Helping 25
1. d, f
2. a
3. c

Helping 26
1. e
2. a, b, c, d

Helping 27
1. a, c, e, g
2. c
3. b

Helping 28
1. a, c, e, g, h

2. c
3. a, c, d, e, f

Helping 29
1. c
2. a, b, c, e, f, g
3. b

Helping 30
1. b
2. b
3. c

Helping 31
1. c
2. b
3. a, b, c, d, e

Helping 32
1. b
2. f
3. a, c

Helping 33
1. a, c, e
2. b
3. a, d

Helping 34
1. b
2. a, b, c, d, e
3. b, c, e

Helping 35
1. c
2. b
3. b, c, e

Helping 36
1. d, f
2. c
3. d

Helping 37
1. c, e
2. a, b, c, d
3. b

Helping 38
1. b
2. a, c
3. b

Helping 39
1. a
2. c, d
3. f

Helping 40
1. b
2. a, c
3. b

Helping 41
1. a, b
2. d, e
3. b
4. a

Helping 42
1. b
2. c
3. b

Helping 43
1. a, b, c
2. a, b, c, d, e
3. a, b

Helping 44
1. a, b, c, d, e
2. a, b
3. a, b, c, d, e

Helping 45
1. c
2. e
3. a, b

Helping 46
1. a, b, c, d, e
2. a, c, e
3. a, c, d

Helping 47
1. a, b, c, e
2. a, c, e
3. f

Helping 48
1. a, b, c, d, e
2. a, b, c
3. e

Helping 49
1. c
2. a, c, d, e
3. a

Helping 50
1. b
2. a, c, d
3. a, b, c, d

Helping 51
1. a
2. a
3. a, b, c, d, e

Helping 52
1. a
2. b
3. a, b, c, d, e

Helping 53
1. a, b, e
2. a, d, e
3. c

Helping 54
1. c
2. a, b, e
3. a, b

Helping 55
1. a, b, c
2. b
3. c, d, e

Helping 56
1. a, c
2. b
3. a, c, e

Helping 57
1. a, b, c
2. a, b, c, e
3. b, d, e

Helping 58
1. a, b, c
2. c, d, e
3. a, b, c

Helping 59
1. d
2. a
3. c, d

Helping 60
1. e
2. b
3. a, b

Index